Published by BSA Publishing 2024 who assert the right that no part of this publication may be reproduced, stored in a retrieval system or transmitted by any means without the prior permission of the publishers.

Copyright Barry Faulkner 2024 who asserts the moral right to be identified as the author of this work

Proof Reading/Editing BSA

Cover art Orphan Print, Leominster.

AMERICAN KILLERS

VOLUME 5:
CALIFORNIA
A TO C

. The information in this book is taken from police and court records where available, recorded witness statements, local media reports, the internet, biographies and other reference works. Over time some of the occurrences may have been exaggerated or embellished. Any parts of the book not verified by public record should be treated as allegations. The book is without prejudice.

In the U.S. state of California capital punishment is not allowed to be carried out as of March 2019. Executions were halted by an official moratorium ordered by Governor Gavin Newson. Before the moratorium, executions had been frozen by a federal court order since 2006, and the litigation resulting in the court order has been on hold since the promulgation of the moratorium. Thus, there will be a court-ordered moratorium on executions after the termination of Newsom's moratorium if capital punishment still remains a legal penalty in California by then.

BURTON W. ABBOTT

Born February 8th, 1928 – executed by asphyxiation-gas March 15th, 1957.

Stephanie Bryan was 14 years old when last seen on April 28th, 1955. She was on the way home from school taking her usual short cut through the parking lot of the Claremont Hotel. Her parents reported her missing later that evening and a large-scale search failed to find her.

Then, in July 1955, three months later, Georgia Abbott reported that she had found personal effects she thought belonged to the missing girl, including her purse and an ID card, in the basement of the home she shared with her husband, Burton Abbott, and his mother, Elsie Abbott. In interviewing the Abbotts, the police found that Elsie Abbott had found the purse some time earlier but did not connect it with the case.

Police subsequently dug up the basement and found Stephanie's glasses, a brassiere and other evidence. No one in the family could account for how the victim's personal effects came to be in the basement. Burton Abbott stated he was driving to the family's cabin 285 miles away when Stephanie disappeared. The police alarm bells were already ringing on him and so they took an interest in the cabin and its surroundings. Two weeks later Stephanie's body was found in a shallow grave a few hundred feet away from the cabin. Shortly after, Abbott was charged with her rape and murder.

The trial was one of the mostly highly publicized in California's history. The prosecution hypothesised that Abbott had attempted to rape the victim and killed her when she resisted. Abbott pleaded not guilty.

At the trial all the evidence produced was circumstantial and nothing directly connected Abbott with Stephanie Bryant's death. The prosecution used emotion to overcome the lack of direct evidence by such strategies as showing the jury the rotten clothes from the victim's body and waving her brassiere and panties, making unproven implications.

Abbott explained that in May the basement of the house had been used as a polling site with many people having access. Although the prosecution charged attempted rape, the pathologist testified that the body was too decomposed to evaluate it for evidence of any sexual assault.

Abbott took the stand and testified for four days, testifying in a calm and poised manner. He spoke in a soft voice and was steadfast in his denials of any knowledge of the crime. He said it was all a "monstrous frame-up". The jury was out seven days before it returned a verdict of guilty of first degree murder. The judge imposed the death sentence.

As provided by California law, there was an automatic appeal to the Supreme Court of California. In a detailed opinion describing the facts of the case and reciting the evidence that had been presented at trial, the court affirmed the conviction and the sentence of death.

Abbott was sent to San Quentin to await execution. His lawyers worked to commute his sentence for over a year.

On March 15th, 1957, the day of the execution which was scheduled for 11:00 pm, his attorney appealed to the United States Court of Appeals for a stay, which was denied, and then tried to contact the governor of California, Goodwin J. Knight, but the governor was at sea on a naval ship and out of reach of the telephone. The attorney arranged with a TV station to broadcast a plea to the governor.

At 9:02am Governor Knight granted a one hour's stay by telephone. Within six minutes a writ of habeas corpus was presented to the Supreme Court of California but at 10:42 am the petition was denied. The attorney tried again with an appeal to the Federal District Court but the court refused a further postponement at 10:50 am. At 11:12 am Governor Knight was reached again and agreed to another stay.

At 11:15 am Abbott was led to the gas chamber and strapped in the chair while the governor was contacting the warden by telephone. The executioner pulled the lever three minutes later and 16 pellets of sodium cyanide dropped into the sulphuric acid as Governor Knight reached the prison warden to stay the execution. The warden told him it was too late, and Abbott died at the age of 29.

This case demonstrates the set of confused legal procedures in place regarding appeals. The federal law allows an attorney 90 days to file for a writ of certiorari after a State Supreme Court's refusal of a rehearing.

However, the State Court set the date for Abbott's execution for two weeks *before* the 90-day limit. Thus, Abbott was executed with the writ still on file and, therefore, the possibility still existed that Abbott might have won a new trial.

The case also renewed the debate over the death penalty, especially when it is based on circumstantial evidence alone.

ROBERT JAMES ACREMANT

Born May 9th, 1968 – sentenced to death in Oregon 1997, in California in 2002

Acremant born May 1968 served in the Air Force and earned a master's degree in Business Administration from San Fransico's Golden Gate University in half the time usually required. Later, he worked as a district operations manager at Roadway Trucking in Los Angeles.

Acremant left his job at Roadway Trucking to start his own software business. He became frustrated by the failure of this company, and his own failure to find a job and achieve financial security.

His money frustrations were compounded by depression when he was rejected by a Las Vegas stripper named Alla Kosova (stage name Ecstasy), whom he considered to be his girlfriend, because he did not have enough money to visit her.

In 1990, after enduring increasing homophobia in Colorado, lesbian couple Michelle Abdill, 37, and Roxanne Ellis, 38, moved from Colorado Springs, Colorado, to Medford, Oregon. The couple met in Colorado, where Ellis — divorced with two children — worked as an obstetrics nurse. Abdill got a job in the same doctor's office, and they eventually became life-partners.

The couple started a successful property rental and management business and were elected to the board of their church. They spent their spare time restoring their old Craftsman-style house and visiting Ellis's three-year-old granddaughter. They also worked as activists, fighting two Oregon state ballot initiatives in 1992 and 1993 that were intending to amend the state constitution to declare homosexuality "abnormal, wrong, unnatural and perverse," and to restrict library access for materials related to homosexuality.

On December 4th, 1995, Ellis, 53, went to an appointment with 27-year-old Robert Acremant to show him an apartment. Police believed the appointment was made earlier that day. Ellis allegedly called her daughter, Lorri, at 4:00 p.m. to tell her she was going shopping.

Abdill, 42, left the office at 5:00 p.m. saying that she was leaving to help Ellis jump start her car after receiving a call that the car would not start. Later, Ellis's daughter drove over to the apartment complex where her mother was going to show the apartment and saw her mother's pickup. She said it pulled away from her when she tried to follow it.

Ellis and Abdill were not seen again until their bodies were discovered four days later in the back of Ellis's pickup truck after a cable TV worker reported the vehicle blocking an entry to the police. Both women had been bound and gagged, and shot in the head. The bodies were wrapped in drapes and covered by cardboard removal company boxes.

The discovery of the bodies caused concern in the local gay community. The couple's activism on gay rights issues, and records of an earlier threats against them, roused suspicion that they had fallen victim to a hate crime. The National Gay and Lesbian Task Force wrote to Attorney General Janet Reno to request that the United States Department of Justice assist local authorities in their investigation. The letter cited the Justice Department's guidelines, which said a crime motivated by bias "in whole or in part" should be considered a hate crime.

The nature of the crime, and the couple's activism, led to widespread publicity. Police published a composite sketch of the suspect based on a description of a witness who had seen a man park Ellis's truck and walk away despite being told it was blocking an entry.

The media coverage of the murders reached Acremant's mother, who had moved to Medford three weeks earlier with her son. She rang a police tip line and told police of her suspicion, based on her son's behaviour and his resemblance to the composite sketch, that he may be the killer. She also showed police the labels of cardboard boxes used during her move to Medford with Acremant which matched the address labels to those on the boxes used to cover the women's bodies in the back of the truck.

Police contacted California authorities and found that Acremant was under investigation there for the October 3rd disappearance of one of his friends. He was tracked down to a Stockton motel room and arrested on December 13th, 1995.

When arrested Acremant confessed to the Ellis and Abdill murders, claiming that his motive was robbery to get money to visit his girlfriend.

According to Acremant, after they refused his demand to write cheques made out to him from their business account, he shot both women in the back of the head execution-style, having bound and gagged them with duct tape and forced them to lie down in the back of Ellis's pickup truck.

Acremant also confessed to killing Scott George of Visalia California, on October 3rd, 1995, and dumping his body down a mine shaft located outside his father's ranch near stockton. On December 18th, 1995 police discovered George's remains at the bottom of an abandoned mine shaft in Calaveras County California.

After his arrest, Acremant declared that he wished to be executed by lethal injection. On September 11th, 1996, Acremant pleaded guilty to the murders of Ellis and Abdill.

On October 27th, 1997, an Oregon jury sentenced Acremant to death by lethal injection for the murders of Roxanne Ellis and Michelle Abdill.

On March 15th, 2005, after several appeals, Oregon's high court upheld Acremant's death sentence.

In February 2011, an Oregon court declared Acremant so delusional that he could not assist in his death sentence appeal and his sentence was reduced to life without parole. He died of natural causes in prison on October 16th, 2018. He also faced a death sentence in California after he was found guilty of the killing of Scott George in 2002.

JOSEPH MORENO AGUAYO

Born 1944 - sentenced to death August 8th 1996 for a 1979 murder.

The interesting thing about this case is that Aguayo would have got away with murder but for a cold case review.

He was serving a 60 year old sentence for the kidnapping, attempted murder, rape and robbery of an ex-girlfriend he had left to die in the boot of a car when detectives from Sacramento cold case review team paid him a visit in his cell in 1996 with a charge sheet alleging the murder by strangulation of Eva Chu, 29. Chu, who was seven months pregnant in April 1979, had been abducted with her body found four days later on the banks of Arcade Creek pushed under some large tree roots. She had been sexually assaulted and strangled.

The cold case review of her case had matched the original DNA samples taken from Chu with those of his current case.

Aguayo was convicted of killing Chu and her unborn child and sentenced to death on August 8th 1996.

RODNEY JAMES ALCALA

Born August 23rd 1943 – died in prison July 24th, 2021 aged 78.

Serial killer Rodney James Alcala murdered at least nine women and girls across the United States in the 1970s, though his true death toll could number over 150.
Alcala spent time in prison for sexual assault and other crimes in the 1970s but continued to rape and kill when he was free. Autopsies of some of Alcala victims revealed that he would strangle women, then he would wait for them to regain consciousness before the final kill. Alcala also sometimes posed the corpses of women he'd murdered. In 2010, photos taken by Alcala decades earlier were made public to try to identify other victims. He has been behind bars since his July 1979 arrest for the abduction and murder of a 12-year-old girl. Alcala was sentenced to death in California but died of natural causes in 2021.
Alcala was born as Rodrigo Jacques Alcala-Buquor in San Antonio, Texas, on August 23rd, 1943. He moved to Mexico with his family when he was 8 years old and his father abandoned the family while they were in Mexico. Alcala, his siblings and mother later relocated to Los Angeles.
At the age of 17, Alcala joined the army. He was discharged in 1964, after suffering a breakdown and being diagnosed with an antisocial personality disorder.

He attended California State University before transferring to UCLA. He graduated with a fine arts degree in 1968. After fleeing California that year, Alcala used his John Berger alias to enrol in New York University, where he took a class with Roman Polanski.

After fleeing the scene of his 1968 attack on 8-year-old Tali Shapiro, Alcala travelled to the East Coast. In 1971 he was included on the FBI's Most Wanted list. Girls at an arts camp in New Hampshire recognized their counsellor, who was using the name John Berger, from this FBI list. They told the camp's dean and Alcala was soon arrested, though he was able to plead to the lesser charge of child molestation and served just 34 months.

Alcala managed to land a job with The Los Angeles Times as a typesetter in September 1977.

His past conviction for sexual assault prompted California police to interview Alcala in March 1978 as a potential suspect in the Hillside Strangler killings, a set of serial murders that occurred in California in the 1970s. Alcala was cleared of those crimes, and at the time police did not realize they had actually spoken with a different serial killer.

In September 1978, Alcala appeared as Bachelor No. 1 on The Dating Game, a TV show that had men and women cheekily interview prospective dates, sight unseen. At that time he was a convicted child molester but the show did not run a background check.

Alcala was introduced as "a successful photographer, who got his start when his father found him in the darkroom at the age of 13, fully developed." When asked by Cheryl Bradshaw, his prospective date, to describe what kind of meal he'd be, he answered, "I'm called 'The Banana' and I look really good... Peel me."

Alcala's use of charm and innuendo won him a date with Bradshaw. However, when they met face-to-face she felt Alcala was 'acting really creepy' and opted not to go out with him.

Alcala was a tall and handsome man who often told women he was a fashion photographer who wanted to take photos for a contest. His intelligence and charm could make him persuasive. A woman who missed a date with Alcala because he'd been arrested in 1979 later said, "He was so easy to trust. He had a way of talking to people that really put them at ease."

In the 1970s, Alcala killed Cornelia Crilley, 23, and Ellen Hover, 23, both residents of New York City. Crilley was raped and strangled with her own stockings in her apartment in June 1971. Hover disappeared on July 15th, 1977, leaving behind a calendar that stated she was meeting with "John Berger." Her remains were discovered in New York's Westchester County in 1978. Alcala pleaded guilty to these murders in 2012. He was arrested in July 1979 for the abduction and murder of 12-year-old Robin Samsoe of Huntington Beach, California. He was convicted on these charges in 1980. Four years later this conviction was overturned as the jury had improperly been told about Alcala's criminal record. Another trial in 1986 resulted in a second guilty verdict, but in 2001 this was also overturned on a technicality. While in custody Alcala wrote the book *You, the Jury*, published in 1994, in which he argued he was innocent.

Before Alcala was re-tried a third time for Samsoe's death, advances in the world of DNA and other crime scene analysis provided evidence tying him to more crimes. At his next trial, which took place in 2010, Alcala was again charged with killing Samsoe. Part of the case against him was a pair of gold earrings linked to Samsoe that had been found in his Seattle storage locker. Alcala played clips from The Dating Game that he said proved he was already wearing gold earrings in 1978, but these didn't convince the jury.

In addition, he faced charges for assaulting and strangling four women in California in the late 1970s: 18-year-old Jill Barcomb, who was killed in November 1977, 27-year-old Georgia Wixted, 27, who was raped, beaten and strangled in December 1978, 32-year-old Charlotte Lamb, who was killed in June 1978 and 21-year-old Jill Parenteau, who was killed in June 1979. Alcala opted to represent himself during these court proceedings. In February 2010 he was found guilty of all five murders. He was sentenced to death in March 2010.

In 2016 Alcala was charged with the 1977 killing of Christine Ruth Thornton in Wyoming, though prosecutors opted not to extradite him to stand trial. Authorities also believe he killed Pamela Lambson in the San Francisco Bay Area in autumn of

1977. However, DNA collected at that crime scene was too degraded to test, so he was not charged.

Some Alcala victims survived his attacks. In 1968, a witness spotted Alcala driving off with Shapiro. Concerned, he followed them to an apartment and called the police. The responding officer discovered Shapiro, who'd been raped and beaten with a steel bar but was still alive. In February 1979, Monique Hoyt, then 15, managed to escape after Alcala raped her.

Alcala's exact death toll is unknown. Some authorities believe he murdered around 50 people, others think he may have taken as many as 130 lives.

Following the disappearance of Samsoe, a sketch of a suspect was issued. Alcala's parole officer saw it and recognized him. Police tracked down Alcala, who was arrested in July 1979.

Following Alcala's arrest police found hundreds of his photographs in a Seattle storage locker. These images, some of which were explicit, may include other Alcala victims.

In 2010 police shared many of these photos with the public in the hope of identifying those in the pictures. Some people were alive and came forward. The photos aided in identifying Thornton as one of Alcala's victims.

Alcala died on July 24, 2021, in California while awaiting execution. He was 77.

ANDRE ALEXANDER

Born 1952 – sentenced to death April 23rd, 1996.

U.S. Secret Service Agent Julie Cross was shot and killed during a robbery attempt while she and her partner were working undercover, monitoring a counterfeit suspect near the Los Angeles Airport around 88th St. and Belford Ave. The two assailants in the shooting were unrelated to the agents' investigation. Agent Cross had been in law enforcement for two years with the San Diego Police Department prior to being hired by the U.S. Secret Service in San Diego. She had just been assigned to the Los Angeles Field Office.

At 9:15 p.m. on June 4th, 1980, Agent Cross and her partner, Lloyd Bulman were in their unmarked car when two subjects approached them to rob them. Even though Agent Cross and her partner identified themselves as officers and left their vehicle the men kept their weapons pointed at the officers. Agent Cross' partner struggled with one man while Agent Cross struggled with the other shot her as she tried to flee.

The case, which was featured on the U.S. television show "Unsolved Mysteries," went cold until Agent Cross' killer was captured 12 years later when a detective working on an unrelated the triple murder case involving the killing of a counterfeit money order printer, his girlfriend and another man in Palms recognized Alexander from a composite sketch drawing of the suspect in the Cross murder. They had been at the same Venice High School. Alexander was already serving three life terms for the triple murder when he was charged with the murder of Julie Cross, convicted and sentenced to death. Alexander was 43 years old when he was sentenced on April 23rd, 1996.

On July 15th, 2010, the California Supreme Court upheld Alexander's death sentence on direct appeal.

Other appeals are ongoing.

EDWARD ALLAWAY

Born 1939 – Found insane and confined to State hospital 1977.

The California State University, Fullerton, massacre was a mass shooting committed by their library janitor, Edward Charles Allaway on July 12th, 1976. Seven people were killed as a result. It was the deadliest act of mass murder in Orange County until the 2011 Seal Beach Shooting, in which eight people died.

Allaway had a history of violence and mental illness. He was diagnosed with paranoid schizophrenia and found insane by a judge after being convicted by a jury. He was initially imprisoned at Patton State Hospital under medical care and treatment. In 2016 he was considered to be in remission and transferred to Napa State Hospital.

On July 12th, 1976 armed with a .22 calibre semi-automatic rifle he had bought at a Buena Park Kmart, Allaway killed seven people and injured two others in the library's first-floor lobby and at the building's Instructional Media Centre located in the basement. Witnesses told investigators that Allaway's attack began shortly before 7 am when he reportedly chased down Deborah Paulsen and Donald Karges before killing them, and then shot Bruce Jacobson after Jacobson attempted to subdue him with a metal statue. After shooting Seth Fessenden and Paul Herzberg, he took a service elevator down to the first floor and shot Frank Teplansky but left a visiting high school student unharmed. He then shot Stephen Becker before he ran out of bullets.

An eyewitness who was a part of a high school program stated Allaway was agitated when he saw him. The eyewitness stated that he saw Allaway pass by him and another counsellor who had gone into the hallway to investigate the noises. Allaway reportedly shouted, "He doesn't belong here; he doesn't belong here." before aiming his rifle at the eyewitness and the other counsellor. However, instead of firing at the two individuals Allaway lowered the gun and ran in the opposite direction.

Allaway fled the school campus and went to the Hilton Inn Hotel nearby in Anaheim, where his former wife worked, and from there he telephoned police to report his actions. He told them, "I went berserk at Cal State Fullerton, and I committed some terrible act. I'd appreciate it if you people would come down and pick me up. I'm unarmed, and I'm giving myself up to you."

The deceased victims were Paul Herzberg, 30, Bruce Jacobson, 32, Donald Karges, 41, Deborah Paulsen, 25, Seth Fessenden, 72, Frank Teplansky, 51 and Stephen Becker, 32. The injured victims were Maynard Hoffman, 64 and Donald Keran, 55.

Allaway was found guilty of six counts of first degree murder and one count of second degree murder. A second phase of the trial determined that he was insane. Five different Mental health professionals diagnosed him with paranoid schizophrenia. He had a history of mental illness, and he had tried to commit suicide and been hospitalized and treated with electroconvulsive therapy in the past. He was committed to the California state mental hospital system, beginning at Atascadero State Hospital. He was then transferred and held at Patton State Hospital in San Bernardino. In 2016, he was transferred to the less secure Napa State Hospital. The families of Allaway's victims protested at his transfer to a less strict regime as being against the judge's recommendation at the original trial and sentence.

He was found to have injured a co-worker at a Michigan plant in his past and a short time before the shooting rampage he had threatened his wife with a knife and raped her. Allaway's apparent motive was that he had delusions that pornographers were forcing his wife to appear in movies. The couple had separated over Memorial Day Weekend 1976 after a big row. His wife had filed for divorce shortly before Allaway attacked the workers at the university.

The defence said Allaway alleged that library staff members screened commercial pornographic movies before library opening hours and in break rooms, and Allaway's wife was in them. The allegation was unproved.

After a 1977 jury convicted Allaway of murder but deadlocked in the sanity phase of the trial, a judge found Allaway not guilty by reason of insanity. By law, defendants found insane are committed to a mental institution until they are found sane. Allaway remained institutionalized at Patton State Hospital for a number of years. During his time at Patton he made several failed petitions to the courts asking for his release. He was eventually transferred to Napa State Hospital in 2016 where he currently resides in 2024 age 65.

In the summer of 2009, officials at Patton indicated that Allaway was asymptomatic, had not needed medication, and they would recommend his release. The district attorney contacted the governor and the state mental health director to protest the hospital's planned action, given his history of violence and the mass murder. Patton withdrew the recommendation for release a few months later.

CLARENCE RAY ALLEN

Born January 16th, 1930 – executed by lethal injection in California January 17th, 2006.

Clarence Ray Allen was a convicted murderer with multiple violent felony convictions serving a life sentence when he conspired to murder eight witnesses that testified against him in his 1977 trial for the murder of Mary Sue Kitts. Kitts was a young girl who informed on him about a burglary of Fran's Market in 1974. As a result of Allen's plot, a former witness and two young, innocent bystanders were murdered during the burglary. On June 1st, 1981, the State of California charged Allen with the murder of Bryon Schletewitz, Douglas White, and Josephine Rocha, and conspiracy to murder Bryon Schletewitz, Ray Schletewitz, Lee Furrow, Barbara Carrasco, Benjamin Meyer, Charles Jones, and Carl Mayfield. In 1982, Allen was convicted of the crimes and the jury sentenced him to death.

The events underlying these crimes were set in motion in June 1974, when Clarence Ray Allen decided to burglarize Fran's Market in Fresno, California. Allen had known the owners of Fran's Market, Ray and Frances Schletewitz, for more than a decade. Allen enlisted the help of his son, Roger, as well as Carl Mayfield and friend Charles Jones, both were employees in Allen's security guard business who were frequent co-conspirators in prior criminal pursuits.

On the night of the burglary, Roger Allen invited the Schletewitz's 19-year-old son, Bryon, to an evening swimming party. The keys to Fran's Market were then taken from his trouser pocket while Bryon was swimming. Later that evening, while Bryon was on a date arranged by Allen with 17-year-old Mary Sue Kitts, Allen, Mayfield, and Jones used Bryon's keys to burglarize his parents' market. They removed a safe from the market and divided the $500 in cash and over $10,000 in money orders found inside. The money orders were later cashed with the help of Roger Allen, Shirley Doeckel, Kitts, Barbara Carrasco and Eugene Leland Furrow.

When Kitts later disclosed her involvement in the burglary to Bryon, the young man confronted Roger Allen, who, in turn, told his father, Clarence Ray Allen. As a result, Allen ordered the murder of Kitts, which was carried out, through strangulation by Furrow. Allen's compatriots then dumped Mary Kitts' body in the Friant Kern Canal. Her fate was unknown for three years before the body was found.

Throughout these events, Allen repeatedly issued threats to his criminal accomplices that any "snitches," or those not obeying his orders, would also be killed. Allen was eventually arrested when the last in a series of store robberies went awry, resulting in the shooting of a bystander.

Ultimately, in 1977, Allen was convicted of the burglary and the related first-degree murder of Mary Sue Kitts. It was while he was serving a life sentence at California's Folsom Prison for Kitts's murder that Allen committed more crimes in an effort to silence the witnesses who testified at the 1977 Fran's Market/Kitts murder trial by threatening to have them killed which resulted in his death sentence. During the Kitts murder trial, Bryon and Ray Schletewitz supplied the crucial testimony about Allen's motive - that Mary Kitts had told them that Allen burglarized Fran's Market and she had to be silenced.

Five years later on August 22nd, 1982, a jury in Glenn County found Allen guilty of the first degree murders of Bryon Schletewitz, Josephine Rocha, and Douglas White. The jury found that Allen had a prior murder conviction (the murder of Mary Sue Kitts), had committed multiple murders, and had intentionally killed Bryon Schletewitz in retaliation for his prior testimony in 1977 and to prevent his future testimony. Allen admitted that he had previously been convicted of murder. Eight days later, the penalty phase began and the death sentence affirmed..

On September 10th, 1982, the jury returned three death verdicts. Allen was 52 years old. His appeals rattled on until January 17th 2006 when he was executed at California after his final appeal was dismissed by the U.S. Supreme Court. He was 76 years old.

SHAREEF ALLMAN

Born 1963 – committed suicide by shooting himself on October 5th, 2012.

47-year-old Shareef Allman, worked as a truck driver at Lehigh Hanson's Permanente Cement Plant quarry. The site of the quarry was in the hills to the west of Cupertino. He had worked there for 15 years.

Allman was married to singer Qwen Mejia also known as Valeri Allman. Their marriage was strained by a series of violent incidents perpetrated by Allman against his wife. According to court documents Mejia obtained a restraining order against Allman in 1992 and divorced him. Allman had fathered a daughter, Lashae Allman, who was born in 1993.

Shareef Allman resided in the Stonegate Apartments of San Jose. He grew up in East Palo Alto in a family troubled by domestic abuse. Friends described him as a community activist and a happy, comedic man, and that he was never known to be violent and would advocate against violence, especially domestic abuse and gang activity.

Allman had been a producer for CreaTV, a San Jose-based public access broadcasting company, where he hosted a show entitled "Real 2 Real." In his show, Allman interviewed famous activists and figures such as Reverend Jesse Jackson. He had written a novel, Amazing Grace, about a fictional victim of domestic abuse who overcame her tribulations with the help of God. Allman had also worked as a bouncer for a nightclub in Sunnyvale and was trained in mixed martial arts.

Neighbours and friends of Allman said that he grew unhappy about being treated unfairly by co-workers, experiencing racial discrimination, and having his job being moved to a night shift. The weekend prior to the attack, a friend said Shareef Allman visited him in Sacramento and showed him his car boot that had an AK-47 inside and said that he had racist co-workers and it was protection. The friend said that he thought Allman was joking and did not take the statement as a threat.

On October 5th, 2011, at 4:00 a.m. Allman attended a safety meeting inside a trailer of Lehigh Hanson's Permanente Cement Plant, and got into a confrontation with his co-workers. He left and went to his car, armed himself, and walked back into the trailer.

Allman opened fire with a .223-caliber semi-automatic rifle and .40-calibre handgun at his co-workers, killing three and wounding six others. After the shooting Allman trapped his co-workers inside the trailer by placing a piece of plywood and a rope over the door to jam it shut. At 7:00 a.m., he attempted to carjack a 60-year-old woman five miles away at a parking lot of Hewlett Packard's campus, and shot her in the leg. She was hospitalized and recovered.

Allman fled on foot in a Sunnyvale neighbourhood where he eluded police in a manhunt that lasted one day. The shootings caused a variety of schools, such as Lawson Middle School, and

Stratford Middle School to go into lock downs. Fremont High School and Lynbrook High School were put into "Code Blue." Peterson Middle School, in Sunnyvale, was put on lock down for several hours and they had to hold their students after the end of school.

On the morning of October 6th, 2011, police confronted a man who fitted the description of Allman hiding behind a car parked in front of a house in the Birdland neighbourhood of Sunnyvale, bordering Cupertino. Allman was asked to put his hands in the air by officers, and raised his handgun towards them. Officers responded with fire. It was initially reported that Allman died from the police officers' multiple gunshots, but an autopsy later showed that Allman's fatality was caused by a self-inflicted gunshot wound. He was 47 years old.

LORENZO ALVARADO

Born 1982 – committed suicide April 27th, 1999.

Only the autopsy report is available as no court room activity was necessary in these killings because the killer committed suicide the same day.

Lorenzo Alvarado had frequent heated arguments with his father and step mother about his continual use of marijuana in their apartment which the adults were worried would have an effect on their other children.

Police believe these arguments were the cause of Alvarado, 16, shooting and killing his father, 40, step-mother, 36, and 5 year old step brother on April 27th, 1999 before turning the gun on himself.

The bodies were discovered by his 17 year old brother and 10 year old half-sister when they came home from school. Each victim was killed by a single shot to the head from a revolver Alvarado had bought several weeks previously.

JUAN MANUEL ALVAREZ

Born February 26th 1979 – sentenced to 11 consecutive life sentences August 20th, 2008.

Juan Manuel Álvarez, a construction worker from Compton, California caused the Glendale train crash, a collision between a passenger train, another passenger train, a freight train, and a car in Glendale, California, a suburb of Los Angeles, on January 26th, 2005.

He parked his gasoline-soaked Cherokee sport-utility vehicle on the tracks and waited for a southbound Metrolink commuter train in a suicide plan. At the approach of the train he changed his mind, allegedly unable to move his vehicle from the tracks, he got out and ran off, apparently abandoning his suicide attempt, and then he watched the train from a safe distance colliding with his SUV causing it to derail.

The derailed train then hit a Union Pacific Railroad freight train parked on a siding, as well as a northbound Metrolink train running on the third track. The collision left 11 people dead and nearly 200 injured.

Alvarez was a known methamphetamine addict, prone to delusional behaviour. At the time of the crash, Alvarez, the father of two young children, was experiencing marital difficulties and had apparently already botched a suicide attempt previously.

He was tracked down pretty quickly by his ID cards found in the wreckage at the scene and located at a friend's house in Atwater village close to the crash site. He displayed stab wounds to his chest and slashes to both wrists which could not be placed as having been done before or after the crash. Police said their investigations indicate Alvarez may have intended to cause the crash without committing suicide to draw sympathetic attention from his estranged wife. Authorities filed additional charges against him for murder with intent. He was charged with, and subsequently convicted of 11 counts of murder.

Prosecutors sought the death penalty for his crimes under a seldom-used law making train wrecking, causing a person's death, a capital offense. This 1873 law was created to prosecute Old West train robbers who were known to blow up the tracks to rob a train.

On June 26th, 2008, Alvarez was found guilty of 11 counts of first degree murder with special circumstances and one count of arson related to the incident. He was acquitted of the train wrecking charge.

On July 7th, 2008, the hearing for sentencing for Juan Manuel Álvarez started.

On July 15th, 2008, the jury recommended a sentence of life imprisonment without the possibility of parole.

On August 20th, 2008, Alvarez was sentenced to 11 consecutive life sentences.

Immediately following the accident, Metrolink temporarily roped off the first cars in all of their trains preventing passengers using them. Seating started in the second car. They gradually modified this policy, and as of 2007, the line permitted passengers to sit in a portion the first car when in "push mode" that is the engine unit pushing the train from the rear not pulling from the front. Seating was not permitted in the roped-off forward most section of the first car just behind the engineer's cab.

MANUEL ALVAREZ

Born 1960 – died from COVID in San Quentin July 3rd 2020 age 59.

Manuel Machado Alvarez was a Cuban murderer who was on parole for voluntary manslaughter when he murdered a man during a robbery, a crime for which he received the death sentence.

In 2020, Alvarez became one of a dozen California death row inmates to die in the span of less than two months as the result of a COVID 19 outbreak at San Quentin State Prison. He died on the same day as Scott Erskine, who also died from COVID-19.

Born in Cuba in 1960, Alvarez suffered a serious head injury as a child which may have contributed to brain damage which caused violent behaviour as he grew up. His mother died when he was young, and his stepmother was abusive and neglectful.

Alvarez arrived in the United States in the Mariel boatlift in 1980. After initially being detained at several camps, he went to Richmond Virginia, in 1981, under the sponsorship of a married couple with young children. He lived with the family for about two months, and displayed mixed behaviour of both kindness and anger.

Alvarez moved to California in late 1981, where he would later commit his crimes. He struggled to adjust to life in a different country, and was able to make just a few friends.

On December 27th, 1981, 21-year-old Pedro Ramirez ran into a liquor store in Hollywood, Los Angeles with Alvarez chasing him with a butcher's knife. Ramirez stopped and put his hands up to protect himself. Alvarez fatally stabbed him through the throat, and then approached one of the store's clerks, but fled when the man pulled out a shotgun and told him to stop. Alvarez later said he killed Ramirez out of revenge for him burglarizing the house of his male lover.

Alvarez was convicted of voluntary manslaughter with a deadly weapon and assault with a deadly weapon and sentenced to four years in prison. In December 1982, he escaped from a maximum security prison with two other Spanish-speaking inmates. They surrendered several hours later, and each of their sentences was extended by 16 months. Alvarez was paroled in 1986.

In March 1987, in violation of his parole, Alvarez moved from Los Angeles to Sacramento. There, he lived on and off with Leslie Colyer and Neetelfer Hawkins, two friends of his. He spent most of his time using drugs and drinking alcohol.

On May 12th, 1987, Alvarez made sexual advances toward Sandra S., a local sex worker, near her apartment building late at night. Sandra rejected his advances returned to her room and went to sleep. She awoke at noon to see Alvarez masturbating at the foot of her bed. She called for her boyfriend's help, but neither he nor Sandra's son were home. Alvarez started raping Sandra when Percy Spence, one of her friends, walked in. Spence asked her if she was 'working'. Sandra said no, but Alvarez said yes, prompting Sandra to keep saying no. Spence became confused and left. By the time another one of Sandra's friends, Anthony Simpkins, arrived, Alvarez had finished raping her. As Simpkins was entering, he passed Spence and Alvarez. When Simpkins asked him what was happening, Spence said "Oh, just let it be." Sandra then ran to Simpkins and said Alvarez had raped her, prompting Alvarez to flee. He stole the nearby car of one of his acquaintances, Edwin Glidewell, and drove off.

On May 15th, Alvarez met a woman named Belinda Denise Ross as she was cashing a welfare check. They became acquainted, got in the car together, and, over the next few days, together set out to obtain drugs and alcohol.

On May 17th, he had Ross drive to an office of the Golden Credit Union, where he got out. Around this time, 35-year-old Allen Ray Birkman, a technician for the Sacremento Police Department, withdrew $60 from his wife's account at an ATM. Alvarez approached Birkman and demanded the money, the two got into a struggle. Alvarez stabbed Birkman in the heart and fled the scene with Ross. Before Birkman was taken to a hospital, he gave a description of Alvarez. Birkman died from his injuries the following day.

Later that day, Alvarez and Ross drove to the apartment of Gail Patton, one of Ross's friends. The two entered the apartment, with Ross holding the knife. Shortly after, police officers arrived at Patton's apartment having followed Alvarez who they suspected of the Birkman murder. Alvarez and Ross told Patton not to say anything. The officers told Patton they were investigating the stabbing at the Golden Credit Union and asked her if she knew anything about the car used by the perpetrators which was parked outside. She said no and the police left. Patton then told Alvarez to leave, which he did leaving behind the knife and the car. Ross did not go with him, and she was arrested several days later.

Not long after leaving the house, Alvarez robbed and assaulted 78-year-old Greta Slatten. Slatten had driven to a store with no cars in the parking lot and no people around other than Alvarez. She stayed in her car with doors locked until Alvarez appeared to walk to a payphone. When Slatten passed by him he knocked her unconscious before stealing her car and purse. He was arrested in Mississippi on May 27th, after a high-speed chase. Alvarez was soon returned to California to face criminal charges, including murder. While awaiting trial, he punched fellow inmates on two different occasions. These assaults were later used against him at the sentencing phase of his trial.

Alvarez was charged with first degree murder with special circumstances, rape, robbery, and attempted robbery, while Ross was charged with first degree murder and attempted robbery. The two were tried jointly in 1989, with the prosecution seeking a death sentence for Alvarez.

At trial, he denied everything. He said he had consensual sex with Sandra and that Glidewell's car was given to him as debt security. He proclaimed his innocence in Birkman's murder, saying he had been mistakenly identified. Ross admitted being the getaway driver in Brinkman's murder, but denied knowing that Alvarez was going to rob and kill Brinkman.

On June 9th, 1989, Alvarez was found guilty on all counts. Ross was only convicted of attempted robbery and being an accessory to murder after the fact. She received a sentence of 3 years and 8 months, and an additional 5 years as a serious felony enhancement due to a prior robbery conviction. She was released from prison in the 1990s.

During the sentencing phase for Alvarez, the prosecution pointed to his prior convictions and history of violence as aggravating factors. His defence team discussed his troubled upbringing and gave examples of times when he'd shown kindness.

On August 3rd, 1989, the jury recommended a death sentence for Alvarez and he was formally sentenced to death on September 14th, 1989. Brinkman's family, who gave victim impact statement in court, were mostly indifferent to the question over whether he should be executed, saying all that mattered to them is that he die in prison. Alvarez was sent to death row at San Quentin State prison.

He did die in prison. He died on July 3rd, 2020, at the age of 59, after contracting COVID-19 during the COVID-19 pandemic in California. He had been hospitalized before his death.

CURTIS DEAN ANDERSON

Born 1961 – sentenced to 301 years in prison in 2005, died age 46 in prison on December 9th, 2007.

Curtis Dean Anderson was already a notorious paedophile and child murderer by the time he died in a state prison in 2007.

Anderson was convicted of the 1999 murder of 7-year-old Xiana Fairchild of Vallejo and of kidnapping another girl from the same city the next year. In late 2007, dying of liver and kidney problems, Anderson confessed that he also abducted 7-year-old Amber Swartz-Garcia from outside her Pinole home in 1988, drove her to Arizona and killed her.

After investigating his story for a year and a half, the FBI and Pinole police concluded he was telling the truth.

"This guy is a true psychopath," said FBI Special Agent Marty Parker, one of those who interviewed Anderson behind bars.

The question was then whether Anderson was responsible for the vanishings of other children, including two girls snatched within seven months of him taking Amber.

Before he died, Anderson "confessed to a number of other open homicide cases authorities" said Pinole Police Chief Paul Clancy at a news conference, without providing details.

Anderson, in a 2001 interview in Solano County Jail said that he had killed "many girls, and you'll never find them all".

Amber vanished on the afternoon of June 3rd, 1988, as she skipped rope outside the home she shared with her mother, Kim Swartz, on Savage Avenue. Anderson didn't live in Pinole but was familiar with its streets, having worked as a cabdriver and as someone who returned lost luggage to airline passengers.

"He said he was driving to Arizona and decided to take someone with him for company," Police Chief Clancy said. "In a case of tragic timing, Amber was standing in front of her house at the exact moment Anderson randomly drove through her neighbourhood. He opened the car door and pulled her in."

Anderson drugged the girl with root beer schnapps, explaining that "it was better than duct tape," the chief said.

Anderson said he then killed Amber in a motel in the Tucson area and dumped her body in the desert not far from his aunt's ranch in Benson, off Interstate 10. Her body hasn't been found and may have been carried away by wild animals.

Anderson showed no remorse when he was interviewed by FBI agents at Corcoran State Prison on November 5th, 2007. Pinole police were present during the 5 hour interview. Anderson died Dec. 11th, 2007, at the age of 46 before a second interview could be conducted.

Anderson was already serving a 251-year sentence for the 2000 abduction and sexual assault of an 8-year-old Vallejo girl when he was charged with the kidnapping, sexual assault and murder of 7-year-old Xiana Fairchild. She disappeared as she walked to school on December. 9th, 1999, and her skull was found in the hills west of Los Gatos two years later. Her initial disappearance sparked a wide-ranging search in the Bay Area.

Police released a copy of Anderson's handwritten confession to Amber's killing. It read, "I, Curtis Dean Anderson, under no threats, coercion or promise, make the following statement. If there is no pursuit of the death penalty, I will freely admit my role in being responsible for the death of Amber Swartz-Garcia."

Amber was the first of three girls in the Bay Area to be abducted over a string of eight months. Nine-year-old Michaela Garecht was snatched in a Hayward grocery store parking lot on November 19th, 1988, by a stranger in an older-model vehicle. On January 30th, 1989, 13-year-old Ilene Misheloff vanished while walking to her Dublin home.

The FBI say that the girls' disappearances remain open cases.

The lead investigator in Ilene Misheloff's case, Dublin police Sgt. Nate Schmidt, said that Anderson had been looked at years before but that police had been unable to link him to the case.

Notable cases of kidnapped children in the Bay Area and surrounding region now on the cold case file for which no arrests have been made as yet are;

Christina Williams, 13, of Seaside (Monterey County): kidnapped June 12th, 1998, while walking her dog. Her body was found seven months later near the former Fort Ord Army base.

Amanda "Nikki" Campbell, 4, of Fairfield: abducted December 27th, 1991, while riding her bicycle. She has never been found.

Ilene Misheloff, 13, of Dublin: disappeared January 30th, 1989, while walking home from school. She has not been seen since.

Michaela Garecht, 9, of Hayward: taken November 19th, 1988, outside a neighbourhood market. She has not been found.

Kevin Collins, 10, of San Francisco: vanished February 10th, 1984, from a bus stop. He was never seen again.

Mitchell Owens, 7, of Menlo Park: taken February 3rd, 1983, from his home. He has not been found.

STEPHEN WAYNE ANDERSON

Born July 8th, 1953 – executed by lethal injection in California on January 29th, 2002.

Stephen Wayne Anderson was convicted of one count of first-degree murder with special circumstances and one count of residential burglary in the May 26th, 1980 murder of Elizabeth Lyman. A San Bernardino County jury sentenced Anderson to death on July 24th, 1981.

Elizabeth Lyman was an 81-year-old retired piano teacher, who lived by herself in Bloomington, San Bernardino County. About an hour after midnight on Monday, May 26th, 1980, Anderson, a 26-year-old escapee from Utah State Prison, broke into her home believing no one was at home, and cut her telephone line with a knife.

He was startled when she woke up in her bed and shot her in the face from a distance of between eight and 20 inches with his .45 calibre handgun as she lay in her bed.

Anderson then covered her body with a blanket, recovered the expelled casing from the hollow-point bullet that killed her, and ransacked her house for money. He found less than $100.

Anderson then sat down in Mrs. Lyman's kitchen to eat a dinner of noodles and eggs. His meal was interrupted, however, by sheriff's deputies called to the scene by a suspicious neighbour who had been awakened by barking dogs and had seen Anderson inside Mrs. Lyman's house through a window. The deputies arrested Anderson at 3:47 a.m., and took him to the San Bernardino Sheriff's Substation in Fontana.

Anderson was an escapee from Utah State Prison at the time of Mrs. Lyman's death. He escaped on November 24th, 1979, and had been in prison for one count of aggravated burglary in 1971 and three counts of aggravated burglary in 1973.

While incarcerated at Utah State Prison, Anderson murdered an inmate, assaulted another inmate, and assaulted a correctional officer. Anderson also admitted to six other contract killings in Las Vegas, Nevada that happened prior to the crime for which he received the death sentence.

Anderson's attorneys lost a last-ditch battle for the life of the man they said had redeemed himself on death row, learning Latin and writing poems of repentance. As Anderson was lying on the gurney in the death chamber, his public defender, Margo Rocconi, mouthed the words "I love you" 3 times to the condemned man. Witnesses said he responded by mouthing, "Thank you."

The U.S. Supreme Court refused to halt the execution. The nation's highest court voted 8-0 to reject Anderson's request for a stay of execution and a request to rehear the case with Justice Antonin Scalia not participating. Anderson's defenders had asked Gov. Gray Davis to spare his life, saying he didn't get a fair trial because of a bad lawyer and noting that some family members of the victim did not support the death penalty.

Expecting clemency to be denied -- the last California governor to grant clemency was Ronald Reagan in 1967 -- the defence team unsuccessfully waged a separate legal battle arguing that Governor Davis' tough-on-crime platform locked him into an intractable position on clemency. Anderson's lawyers filed a new appeal claiming Davis' 34-page opinion showed his bias. That argument also was rejected by the courts.

At 12:18 a.m., January 29th, 2002, the execution by lethal injection of Stephen Wayne Anderson began in San Quentin State Prison's execution chamber. He was pronounced dead at 12:30 a.m. When asked by the Warden if he had any last words, Mr. Anderson was very adamant that he did not.

ROGELIO ANDRADE

Born 1976 – charges dropped by insufficient evidence available in January 2000.

In November 1998, more than five years after one of the city's worst arson fires killed three women and seven children in a tenement building west of downtown Los Angeles, prosecutors filed multiple murder charges against two members of the notorious 18th Street gang.

Prosecutors charged Rogelio Andrade and Allan Lobos, both then 22, for the fire, which they allegedly ignited to intimidate an apartment manager who had tried to drive drug dealers off her property in May 1993.

The two men pleaded not guilty in Eastlake Juvenile Court. The 1993 fire exposed the substandard condition of many buildings crammed with immigrant families in the Westlake-Pico Union neighbourhood and revealed that the Fire Department inspected the area infrequently and haphazardly.

Investigators said they suspected from the beginning that gang members set the deadly fire. But they could not identify the perpetrators until now in 1998, when a gang member arrested in an unrelated murder told Rampart Division police that he knew who started the so-called "Burlington fire" and gave them the names Rogelio Andrade and Allan Lobos.

Police arrested Andrade at his home in Hollywood. Lobos was already in state prison, serving 15 years to life for a 1997 murder in the same neighbourhood.

"It was just a matter of time" before the crime was solved, said Thomas L. Derby, an arson investigator for the Los Angeles City Fire Department. "Gang members love to brag about what they did. If you don't catch the person today, you'll get them tomorrow."

Both fire and police investigators said they were particularly determined to find the killers because of the ages of seven of the victims who were 11 or younger.

Investigators had declined to discuss the new evidence in the case, except to say that details from the informant was corroborated by facts known from the scene.

They insisted that the informant was not offered special treatment for making his statement against Andrade and Lobos.

The 69-unit apartment building at 330 S. Burlington Ave. was one of many in the poor Westlake community beset in those days by gang members at the time of the fire on May 3rd, 1993. Authorities had said that just hours before the blaze erupted, the apartment's manager had ordered two men out of the building, suspecting that they were dealing drugs.

The flames spread quickly through the building left unchecked because a series of fire doors were either propped or nailed open. Most of the victims could not escape the second and third floor hallways, where they suffocated.

In 1998 investigators would not say whether they believe that the two men driven from the building by the manager were Lobos and Andrade or their associates.

But other LAPD officials had confirmed that about the time of the deadly blaze, the apartment building was a hot spot for a lucrative 18th Street gang-controlled drug trade. Drug dealers in the neighbourhood were making thousands of dollars a day, much of it coming from the Burlington building.

Many of the buildings had serious fire safety violations, such as missing fire extinguishers and padlocked emergency exits. The Burlington building had earlier been the target of an arson attempt, and inspections had detected a series of safety violations there--but they were not corrected.

As a result of the Burlington blaze, the Fire Department implemented a computerized inspection system to help track building inspections. An inspector immediately was added to the neighbourhood's Station 11.

Authorities said that Andrade and Lobos were hard-core members of the 18th Street gang and had had numerous run-ins with police. The most serious occurred in 1997, when Lobos shot and killed a 16-year-old boy, Alexandro Garcia, who was waiting for a bus to school. A jury had convicted Lobos of second-degree murder in February 1997 and he was sentenced to 15 years to life for the killing, which he committed within sight of the LAPD's Rampart Division headquarters.

In the 1998 Burlington arson trial, Lobos and Andrade were each charged with 12 counts of murder and one count of arson. They were charged with one count for each child and adult murdered plus two additional counts because Olga Leon, 32, and Rosalia Ruiz, 21, were both pregnant when they died inside the Burlington building.

In a twist to the case all charges against Andrade and Lobos were dropped in January 2007 due to 'insufficient evidence' to prove they actually ignited the fire. The case remains open.

A civil case related to the fire was settled in 1997 when insurance companies for the building's owner and managers--Richard I. Kaufman and Yale Management Services Inc.--agreed to pay $2 million to the survivors.

After attorneys' fees, some of the survivors got as little as $198.

ROSCOE 'FATTY' ARBUCKLE

Born March 24th, 1887 – died June 29th, 1933 age 46.

Roscoe Conkling "Fatty" Arbuckle was an American silent film actor, director, and screenwriter. He started at the Selig Polyscope Company and eventually moved to Keystone Studios, where he worked with Mabel Normand and Harold Lloyd as well as with his nephew, Al St John. He also mentored Charlie Chaplin, Monty Banks and Bob Hope, and brought vaudeville star Buster Keaton into the movie business. Arbuckle was one of the most popular silent stars of the 1910s and one of the highest-paid actors in Hollywood, signing a contract in 1920 with Paramount Pictures for $1,000,000 a year (equivalent to $16.6 million in 2024).

Arbuckle was the defendant in three widely publicized murder trials between November 1921 and April 1922 for the rape and manslaughter of actress Virginia Rappe.

Rappe had fallen ill at a party hosted by Arbuckle at San Franciso's St Francis Hotel in September 1921, and died four days later. A friend of Rappe accused Arbuckle of raping and accidentally killing her. The first two trials resulted in hung juries, but the third trial acquitted Arbuckle. The third jury took the unusual step of giving Arbuckle a written statement of apology for his treatment by the justice system.

Despite Arbuckle's acquittal, the scandal has mostly overshadowed his legacy as a pioneering comedian. He was publicly ostracized and was faced with the moral outrage of various groups such as the Lord's Day Alliance, the powerful Federation of Women's Clubs and even the Federal Trade Commission to curb, what they perceived as, Hollywood debauchery running amok and its effect on the morals of the general public. Arbuckle only worked sparingly through the 1920s. In a deal with Buster Keaton, Keaton promised to give him 35% of the Buster Keaton Comedies Co. profits. He later worked as a film director under the pseudonym William Goodrich. He was finally able to return to acting, making short two-reel comedies in 1932–33 for Warner Bros.

Arbuckle died in his sleep of a heart attack in 1933 at age 46.

WILLIAM DALE ARCHERD

Born 1912 – sentenced to death 1968, commuted to life in prison 1972, died in prison 1977.

William Archerd was fascinated by medicine and worked as a hospital attendant handling drugs. In 1940 and 1941 he was employed at Camarillo State Hospital in California working in the wards where insulin was prescribed for mental illness. He received 5years probation in 1950 for illegal possession of morphine. A second offence revoked the probation and he was sent to jail escaping in 1951. On being recaptured he was sent to San Quentin and freed on parole in late 1953.

He was married seven times in fifteen years with three of his wives dying from bouts of undefined mystery illnesses between 1956 and 1966. Some other friends and relatives suffered the same fate. When finally arrested Archerd was accused of murder by the use of insulin.

The list of Archerd's wives, relatives and acquaintances who died after manifesting symptoms of insulin poisoning is indeed striking.

The first was William Jones Jr., 34, in 1947, who died the day after Archerd paid a visit to his hospital sickbed. The motive, if any, is unknown.

The second-and certainly the weirdest case, was that of bride No. 4, Zella, 48, who died in 1956. Two months after their marriage. Archerd told police in the Los Angeles suburb of Covina, two burglars had entered their house with guns in one hand, hypodermic needles in the other. Archerd said they injected both himself and Zella with a drug and then made off with $500 in cash, overlooking jewellery and other valuables. Archerd was unaffected by the unsought medication, but his wife went from convulsions into a coma and died. If they found anything odd in such a story, Covina police found no cause for investigation or arrest.

The third unfortunate, in 1958, was Juanita Plum Archerd, wife No. 5. Two days after their marriage in Las Vegas, Juanita was taken to the hospital, suffering from what was described as an overdose of barbiturates. She died the next day of a condition that looked strangely like insulin poisoning.

Frank Stewart, 54, was the fourth, in 1960. Taken to the hospital after apparently faking a fall in an airport rest room to collect on insurance, Stewart was visited by the ever-solicitous Archerd and then died after the usual convulsions that night. Archerd, recipient of the insurance, tried but failed to collect.

At about this time, Archerd's brother Everett died at his job, and Archerd and his mother were entrusted with $5,000 in his will for Everett's son, Burney, age 15.

In August 1961, Burney was taken to the hospital, where he reported that he had been hit by a car, though an investigation showed no such accident had taken place. Burney nonetheless remained in the hospital, where he was visited by his kindly Uncle William. He died soon thereafter. The symptoms were those of insulin poisoning.

Archerd's mother, co-trustee of the $5,000, herself died three weeks later of causes not disclosed by the investigation.

In April 1965, Archerd—calling himself James Lynn Arden—took Bride No. 7. Marriages Nos. 1, 2, 3, and 6 ended in divorce or annulment. His new wife was Mary Brinker-Post, 59, a widow with grown children, a successful author of short stories and novels for women and a public relations professional.

Mary was admitted in a coma to Pomona Valley Community Hospital in November 1966 and died next day of hypoglycemia—shortage of blood sugar.

Her death was one coincidence too many, and the Los Angeles County sheriff's department finally put eight detectives on the trail of Archerd, who had been convicted of peddling narcotics in the early '50s, more than 25 years previously, when he had worked as an orderly in the insulin-shock ward at the Camarillo State mental hospital.

On March 6th, 1968 Archerd was convicted on three counts of murder and given the death sentence. He was the first American killer convicted of using insulin as the murder weapon. His sentence was affirmed by California's Supreme Court in December 1970 and then commuted on appeal in 1972 to life in prison. He died in prison in 1977 age 65

PEDRO ARIAS

Born 1963- sentenced to death February 22nd, 1990.

On June 6th, 1979, Daniel Rypich, then 64 years old, and his wife Lucy were returning to their car after buying groceries in Sacramento when Pedro Arias, then 16 years old, grabbed Daniel around the neck from behind and held a knife to his back. He told Daniel to hand over all his cash or he would be killed. Daniel gave Arias $223. As Arias fled from the scene, a rust-coloured Chevrolet, license CEA 026, picked him up and sped away. A witness provided the police with the license number. Arias was arrested driving the same car the next day. Daniel never saw Arias's face, but two days after the robbery, his wife Lucy positively identified him from a photo line-up. She also emphatically identified him at the juvenile court proceedings arising from the incident. Beatrice Arriaga, Arias's girlfriend at the time, testified he told her "he got $200 from the old man" in Sacramento.

Around 11 p.m. on August 14th, 1981, James Barger was in the driveway of his house on Priscilla Lane. He heard a shot. Moments later, a car turned onto Priscilla Lane from Fruitridge Road. Arias, wearing a long coat, emerged from the back of the car. A female voice shouted, "There he is," whereupon Arias took a rifle from the car and fired into the yard of the corner house, 5571 Priscilla Lane. He then ran in the direction of the house and disappeared from Barger's view. Barger then heard the sound of gunfire five more times.

Barger entered his own house, told his wife to call the police, and returned outside with a .45 automatic. Someone inside the car shouted, "Get out of here," and the vehicle sped away. As it did so, Arias, who was still carrying the rifle, ran past Barger. Barger levelled his pistol at defendant's back and ordered him to freeze. Arias dropped the rifle and approached Barger, who instructed him to lie down in the street and await the police. A crowd of Black and Hispanic youths assembled in between the two, Arias got up and walked around the corner onto Fruitridge Road. Barger followed, keeping him in sight.

When the police arrived, Barger pointed out Arias in the crowd. Arias was arrested, handcuffed, and placed in a police car with another suspect in the incident. In their conversation, which was tape-recorded, Arias threatened to return and kill Barger.

When police entered the back-yard of 5571 Priscilla Lane, they found Andrew Benanato cowering under a bush. Spent shell casings and bullet strafe marks were discovered nearby. What was the relationship between him and Arias is unknown but it wasn't a happy one.

In the early afternoon of July 22nd, 1985, Ernest Daniels, a plainclothes narcotics officer, was parked in an unmarked vehicle on 38th Street at 22nd Avenue, near a house where drug activity was suspected. Arias's car stopped in front of the house. Being suspicious, Daniels emerged from his own car, displayed his badge, announced his identity as a police officer, and approached Arias's car. Arias drove away on 38th Street, a narrow residential road. Daniels gave chase, activating his siren and red light. Another police car tried to cut Arias off at 20th Avenue but was forced to swerve aside to avoid a collision. Arias then ran a stop sign at 21st Avenue and violated a yield sign at 19th Avenue. The pursuit ended at 16th Avenue, where Arias was arrested for resisting an officer. Two locking-blade knives were found on his person.

Late on the evening of February 16th, 1987, Richard Lam was working as assistant manager of the Chief's Auto Parts Store on Broadway in Sacramento. John Geddes was the only other employee in the store. Arias and another man entered, inquired about a part, and left. An hour later, they returned, pressed knives into the backs of Lam and Geddes and ordered them to lie down. Arias attempted to open the register, and when unable to do so, ordered Lam to open it which he did. Arias took the bills from the register and left. Meanwhile, his accomplice tore loose a television set that was bolted to a shelf and carried it out of the store.

On May 23rd, 1987, the evening of the Beacon robbery and murder, Arias and James Valdez went to a house on 20th Avenue to negotiate a $20 purchase of heroin. Among the persons present, according to Valdez, were "this lady" and "this guy named Joe." Valdez indicated he had only $15 and asked for partial credit. The lady refused. Instead, she handed Valdez a bag containing $10 worth of heroin. Valdez immediately injected this entire amount, telling Arias, "Well, I tried to help you, home boy, but I can't. All I got is a dime."

Arias became angry and ran toward the lady, threatening her with a knife. Joe got up to meet him and the two men fell to the floor and a struggle ensued. Joe was cut on the hand while defending himself from Arias's knife. When the lady screamed for Valdez to "do something," Valdez replied, "See, I told you, you should have gave us the dope." The lady handed Valdez another bag of narcotics. Valdez then approached Arias, who was still struggling with Joe, and said, "Hey, Pete, Pete, I got the dope." Arias stopped fighting, jumped up, snatched "all the dope and money," and ran out to the car.

With Arias driving the Plymouth, the two men arrived at the Beacon gasoline station at 44th Street and Fruitridge Road. The station includes a small convenience store. Two clerks, Tina Cheatam and John Waltrip, were on duty inside the store. Each clerk was responsible for a particular cash register and had the only key for that register. Also in the store was Lawrence Galvin, a district manager for the Beacon chain.

Around 8 p.m., Waltrip and Galvin were in the rear of the store, restocking the display of cold beverages. Waltrip, who was out of sight in the storage cooler, was passing merchandise through to Galvin, who was standing in front of the beverage cases. Arias and Valdez entered the store and walked toward the beverage cases. Valdez grabbed a 12-pack of beer and ran out of the store.

As Cheatam yelled for Valdez to stop, Arias grabbed her from behind and held a knife to her hip. Galvin began to move forward, and Arias told him to "freeze." and then ordered Cheatam to open her register. Cheatam was standing in front of Waltrip's register and tried to tell Arias she did not have the key to open it. He grew angrier, shouted obscenities, and continued to demand she open it.

Cheatam became hysterical, pounded hopelessly on Waltrip's register, and indicated to Arias that the "other clerk" would have to open it. Arias told her to, "Get the guy out here." Cheatam then screamed "several times" for Waltrip who emerged from the back room and said, "Here I am." Approaching from behind Arias, Waltrip stepped up onto the slightly elevated register area, causing the floor to creak. At this moment, according to Galvin, Arias turned, placed his left hand on Waltrip's right shoulder, pulled Waltrip toward him, drew back his right elbow to a 90-degree angle, and "very, very violently" thrust the knife into Waltrip's stomach. Waltrip doubled over and stumbled into the store's back office.

Meanwhile, Cheatam had managed to open her own register. Arias reached in and took the cash out of the till. In doing so, he triggered a hidden camera, which sequentially photographed the rest of the holdup. While the robbery was in progress, Edgar Calderon entered to pay for some gas, but Calderon withdrew when Arias t told him to "get the hell out." After cleaning out Cheatam's register, Arias brandished the knife at Galvin and forced him to lie down on the floor and then left the store.

Outside, Valdez was waiting in the passenger seat of the Plymouth, anxious to depart with the stolen beer. When Arias approached the car at a run, Valdez slid behind the wheel and Arias got in the passenger side. They sped away northbound on 44th Street. At the first intersection, Valdez started to turn right, but Arias told him it was a dead end so Valdez swerved back onto 44th Street. As he did so, Edgar Calderon, who was keeping the vehicle in sight, saw the passenger door fly open.

Back at the store Galvin locked the front door and entered the back office. There Waltrip was lying unconscious with the telephone in his hand. Galvin took the telephone and called the police.

Waltrip died of his wound later during emergency surgery. The cause of death was loss of blood. The knife had penetrated to a depth of nine or ten inches, passing completely through his abdominal wall and liver and piercing the front wall of the aorta.

Arias and Valdez returned to the Lemon Hill house and divided the money from the robbery, $90. Valdez heard Arias tell Gomez he had robbed the Beacon store. Gomez's friend Sonya White also overheard this comment and Arias implied that White should forget what she had heard.

Later the same evening, Arias and Victor Trejo went on a quest to obtain drugs. They were driving a van owned by Trejo's father. Arias had avoided using the Plymouth because it was "a little warm." At one point, Trejo wanted to return the van to his father, but

Arias pulled a knife and held it to Trejo's neck and told Trejo he did not want to have to make a "movita," or move, on Trejo, "like he already did to someone else." Trejo complied with Arias's demand to continue on in the van.

Trejo eventually dropped Arias off at the Lemon Hill house. At Arias's request, Valdez then went with him in the Plymouth to obtain still more drugs. Late that night, Arias discussed the Beacon Store robbery and told Valdez, "I think I killed somebody."

The next day, Ariast and Valdez walked to a nearby store and bought a newspaper. The paper contained an account of the Beacon Store robbery, including a description of the red Plymouth. Arias read the story and told Valdez "The guy died at the gas station."

When they returned Arias moved the Plymouth into the backyard of the Lemon Hill house, where the police later found it. Valdez asked him what he had done with the knife he used to kill Waltrip. Arias went to the kitchen and grabbed a knife, which Valdez described as about 12 inches long. Valdez took the knife and broke it up with his hands. Valdez then made plans to leave the Lemon Hill house immediately.

Sometime after the Beacon Store incident, Arias met his mother, Adeline Rodriguez, in a park. He told her he had robbed the Beacon Store and killed a man there, though he "didn't mean to do that." According to Arias, somebody had grabbed his shoulder from behind, and he turned and stabbed him.

He said he did not want to go to prison and needed time to get away and think. A couple of days later, Arias called Rodriguez and asked for money.

About two weeks after the Beacon Store incident, Valdez saw Arias who told Valdez, "Don't worry about nothing, home boy, I ride my own beef." He acted paranoid, said homicide detectives were at his house, and indicated he wanted to go to Mexico.

On June 5th, 1987, 13 days after the Beacon incident, Arias borrowed a brown 1970's Plymouth owned by Nelda Smith. About 3 p.m. that day, Judy N. was driving eastbound in her 1986 Honda on highway 50, a freeway in Sacramento. Arias, driving the brown Plymouth, came into her lane from the right and bumped the right front fender of her car. She signalled defendant to pull over, and they both parked on the shoulder just west of the 51st Street overpass.

After they inspected the minor damage, Arias told her that he had no insurance. Ms. N. suggested they exchange names and telephone numbers. She got back into her car to obtain writing paper and a pen. She offered Arias the pen, which he refused. She then used the pen to write her own name and telephone number, as well as the license number of his car. She tore off the license number and began to hand him the remainder of the paper. As she did so, he reached in the driver's window pointing a revolver at her.

Arias demanded Ms. N.'s purse and wallet. She said she had only 23 cents with her and opened her wallet to show that it contained no cash. He asked if she had automatic teller machine (ATM) cards, and she acknowledged that she did. She then complied with his instructions to bring her purse and wallet, follow him, and get into the passenger seat of the brown Plymouth. Arias got in the driver's side and placed the gun in his lap, pointed at her. He asked the location of the nearest machine that would accept her ATM card. She mentioned the "college campus" nearby and said she would try to direct him from the next freeway exit, at 59th Street.

Arias began to drive, meantime instructing Ms. N. to remove all her clothing below her waist. He said this was to keep her from trying to run away. She took off her shoes, jeans, pantyhose, and underpants.

Arias left highway 50 at the 59th Street exit, but then doubled back westbound on South Street, which runs parallel to the south side of the freeway. Near the intersection with 55th Street, he parked and told Ms. N. they were going to return to her car. At his direction, she put her jeans and shoes back on, and he put her underpants in his pocket. The two then climbed over a chain link fence and clambered down a steep embankment to the freeway and to her vehicle.

Arias directed Ms. N. to get behind the wheel, again remove her jeans and shoes, and begin driving. She did so. He asked about her husband and children, the family's financial status, and their credit and ATM cards. Because she feared for their safety, she told defendant falsely that she had no children. She also advised, among other things, that she and her husband had ATM cards for Golden One Credit Union and Sacramento Savings. Arias said, "We'll go to the

Golden One. I know where there's a Golden One." He began to direct her, by freeway and surface road, in a south-westerly direction through Sacramento.

As they drove, Arias demanded Ms. N.'s watch and wedding ring. She handed them over. Arias pulled out her underpants, began to fondle them, and asked questions about her sex life. While they were en route, they passed a number of police cars, and this caused Arias to become more and more agitated. On several occasions, he advised Ms. N. to drive carefully and avoid attracting attention. Each time, he warned that he had killed before, and it would not bother him to kill again. He indicated that the killing had occurred about two weeks before, and he asked if she had read about it in the newspaper.

At length, they were travelling westbound on Florin Road, and they seemed to be headed toward the Golden One branch at Florin Road and interstate 5. Before they reached that location, however, Arias instructed Ms. N. to turn left. When she said, "I thought we were going to the credit union," he replied with a smirk, "We'll get there."

Eventually they crossed the Sacramento River into Yolo County. In a rural area, they left the paved highway and travelled on a dirt road. Finally they arrived at an isolated clearing. At Arias's direction, Ms. N. got out, went to the back of the car, placed her hands on the bumper, and leaned over. Arias sexually assaulted and raped her. (graphic details of this are in the court papers but add nothing to the basic case so I have not included them.) During the assault she lost an earring.

Afterwards Arias and Ms. N. then returned to her car. He opened the trunk, got out her purse, and removed ATM cards for two different Golden One accounts. At his direction, she told him the personal identification numbers for these cards, and he wrote the numbers down. He then tied her hands with his belt and put a gag in her mouth before he ordered her into the trunk.

From inside the trunk, Ms. N. felt the car return to the paved road, re-cross the bridge into Sacramento County, and continue. After a while, the car stopped for several minutes, then began moving again. When it stopped a second time, Arias got out and opened the trunk. They were back in Yolo County, at the isolated clearing where the sexual assaults had occurred.

Arias ordered Ms. N. out of the trunk and untied her hands. At his direction, she put her T-shirt back on and got behind the wheel. He told her to remove the gag. In doing so, she dislodged her other earring.

Ms. N. then began driving back toward Sacramento, as he instructed. Before they reached the bridge, he ordered her to stop on the shoulder. He said he had already gotten money from one of her ATM cards, and he showed her the receipt. He asked where her Sacramento Savings card was. She said it had been on the passenger seat when their collision occurred and must have fallen on the floor of the car. At his direction, she put her jeans back on, searched for the card, and found it. He asked how much money he could get with this card, and she said $900.

Arias noticed she was wearing a gold necklace with a Disneyland pendant. He told her to take off the necklace and put it around his neck. Her hands trembled, so much she could not work the clasp. Arias unfastened the necklace himself.

Arias ordered Ms. N. to remove her jeans again and resume driving. He directed Ms. N. to the Golden One branch located in a shopping centre at Mack Road and Franklin Boulevard in Sacramento. He ordered her to park and wait. He cradled the revolver in his left arm and draped his T-shirt over it. He then emerged from the car and got into the ATM line. Ms. N. noticed a security guard nearby and a chance to escape. Still naked from the waist down, she snatched her jeans, got out of the car, pointed to Arias and shouted that he had a gun. She then ran into a nearby hardware store.

Around 6 p.m. on June 5th, 1987, Linda McCord had parked her yellow 1974 Ford pickup next to the same Golden One ATM at Mack Road and Franklin Boulevard. She did some grocery shopping, returned to the truck with her purchases, placed them in the truck bed, and got into her vehicle. As she started her engine, she heard a loud thump and felt the truck move. She looked around and saw a man with a gun in the bed of the truck. At the same time, she heard voices shouting, "He has a gun," and saw people ducking behind cars. The man told her to get out of her truck. He then came around to the driver's window brandishing the gun. He opened the door and slid into the driver's seat. As he did so, McCord escaped out the passenger door, leaving her keys in the ignition.

Shortly after 6 p.m. on June 5th, 1987, Sacramento police officers Steven Spillmer and Henry Luckie, in separate cars, were parked in the Mack Road shopping centre. A man approached and told the officers about a naked woman and someone with a gun near the Golden One ATM. Spillmer responded. When he reached the ATM, witnesses told him that the gunman had fled northward on Franklin Boulevard. Spillmer drove off that way soon spotted a yellow pickup travelling erratically at high speed. Spillmer followed with his siren and blue lights on, keeping the pickup in sight through several turns until the truck hit a curb in a residential neighbourhood and rolled over. Other officers arrived and Arias was arrested in the truck, which belonged to Linda McCord. Various items of Ms. N.'s property, including the ATM cards, were found on his person at the scene. A loaded handgun was also recovered from the truck.

Arias was taken to a hospital for treatment of injuries sustained in the rollover. Ms. N. was taken to the same hospital for a medical examination. While there, she saw Arias and identified him as her assailant. She identified him again at his trial.

Police recovered $423 in cash from under the mattress of Arias's hospital bed. Also retrieved from his person or clothing at the hospital were Ms. N.'s necklace, watch, and wedding ring, an ATM receipt on Ms. N.'s Golden One account, and a live .22-calibre bullet.

An employee of Golden One confirmed that between 5:21 p.m. and 5:24 p.m. on June 5th, 1987, ATM withdrawals of $200 each, the maximum daily allowance, were made from two separate accounts belonging to Ms. N. and her husband. The cash was supplied in $20 bills. The withdrawals were made from the Florin Road branch, and the person who made them was videotaped. Six unsuccessful attempts to withdraw money from the same accounts were made at the Mack Road ATM between 6:18 p.m. and 6:21 p.m. the same day. These transactions were also videotaped. Neither Ms. N. nor her husband used their Golden One ATM cards on June 5th, 1987.

Arias's fingerprints were found on the brown Plymouth. They were also found on several places on Ms. N.'s Honda. Her earring was located at the remote Yolo County location she described as the site of the sexual assaults.

Arias was convicted of first degree murder of Herbert J. Waltrip, kidnapping, seven sex crimes and three robberies. He was sentenced to death on February 22nd, 1990. Arias died in prison from COVID complications in 2020.

DAVID WAYNE ARISMAN

Born 1948 – sentenced to death January 15th, 1999, died in prison September 5th, 2009 age 61.

Redonda Beach, 26, had only set up her estate agent business called 'Answers' at 856 Manhattan Beach Blvd a fortnight before Arisman, 47, walked in and asked for a list of real estate listings on April 25th, 1997. As she produced them he pulled a gun and forced her into a back room where he tied her up and sexually assaulted her.

A delivery interrupted him when deliverymen Michael Trinidad and Richard Moriel arrived with furniture for the new office. Arisman held them up with the gun, tied them up and for some reason shot Trinidad in the heart. Redonda Beach managed to free herself and fought off Arisman and ran out into the front office shouting toward a parking officer outside.

Arisman fled but was soon cornered by a police dog, caught and arrested. He was sent to trial where it was revealed that he was a parolee with a history of violence. He was given the death sentence on January 15th, 1999 and sent to San Quentin State Prison where he died on September 5th, 2009 age 61 from natural causes.

TROY ADAM ASHMUS

Born March 26th, 1962 – sentenced to death July 25th, 1986.

About 4 o'clock on the afternoon of Saturday, May 19th, 1984, Marcella (Marcie) D., who was seven years of age, rode to Howe Park in Sacramento on her bicycle. There she met her brother Arby, age 10, who was responsible for her, and Arby's friend Ernesto (P.J.) G., age 9. Arby and P.J. walked to a pond to fish from a dock, and Marcie went to play with some friends within a few feet of the boys.

Troy Ashmus, who was 22 years old, approached Arby and P.J. as they were fishing. For the past few days he had been camping in an area in adjacent Santa Anita Park called Stoner's Pit, a site that was filled with litter but also secluded and covered with vegetation. He gave the boys advice with their fishing, and stayed nearby.

About 5 or 5:30 p.m., Arby and P.J. walked to the park clubhouse. Marcie soon rode up. She said that she was going off to Santa Anita Park with Ashmus as he had told her that he knew of a duck's nest there, and that he would give her a duckling if any had hatched. The boys said that she should return in about an hour.

Ashmus and Marcie proceeded to Stoner's Pit. Once there, he subjected her to a fatal attack. He raped her and perhaps also penetrated her with some foreign object, making a very large tear through the length of her vagina to within a quarter of an inch of her rectum. He sodomized her, inflicting two small wounds in the anal or rectal tissue. He possibly committed oral copulation by inserting his penis into her mouth. He evidently ejaculated over her body. He stuffed material into her mouth and throat including two plastic bags, a piece of cellophane about six inches long and two to three inches wide, and a pair of red shorts she had been wearing; the bags were wedged side-by-side in separate tight wads deep in her throat with the cellophane in between; the shorts were tightly compressed within her mouth; the bags obstructed her throat and caused her to die by asphyxiation. Covering her naked body with a carpet remnant he had used for a sleeping mat during his stay at Stoner's Pit, he then fled the scene.

When Marcie did not return as she had been told, Arby and P.J. became concerned. They searched without success. Arby telephoned his father. He too searched without success. The police were called in. About 8:30 p.m., a neighbourhood man who was assisting the officers found Marcie's body. Within a few hours, Ashmus was arrested. He had fresh abrasions on at least one of his hands. It does not appear that the duck's nest of which defendant spoke had ever existed.

Although most of the basic facts were essentially undisputed, one was strongly contested: the intent to kill. The People sought to prove intent by evidence including the manner and means Asmus used to kill Marcie. By contrast, Ashmus, who took the stand himself, expressly denied intent. In his testimony, he generally confessed his culpability, admitting that he had lied in extrajudicial statements to the police and others in which he attempted to avoid responsibility and even tried to shift blame to his brother Tracy, who was three years younger. All the same, he asserted that Marcie's death was accidental.

He went to trial in July 1986 charged that on May 19th, 1984, he murdered Marcella D. in violation of Penal Code section 187. It was alleged that he committed the offense under the following special circumstances: (1) felony murder in the course of rape under Penal Code section 261, within the meaning of Penal Code section 190.2, subdivision (a)(17)(iii); (2) felony murder in the course of sodomy under Penal Code section 286, within the meaning of Penal Code section 190.2, subdivision (a)(17)(iv); and (3) felony murder in the course of a lewd or lascivious act on the person of a child under 14 years of age under Penal Code section 288, within the meaning of Penal Code

Trial was by jury. On July 25th, 1985 the jury returned verdicts finding Ashmus guilty as charged, determining the murder to be of the first degree, and found all the special circumstance allegations true. It subsequently returned a verdict of death. The court entered judgment accordingly, sentencing defendant to death for the murder and to full, separate, and consecutive middle terms of six years in prison for each of the three non-capital offenses.

In their case in aggravation, the People introduced evidence to prove that Ashmus suffered two felony convictions: the first, in 1981, for burglary in the second degree in violation of Penal Code sections 459 and 460, in Kern County; and the second, in 1985, for assault with intent to commit rape in violation of Penal Code section 220, in Sacramento County. They also presented evidence to establish the facts underlying the latter conviction. Lisa Cronin, the victim, testified that in the early hours of May 19th, 1984 -- the date of the crimes against Marcie -- defendant attacked her, and in fact bruised and sprained one of her arms; he announced his intent to commit rape; but he fled without accomplishing his purpose when bystanders came to her aid.

In his case in mitigation, Ashmus introduced evidence to generally describe his background and character, from before birth up until the time of trial. The testimony, given by lay witnesses as well as psychiatric and psychological experts, painted the following picture: Ashmus had suffered abuse and neglect from his earliest years at the hands of his father and mother; his parents had a troubled and unhappy marriage, which was dissolved. When he was about 17 or 18 years old; he was an emotionally and behaviourally disturbed child, youth, and adult; over the years, he had been cruel to animals and hurtful to his peers; he had experimented with drugs; he was friendless, angry, and refractory; and he may have experienced organic brain damage or impairment. Further, the evidence supported an inference that he may have been under the influence of some mental or emotional disturbance at the time of the crimes. It also showed that his burglary conviction arose from petty, nonviolent criminal conduct. In addition, it suggested that he would not be dangerous in prison if his life were spared.

In rebuttal, the People introduced evidence through the testimony of a psychologist, who opined that defendant had not, in fact, experienced organic brain damage or any impairment.

Ashmus died of COVID-19 complications on San Quentin death row on July 20th, 2020.

As an aside; The California Department of Corrections and Rehabilitation said at the time 'There are 925 inmates at San Quentin with active infections, with 402 new infections within the last two weeks. Another 36 infected inmates have been released and 1,112 inmates have recovered from being infected with the virus.'

On July 10th, 2020, Governor Gavin Newsom announced that some 8,000 prisoners would be released to try to contain the COVID-19 outbreak at state prisons. The governor's plan applied to low-level offenders with 180 days or less remaining in their sentences and those who were at risk of COVID-19-related complications.

DAVID EDWARD ATTIAS

Born May 6th, 1982 – found to be insane and sentenced to be detained in a mental hospital June 11th, 2002. Released on an outpatient treatment program September 4th, 2012.

On the evening of February 23rd, 2001, just after 11:00 p.m., UCSB student David Attias, the 18-year-old son of television director Dan Attias, drove his father's 1991 Saab 9000 down the 6500 block of Sabado Tarde Road at a speed of 50 to 65 miles per hour hitting parked cars and pedestrians. Four people were killed and a fifth was critically injured. According to a police statement, "All five victims were thrown forward, some being knocked out of their shoes."

According to witnesses, Attias got out of the vehicle and yelled "I am the Angel of Death!" He continued to taunt a growing crowd, until he was subdued by the first CHP officer to arrive on the scene. In the initial aftermath, it was unclear if Attias was affected by taking drugs, or if the attack was intentional. Blood tests later showed that he was under the influence of marijuana and Lidocaine, but neither were deemed significant to the incident.

Four people were killed at the scene: 20-year-old UCSB students Nicholas Bourdakis and Christopher Divis, 27-year-old Dan Francisco resident Elie Israel, and 20-year-old Santa Barbara City College student Ruth Levy. A fifth person, Albert Arthur Levy, 27, brother to Ruth, was critically injured but survived. His injuries consisted of crushed legs and a severely battered head, and he died in October 2016 after having seizures for years caused by the injury.

Attias was charged with four counts of murder, four counts of vehicular manslaughter with gross negligence, and five counts of felony driving under the influence. Residents of his hall told police and the campus paper that Attias had been known for his erratic behaviour, including stalking another student. Several students referred to him as "Crazy Dave" and "Tweaker."

The case received additional media attention because David Attias is the son of Dan Attias, a prominent Hollywood TV director. Attias pleaded not guilty by reason of insanity, and his trial sparked significant interest.

At trial on June 11th, 2002, Attias was convicted by a jury of four counts of second-degree murder. He was acquitted of driving under the influence. One week later, the same jury found that Attias was legally insane. This resulted in a sentence of up to 60 years at Patton State Hospital in San Bernardino.

A memorial to the victims was installed in Little Acorn Park. The park borders the intersection where Attias struck and killed them.

While at Patton Hospital, Attias was treated for substance abuse, bipolar disorder and pervasive developmental disorder. In May 2012, his lawyers asked the courts to transfer him from Patton to an outpatient psychiatric facility, stating he has his bipolar disorder under control. The news of this request prompted expressions of concern about his potential risk of relapse and danger to the public from survivors and the families of his victims at court hearings on this proposed action. Testimony was heard from mental health professionals. Attias was given a conditional release from Patton State and transferred to a supervised "unlocked outpatient treatment program" on September 4th, 2012 where he still resides.

JORJIK AVANESIAN

Born 1953 – sentenced to life imprisonment July 1st, 1999. Committed suicide by hanging May 14th, 2005.

The night before Jorjik Avanesian set his family's Glendale apartment on fire he told police he had pleaded with God to send him a dream to keep him from becoming a murderer.

But when he awoke before dawn on February 6th, 1996, with no overnight reply from God, he went ahead with plans to kill his wife and six children.

In an interview with Glendale police hours after the fire, he said he had planned to stab his youngest children to death to spare them the pain of the flames.

"I figured the little ones, they would suffer," Avanesian said through an interpreter. "I didn't want them to suffer."

Avanesian's wife, Turan, 37, and their six children, ages 4 to 17, died of smoke inhalation in the fire that engulfed their Harvard Street apartment in Glendale.

Avanesian was described by his defence attorney as "delusional," a man who thought his wife and children were tainted by drugs, despite no evidence to support those claims.

But prosecutors raised another motive for the killings: Avanesian's wife had refused to divorce him.

Avanesian described how the day before the fire, he bought a $2.50 axe and a 69-cent knife at a local store. He then filled a water container with gasoline at a filling station. He returned to his apartment and hid the gasoline and weapons.

Rising at 4 a.m. the next day he poured gasoline onto a kitchen towel and went into the room where his children and wife slept. He said he lit the towel and tossed it into the room.

"I wanted us all to die," Avanesian told police.

But when detectives pressed him about why he fled the apartment instead of perishing with his family as he had planned, he gave a rambling reply about being confused and "not thinking."

As homicide investigators had attempted to get him to explain why he wanted to kill his family, Avanesian talked instead about the Muslim regime giving drugs to Armenians in his former country of Iran.

Local drug dealers, he insisted, were also trying to control his family.

Investigator Dennis Smith of the Glendale Police Department testified he found traces of gasoline on a living room rug in the family's apartment.

Smith said he also found the axe and knife allegedly bought by Avanesian and tossed into a nearby laundry room. Fingerprints on the axe, Smith said, matched Avanesian's.

Witness Vickie Carrillo said she was at a Verdugo Road gas station on February 5th when she noticed Avanesian struggling at a gas pump with the water container. She assisted him, she said, then she drove off. After the fire the next day she recognized Avanesian on the TV news and notified the police.

Another prosecution witness, Nancy Flack, said she stepped outside her home about 5:45 a.m. on February 6th when she noticed Avanesian staring from across the street.

He later turned and calmly approached her showing her his burnt hands and asking for some oil. When she said she didn't have any, he walked away, she said.

By then, smoke had begun to curl out of the apartment complex round the corner in the next street.

Avanesian then went to the offices of Asre Emrooz, a Farsi Newspaper and told the owner that he had burnt his home down to scare his wife. He said he wanted a divorce and hoped to have her deported. He didn't mention the family inside the home when he set it on fire. When news of the deaths came through the paper notified the police and Avanesian was arrested.

Unanswered questions remain about the killings. Why did the family not flee the building? Why were three bodies found in the bathtub, another on the bathroom floor and three in the bedroom. All were burnt so much that forensic and pathology reports were very scant.

Avanesian was charged with seven counts of murder and one count of arson. He was sentenced to life imprisonment on July 1st, 1999, and hung himself from a bedsheet in the prison infirmary on May 14th, 2005.

ALEJANDRO AVILA

Born 1975 - sentenced to death July 22nd, 2005.

On July 15th, 2002, Samantha Runnion, age 5, was playing with a friend, Sarah Ahn, in her front yard when a man approached them asking for help in finding a lost dog. After a short conversation, he grabbed Samantha, forced her into his car, and drove away. Sarah was able to provide a portrait via a police artist of the abductor. A Hispanic male with a moustache, slicked back black hair and glasses between 25 and 35 years old who drove a green Honda car.
    A day later, Samantha's nude body was found 50 miles south in Cleveland National Forest. She had been sexually assaulted and strangled. Police said that the killer was "extremely sloppy" and had left behind "mountains of physical evidence connecting him to the crime".
    A tip off to the police gave Avila's name and he was arrested three days after the abduction. His DNA was found on Samantha's body, and her DNA was found in his car. Avila had previously visited his girlfriend in the condominium complex where Samantha lived and had been previously been acquitted of sexually molesting his girlfriend's daughter and her niece in 2001. Police found child pornography on Avila's laptop computer, and he had booked a motel room on the day of the murder, where it was believed that Samantha was killed. He could not account for his movements on the day she

disappeared and both his mother and sister with whom he lived testified that he came home very late that night.

Avila was charged with Samantha's murder on July 23rd, 2002. On May 16th, 2005, a jury returned a guilty verdict, and Avila was sentenced to death. He is incarcerated at San Quentin State Prison on death row.

MANUEL PINA BABBIT

Born May 3rd 1949 - executed by lethal injection May 4th, 1999.

Manuel Pina "Manny" Babbitt was a U.S. Marine veteran of the Vietnam War who was convicted of the murder of a 78-year-old Leah Schendel during a burglary in Sacramento, California on December 18th 1980. Schendel died from a heart attack after Babbitt beat her and attempted to rape her. The following night, December 19th, 1980, Babbit attempted to rape another Sacramento woman, whom he grabbed and beat unconscious before robbing her of money and jewellery. Following his arrest, Babbit did not deny committing the crimes, but said he had no memory of what happened. However, several items of Mrs. Schendel's property were found in his possession, linking him to her murder. He was executed by the state of California by lethal injection at San Quentin State Prison, one day after his 50th birthday.
Babbitt had been wounded at the bloody 1968 Battle of Khe Sanh in Quang Tri Province, South Vietnam and as part of his defence, he claimed he suffered from Post-Traumatic Stress Disorder (PTSD) which he claimed caused him to commit his crimes and to later lose all memories of those crimes.
One year before his execution, whilst on death row, Babbitt was awarded a Purple Heart medal for the wounds he had received at the Battle of Khe Sanh.

Babbitt refused his last meal and asked that the $50 allotted for it be given to homeless Vietnam veterans. He was buried in his native Wareham, Massachusetts, on May 10th, 1999, with full military honours.

The movie Last Day of Freedom, nominated for an Oscar in 2016, depicts his brother's narrative of the events that led to Babbitt's execution.

STANLEY DEAN BAKER

Born 1948 – sentenced to life in prison 1970, released in 1985.

At three o'clock in the afternoon of Saturday, 11th July 1970, a man out fishing on the banks of the Yellowstone River in Montana snagged a human body on the end of his line. He drove in shock to the nearest ranch to telephone the police, and Deputy Bigelow, who was, stationed at the entrance to Yellowstone National Park, responded to the call.

With the aid of some local men, the deputy waded into the turbulent river and dragged the body to shore. Although accustomed to routine drowning cases, Bigelow knew immediately that this was a murder. The head of the body was missing.

Bigelow called Sheriff Don Guitoni, who drove Coroner Davis to the scene. All three men crouched over the body, which was clad only in shorts. It was that of a male. Apart from the missing head, the arms had also been severed at the shoulders and the legs chopped off at the knees. The abdomen and chest were covered with stab wounds, with a particularly large ugly hole in the chest.

The coroner looked shocked when he concluded his examination. 'I never saw anything like it,' he said grimly. 'The poor fellow's been stabbed about twenty-five times and I figure he's been in the water about a day. He was a young fellow, probably in his early twenties. There's one other thing,' he said.

'The heart is missing!' The chest had been cut open and the heart removed.

For the sheriff it was a major headache. All normal means of identifying the body - the head and hands, had been deliberately removed. But why the butchery of the rest of the body? Why cut off the legs? Why remove the heart?

The only thing it suggested was that it was some form of cult murder. The Sharon Tate case had grabbed the headlines, and copy-cat killings were going on all over the USA.

The torso was taken by ambulance to the morgue in Livingston for a proper autopsy to be carried out whilst police sent details of the victim to Wyoming and other neighbouring states. It was impossible to tell where the body had been dumped in the river. The Yellow stone passed through Wyoming before entering Montana and the National Park. Although police searched the river and along its banks for many miles, no traces of the missing limbs were found.

The results of the autopsy indicated that the victim had been stabbed twenty-seven times with a sharp-pointed blade of at least five inches in length. The removal of the head and limbs had been crudely performed, possibly with the knife used to inflict the stab wounds. The victim was in his early twenties and had been dead for twenty-four hours when found. Police had to wait until someone was reported missing.

Two days later on the Monday morning a teletype message came into the sheriff's office in

Livingston, concerning a missing person who resembled the description of the torso. James Michael Schlosser, aged twenty-two, had been reported missing from the town of Roundup, a hundred miles away, that same morning.

Schlosser had set out on the Friday to drive to Yellowstone Park in his Opel Kadett sports car, but had not turned up for work on the following Monday. When his office colleagues got in touch with his landlady, they discovered that the popular young social worker had not returned from the trip.

Schlosser was described as being six feet tall and weighing two hundred pounds. The age, height and weight fitted the torso. Sheriff Guitoni put out an alert for sightings of his Opel Kadett car, which might have been dumped in the area. It was a 1969 vehicle, yellow, with black racing stripes.

An hour later that same car was in a collision with a pick-up truck on a dirt road in Monterey County, California, just a few miles from the Pacific Ocean. The car had been travelling at speed on the wrong side of the road. The truck suffered only a dented bumper, but the car was a write-off. The driver of the truck was a businessman from Detroit on holiday. He got out of his truck and approached the car, from which two large young men emerged. Both men were typical Californian hippies, with long hair and beards.

One was blond, the other dark. The blond man was about six feet tall and very powerfully built, with shoulder-length golden hair. He wore a leather waistcoat and bell-bottom trousers, topped with an

Army fatigue jacket. His companion wore cowboy boots and a green Army field jacket. The businessman might have expected trouble, but the pair were friendly.

The businessman wanted to exchange driver's licences, but neither man had one, so he took the registration number of their vehicle and suggested he should drive them both to the nearest telephone so the police could be notified of the accident. The pair were agreeable to this and got into his truck. But when he drove into a service station in the town of Lucia, both men got out and ran off into nearby woods.

The businessman phoned the police and told them about the incident, giving the registration number of the other vehicle. It was that of the car belonging to the missing James Schlosser, and the California Highway Patrol were alerted to keep an eye out for the two men, wanted in connection with a homicide.

Patrolman Randy Newton was out cruising the Pacific Coast Highway when he got the call over his radio, and he turned off into a dirt side-road, figuring that the two fugitives could not have got far.

He came on the suspects walking along the road just two miles out of Lucia, trying to hitch a lift. The two men had no identification, but readily admitted having been the two men in the Opel Kadett involved in the accident. Newton arrested both men and radioed for assistance. When fellow officers arrived, the two suspects were handcuffed and advised of their rights.

The blond man seemed anxious to talk identifying himself as Stanley Dean Baker, aged twenty-three, and his companion as Harry Allen Stroup, aged twenty, Baker said they were both from Sheridan, Wyoming, and had been travelling together since 5th June, hitching lifts when they could.

They were searched, and in Baker's pockets police found small lengths of bone. Officer Newton studied them curiously and asked Baker what they were.

Baker told him, 'They ain't chicken bones. They're human fingers.' Then he added, memorably and in typically American phraseology, 'I have a problem. I'm a cannibal.

Both men were taken to the police station in Monterey with Baker continuing to talk in the patrol car about his compulsion to eat human flesh. He claimed to have developed a taste for it after having electric shock treatment for a nervous disorder when he was seventeen, and referred to himself as 'Jesus'.

At the police station Detective Dempsey Biley took over the questioning. Baker almost boasted of how he had killed the owner of the Opel Kadett, saying Stroup had not been with him at the time. He and Stroup had split up when they reached Big Timber, a few miles from Livingston, because Baker had managed to hitch a ride with James Schlosser.

When Schlosser had said he was going to the Yellowstone Park for the weekend, Baker had asked to go along, and the two men had set up camp for the night close to the Yellowstone River.

In the middle of the night Baker had crept over to his sleeping companion and shot him twice in the head with a .22 pistol he habitually carried. Then he had cut up the body into six parts, removing the head, arms and legs. When asked what he had done with the dead man's heart, Baker replied: 'I ate it.'

He explained that he had cut off the dead man's fingers to have something to chew on, and dumped the remainder of the body in the river, along with the pistol, before driving off in Schlosser's car.

Later he had met up with Harry Stroup along the road and offered him a lift. He insisted that Stroup had not been involved in the Schlosser murder.

Both men were searched thoroughly and among Baker's possessions was a recipe for LSD and a paperback book called The Satanic Bible, which was a handbook of devil-worship with instructions on how to conduct a black mass.

Baker described the location of the camp where he had killed Schlosser, and when police officers located it and searched it, they found evidence that murder had indeed taken place at that spot. The earth was splattered with human bone fragments, teeth, skin and a severed human ear.

The pair were taken before a judge in California and waived extradition. Subsequently they were flown back to Montana, where they were arraigned before District Judge Jack Shamstrom on 27th July. The pair were remanded in Park County jail, but on 4th August Judge Shamstrom approved a motion that Baker be sent to Warm Springs State Hospital for psychiatric evaluation. Harry Stroup had remained silent throughout, apparently guilty of nothing more than having befriended a homicidal maniac and devil-worshipper. Those short lengths of bone found on Baker were sent to a pathologist for examination and proved to be bones from a human right index finger.

The case was grim enough, but Baker was not finished talking. According to his statement, he had been recruited by Satanic cultists from a college campus in his home state of Wyoming. An alleged member of the homicidal "Four Pi movement," Baker had sworn allegiance to the cult's master -- known to intimates as the "Grand Chingon" -- and he had committed other slayings on the cult's behalf. There had been human sacrifices, he reported, in the Santa Ana Mountains, south of Los Angeles.

Displaying supposed cult tattoos, Baker also confessed his participation in the April 20th, 1970 murder of Robert Salem, a 40-year-old lighting designer in San Francisco. Salem had been stabbed 27 times and nearly decapitated, his left ear severed and carried away in a crime that Baker attributed to orders from the Grand Chingon. Slogans painted on the walls in Salem's blood -- including "Zodiac" and "Satan Saves" -- were meant to stir up panic in an atmosphere already tense from revelations in the Manson murder trial.

Baker, 22, and Stroup, 20, were returned to Montana on July 20th to stand trial. Convicted of murder, both were sentenced to prison, where Baker continued his efforts on behalf of the cult. Authorities reported that he actively solicited other inmates to join a Satanic coven, and full moons seemed to bring out the worst causing him to howl like an animal.

He sometimes threatened prison guards, and was relieved of homemade weapons on eleven separate occasions.

Stanley Baker was paroled in 1985 in Wyoming with his whereabouts remaining confidential to the parole board. He died in 1994.

Harry Stroup was given a short sentence of ten years and released in two. He continued a life of crime and was serving a sentence of five years for drug possession when he died aged 69 in 2019.

ROBERT JOHN BARDO

Born January 2nd 1970 – sentenced to life in prison without parole on December 20th, 1991.

Robert John Bardo is an American man convicted for the July 18th, 1989, murder of American actress and model Rebecca Schaeffer, whom he had stalked for three years.

Bardo was the youngest of seven children. His mother was Korean, and his father Philip was a non-commissioned officer in the United States Air Force. The family moved frequently and eventually settled in Tucson, Arizona, in 1983.

Bardo reportedly had a troubled childhood, being abused by one of his siblings and was placed in foster care after he had threatened to commit suicide. The family had a history of mental illness, and he was diagnosed with bipolar disorder.

At the age of 15, Bardo was institutionalized for a month to treat emotional problems. He dropped out of Pueblo Magnet High School in the ninth grade and began working as a janitor. In the eighteen months prior to Schaeffer's murder, Bardo had been arrested three times on charges that included domestic violence and disorderly conduct. His neighbours also said that he had exhibited strange and threatening behaviour toward them.

Prior to developing an obsession with Schaeffer, Bardo had stalked child peace activist Samantha Smith. These attempts had ultimately failed to establish any contact with Smith.

Bardo had travelled to Maine to meet her, but a run-in with state police over a traffic offence had caused him such concern that he was drawing attention to himself that he was sufficiently discouraged to return home. Bardo had made future plans to stalk Smith until her death in a 1985 plane crash. Bardo claimed he then turned his attention towards pop stars Tiffany and Debbie Gibson, but neither obsession had resulted into stalking as he later admitted to police that he could not find a feasible way to carry out his plans in New York City.

After writing numerous letters to Schaeffer, Bardo attempted to gain access to the set of the CBS television series My Sister Sam, in which she played a starring role. He was denied entrance by security guards who encouraged him to return home. While Warner Brothers had a policy that executives and actors were to be notified about uninvited advances towards them, security later admitted that because Bardo had made very little fuss about the denied access and left when ordered, the encounter was considered too trivial to report to Schaeffer. Ultimately, Bardo obtained her home address via a detective agency, which in turn tracked it for him via California Department of Motor Vehicles records. On July 18th, 1989, Bardo confronted Schaeffer at her home, angry that she had appeared in a sex scene in the film Scenes from the Class Struggle in Beverly Hills; in his eyes, she had "lost her innocence" and become "another Hollywood whore".

After having been turned away by Schaeffer, Bardo stopped at a diner for breakfast, only to return to her apartment about an hour later. When Schaeffer opened the door, Bardo shot her in the chest and fled. He was spotted later that morning in Tucson wandering around aimlessly in traffic and was arrested.

Following his arrest, Bardo was housed in a sensitive needs unit (SNU) for inmates such as gang members, notorious prisoners and those convicted of sex crimes. During his trial, he claimed the U2 song "Exit" was an influence in the murder of Schaeffer, and the song was played in the courtroom as evidence (with Bardo lip-synching the lyrics).

Bardo was found guilty of first-degree murder and sentenced to life imprisonment without the possibility of parole.

Interestingly, Bardo carried a red paperback copy of The Catcher in the Rye when he murdered Schaeffer, which he tossed onto the roof of a building as he fled. He insisted that it was coincidental and that he was not emulating Mark David Chapman, who had also carried a copy of that novel with him when he shot and killed John Lennon on December 8th, 1980. Mark Chapman later claimed in interviews that he had received letters from Bardo before the murder of Schaeffer, in which Bardo inquired about life in prison.

As a consequence of Bardo's actions and his methods of obtaining Schaeffer's address, the U.S. Congress passed the Driver's Privacy Protection Act, which prohibits state Departments of Motor Vehicles from disclosing the home addresses of state residents. After the murder, the first anti-stalking state laws were enacted in the US, including California Penal Code 646.9.

On July 27th, 2007, Bardo was stabbed 11 times on his way to breakfast in the maximum-security unit at Mule Creek State prison in Amador County, California. Two inmate-made knives were found at the scene. He was treated at the UC Davis Medical Centre and returned to prison. The suspect in the attack was another convict, serving 82 years to life for second degree murder.

As of 2024, Bardo is serving his life sentence at the Avenal State Prison in Avenal, California.

JACK BARRON

Born 1962 – sentenced to three consecutive life terms without parole on April 15th, 2000.

From the beginning, there was something suspicious about the death of Irene Barron whose body was found in a bedroom at her Florin-area home in June 1992. She seemed to have just died in her sleep.

But, lacking evidence, no investigation was started and no suspect was arrested until more than three years later, after Jack Barron's two young children and his mother had also died one by one, under similar circumstances.

It was four and a half years later that Barron was arrested, tried and convicted of all their murders and jailed for 3 consecutive life terms.

It started on June 8th, 1992, when Barron telephoned his in-laws from a neighbour's home in south Sacramento.

"He said, 'You gotta get over here quick!' "His mother-in-law Norma Paget, 78, remembered when she took the call in her Citrus Heights home about 9 a.m.

"Why?" Paget asked, startled. "Why?"

"Irene's dead," Barron said curtly and hung up.

Paget and her husband, Jack, sped to 7724 Southbreeze Drive, where their daughter, Irene Barron, 34, had just been found dead on a water bed in the home's master bedroom.

In the months that followed, Jack and Irene Barron's two children -- Jeremy and Ashley, both 4 -- also died mysteriously in their beds at the same address. Then, in February 1995, after Jack had moved in with his mother, Roberta Butler, 52, she was discovered lifeless in her water bed in Benicia, Solano County.

Her death finally prompted an investigation that led to Jack Barron's arrest and convictions. He was assessed by psychiatrists and medical professionals who diagnosed that he was the first killer to suffer from Munchausen-by-Proxy, an illness where a person causes illness or death of a loved one to attain sympathy.

DONALD KEITH BASHOR

Born 15th April 1919 – executed by asphyxiation-gas in California on November 11th, 1957.

On the night of February 18th, 1955, an apartment occupied by three women at 215 South Carondelet Street in Los Angeles was entered while they slept and the sum of $87 was taken from their purses. On the same night, in an apartment at 271 South Carondelet, Karil Graham was beaten to death. The contents of her purse were found scattered on the floor when her body was discovered, and drawers in the kitchen and living room were open. In the opinion of the doctor who performed an autopsy, the multiple head injuries which the victim suffered were caused by repeated blows with a hard object which could have been a piece of lead pipe.

In May of 1956, Laura Lindsay was slain in her home, which was located about two blocks from the site of the previous killing. Her body, which was found at 8:30 a. m., was partially clothed, and there were various articles strewn over the floor. A palm print was discovered on a firewood store which was open, permitting entry from the outside, and it was subsequently determined that the print was made by Donald Bashor. An autopsy surgeon found that the victim had sustained several head wounds which, in his opinion, could have been produced by a hammer.

About two weeks later, the apartment of Lester Olson was entered at night, and his wallet, which contained a $50 bill and other money, was taken while he slept. Shortly after 2 a. m. on that night, two police officers on "stake-out duty" in the vicinity of Olson's apartment saw Bashor, who was barefoot and wearing gloves, standing in the courtyard of an apartment house. He was arrested, and a considerable amount of money was found on his person, including a $50 bill.

In response to questioning by the police, Bashor confessed that he had committed all of the crimes described above. He admitted that the two burglaries were committed in the night-time and that he was armed with a piece of lead pipe when he entered the apartment at 215 South Carondelet Street. With respect to the killing of Karil Graham, Bashor said that he entered the apartment through an unlocked door, and the victim, who was sleeping, awoke and screamed while he was looking for her purse. Bashor took a piece of lead pipe from his pocket and struck her on the head, when she continued to scream, he struck her several more times until she was quiet. He found her purse after a further search and took $20 from it. In confessing the killing of Laura Lindsay, Bashor stated that, armed with a hammer, he entered her home at night through the wood store into the living room. He walked through the house, looking for a purse or a wallet, and came to the bedroom where he saw a woman lying on the bed. When she awoke and started to rise, he took the hammer from his pocket and struck her on the head. She "didn't go down immediately," he said, and so he struck her several more times. She followed him across the room and fell after a struggle in which a table was knocked over. Then, continuing his search, Bashor found a purse from which he removed $25. Before leaving, he washed his hands in the bathroom and wiped the taps with a towel.

Four psychiatrists who were appointed by the court familiarized themselves with the circumstances of the crimes and examined Bashor before they testified that, in their opinion, he was sane when the offenses were committed.

Bashor was sent to trial, sentenced to death and executed at San Quentin on 11th November 1957 age 38. He is buried in Napa State Hospital Cemetery, California.

JASON VICTOR BAUTISTA

Born 1983 – sentenced to life in prison April 8th, 2005.

After killing his mother on January 15th, 2003, Jason Bautista, 20, a graduate of Paloma Valley High School in Menifee, cut off her head and hands to keep investigators from identifying her. The body was found dumped in the mountains off Ortega Highway.

The killing occurred in Riverside, but Orange County prosecutors took over the case because the body was found in Orange County.

Bautista, according to prosecutors, got the idea to cut off his mother's head and hands from an episode of HBO's gritty mob drama "The Sopranos."

The Riverside resident admitted killing his mother, Jane, 41, but claimed it was an act of "accidental self-defence" after she put him in a "life-threatening situation" by coming at him with a knife.

Bautista's bloody thumbprint, however, was found on his mother's throat, and her face was badly beaten.

Bautista, a one-time biochemistry student at Cal State San Bernardino, testified that after his mother was dead, he cut off her head and hands to hide her identity.

The head and hands were later found in a duffel bag in the family's Riverside home.

Bautista testified that his mother became abusive as her paranoia and mental illness got worse over time.

Assistant Public Defender Don Ronaldson told jurors that the abuse Bautista endured included beatings, taunts, threats with a knife and beatings with sticks and clubs, one of which resulted in a visit to an emergency room.

The mother's paranoia left the family homeless at times, as she believed neighbours turned against her and subjected them to abuse. They moved repeatedly and depended on other family members for handouts and financial help living off Jason's wage as a hotel clerk. The mother had no job or income with her second husband having left them.

About three months before her death, the mother had been relatively OK, but then got worse until Bautista said he could no longer tolerate it.

Prosecutors argued that her erratic behaviour cramped her son's lifestyle, and that he wanted to get rid of her.

Bautista's half-brother, Matthew Montejo, who was 15 years old when his mother was slain, testified for the prosecution, saying he did not help kill his mother, but helped dispose of her body.

He pleaded guilty to being an accessory to murder and testified for the prosecution and was sentenced to the 749 days he had already been in jail, and then freed. He testified that Bautista had planned to kill his mother by starting an argument so he could claim self-defence.

The defence attorney argued for a manslaughter charge but the judge insisted on first degree murder and the jury agreed returning a guilty verdict.

On February 4th, 2005, Bautista was sentenced to 25 years to life in prison.

DONALD JAY BEARDSLEE

Born May 13th, 1943. Executed by lethal injection in California January 19th, 2005.

In 1969, Donald Beardslee killed a 52-year-old woman he met in a St. Louis bar by stabbing her in the throat with a knife and leaving her in a bathtub to bleed to death. After serving seven years of an 18-year sentence for that killing, the former Air Force mechanic moved to California to be near his mother.

In 1981, Beardslee picked up a female hitchhiker, Rickie Soria, a drug addict and prostitute. She moved in with Beardslee and introduced him to her friends. One of them, 19-year-old Bill Forrester, claimed that he had been ripped off in a $185 drug deal involving two women, 23 year old Patty Geddling and 19 year old Stacey Benjamin.

Frank Rutherford, another friend of Soria's and a drug dealer portrayed as the group's ringleader, devised a scheme to entice Geddling and Benjamin to Beardslee's apartment, beat them and take any money they had on them. The day before, Beardslee sent Soria to buy duct tape to tie the women's hands when they arrived.

After the pair arrived at Beardslee's apartment Rutherford accidentally wounded Geddling so Beardslee, Soria and Forrester drove her to a remote site in San Mateo County, where Beardslee shot the young mother twice in the head with a sawn-off shotgun.

The next day, Beardslee, Soria and Rutherford, who had remained with Benjamin, used cocaine as they drove 100 miles to a secluded area in Lake County, north of San Francisco.

After the two men unsuccessfully tried to strangle Benjamin with wire Beardslee slit her throat with Rutherford's knife. Before leaving the body, the two men pulled down Benjamin's pants to make it appear that she had been raped.

Beardslee's phone number had been found near Geddling's body and when police called at his apartment he confessed and told them about Benjamin's killing and led them to her body. At the time of this offence, he was still on parole for the 1969 Missouri killing which made him eligible for the death penalty as a repeat offender.

At trial Rutherford was sentenced to life in prison without parole and died there in 2003. Soria pleaded no contest to second-degree murder and testified against Rutherford and Beardslee and was sentenced to 15 years and was paroled in 2015. Bill Forrester was acquitted of charges in the case and charges against a fourth person were dropped before trial. Beardslee was convicted of first-degree murder and sentenced to death.

The defence tried to appeal on the grounds of inadequate defence since the original lawyer had quit the case, and on the grounds of Beardslee having a mental defect due to a head injury from a falling tree in the Minnesota work farm accident when he was 21. Prosecutors noted that he was of above average intelligence although family members testified he had life-long trouble expressing emotion and previous prison records indicate diagnoses of schizophrenia.

He was executed on January 19th, 2005. Beardslee, aged 58, was the first prisoner to be executed in California since Governor Arnold Schwarzenegger took office. Schwarzenegger denied clemency to Beardslee, stating that "we are not dealing here with a man who is so generally affected by his impairment that he cannot tell the difference between right and wrong."

NORMAN BERNARD

Born 1951 – sentenced to life without parole on March 7th, 1984.

Norman Bernard wasa black drifter from Fayetteville, North Carolina, who attempted his first murder there on August 15th, 1983.

Accosting a drunken migrant worker, 58-year-old Manuel Diaz, Bernard shot him once in the head with a small-calibre pistol, and then, for some unknown reason, severed the victim's penis for good measure. Believing Diaz to be dead, which he was not, Bernard fled across country, winding up in Los Angeles, where he quickly resumed his activities.

On October 13th, 1983, Anthony Cody, a 34-year-old drifter, was shot and killed in L.A. with a small-calibre weapon. Precisely one month later, an elderly "John Doe" victim was killed on Skid Row with police ballistics naming the same gun.

The following day, November 14th, 52-year-old Milton Regzarrie was shot twice in the head, but he managed to survive his wounds and give the police a description of Bernard.

On November 20th, Bobby Joe Jones, 45, was killed in Bernard's final attack.

Arrested on November 21st whilst attempting to steal a car, the 32-year-old suspect led police on a tour of the shooting scenes, describing his crimes "in a matter-of-fact way." Bernard professed a desire "to help" homeless men, stating that he was "doing them a favour" by putting them out of their misery.

Surprised to learn that Manuel Diaz had lived through the attack in Fayetteville, and had identified him in a photo line-up, Bernard confessed that crime on November 28th.

Three months later, on March 7th, 1984, he pleaded guilty to three counts of murder "with special circumstances" in Los Angeles and was sentenced to a term of life in prison without parole.

KENNETH ALESSIO BIANCHI

Born May 22nd, 1951 – sentenced to life in prison.

Kenneth Alessio Bianchi is an American serial killer. Bianchi and his cousin Angelo Buono, Jr., together are known as the Hillside Stranglers. He is serving a term of life imprisonment in Washington. Bianchi is also a suspect in the Alphabet murders, three unsolved murders in his home city of Rochester.

Bianchi was born in Rochester, New York, to a prostitute who gave him up for adoption two weeks after he was born. He was adopted at three months by Frances Scioliono and her husband Nicholas Bianchi in Rochester.

Bianchi was deeply troubled from a young age, and his adoptive mother described him as being "a compulsive liar from an early age". Despite having above-average intelligence, he was an underachiever at school who was known to quickly lose his temper. He was diagnosed with petit mal seizures when he was five years old and passive-aggressive disorder when he was 10. After his step-father's' death from pneumonia in 1964, Frances had to work while her son attended high school.

Shortly after Bianchi graduated from Gates-Chili High School in 1971, he married his high school sweetheart; the union ended after just eight months when she left him without an explanation. As an adult, he dropped out of college after one semester, and drifted through a series of menial jobs, finally ending up as a security guard at a jewellery store. This gave him a great opportunity to steal valuables, which he often gave to girlfriends or prostitutes to buy their loyalty. He was found out and sacked from the store and was constantly on the move to avoid arrest because of many petty thefts.

He moved to Los Angeles in 1977, and started spending time with his older cousin Angelo Buono, who was impressed with Bianchi's fancy clothes, jewellery, and stories of getting any women he wanted and "putting them in their place". Before long, they worked together as pimps, and, by late 1977, had escalated to murder. They had raped and murdered 10 women by the time they were arrested in early 1979.

Bianchi and Buono would usually cruise around Los Angeles in Buono's car and use fake badges to persuade girls that they were undercover cops. Their victims were women and girls aged 12 to 28 from various walks of life. They would order the girls into Buono's "unmarked police car" and drive them home to torture and murder them.

Their victims were:
Yolanda Washington, age 19 – October 17th, 1977
Judith Ann Miller, age 15 – October 31st, 1977
Lissa Kastin, age 21 – November 6th, 1977
Jane King, age 28 – November 10th, 1977
Delores Cepeda, age 12 – November 13th, 1977
Sonja Johnson, age 14 – November 13th, 1977

Kristin Weckler, age 20 – November 20th, 1977

Lauren Wagner, age 18 – November 29th, 1977

Kimberely Martin, age 17 – December 9th, 1977

Cindy Lee Hudspeth, age 20 – February 16th, 1978

Both men would sexually abuse their victims before strangling them. They experimented with other methods of killing, such as lethal injection, electric shock, and carbon monoxide poisoning. Even while committing the murders, Bianchi applied for a job with the Los Angeles Police Department and had even been taken for several rides with police officers while they were searching for the Hillside Strangler.

One night, shortly after they botched their would-be eleventh murder, Bianchi revealed to Buono he had attended LAPD police 'ride alongs' and that he was currently being questioned about the strangler case. After hearing this, Buono erupted in a fit of rage. An argument ensued at one point during which Buono threatened to kill Bianchi if he did not flee to Bellingham, Washington. In May 1978 he did flee to Bellingham, joining his girlfriend and son currently living there.

On January 11th, 1979, Bianchi lured two female students into an empty house he was guarding as a security person. The women were 22-year-old Karen Mandic and 27-year-old Diane Wilder, and were students at Western Washington University. He forced the first student down the stairs in front of him and then strangled her. He murdered the second young girl in a similar fashion. Without the help from his partner, he left many clues and police apprehended him the next day. A California driver's license and a routine background check linked him to the addresses of two of the Hillside Strangler victims.

Following his arrest, Bianchi admitted he and Buono, in 1977, while posing as police officers, stopped a young female by the name of Catharine Lorre with intentions of abducting and killing her. But after learning she was the daughter of actor Peter Lorre, they let her go. Only after he was arrested did Catharine learn of the true identity of the men whom she had encountered.

At his trial, Bianchi pleaded not guilty by reason of insanity, claiming that another personality, one "Steve Walker", had committed the crimes. Bianchi even convinced a few expert psychiatrists that he indeed suffered from multiple personality disorder, but investigators brought in their own psychiatrists, mainly the renowned psychiatrist Martin Orne. When Orne mentioned to Bianchi that in genuine cases of the disorder there tend to be three or more personalities, Bianchi promptly created another alias, "Billy". Eventually, investigators discovered that the very name "Steven Walker" came from a student whose identity Bianchi had previously attempted to steal for the purpose of fraudulently practicing psychology. Police also found a small library of books in Bianchi's home on topics of modern psychology, further indicating his ability to fake the disorder.

Once his claims were subjected to this scrutiny, Bianchi eventually admitted that he had been faking the disorder. To acquire leniency, he agreed to testify against Buono. However, in actually giving his testimony, Bianchi made every effort to be as uncooperative and self-contradictory as possible, apparently hoping to avoid being the ultimate cause of Buono being convicted. In the end, Bianchi's efforts were unsuccessful, as Buono was in fact convicted and sentenced to life imprisonment.

In 1980, Bianchi began a relationship with Veronica Compton, a woman he met whilst in prison. During his trial, she testified for the defence, telling the jury a false, vague tale about the crimes in an attempt to free Bianchi and also saying he wanted to buy a mortuary with another convicted murderer for the purpose of necrophilia. Hardly a good defence. She was later convicted and imprisoned for attempting to strangle a woman she had lured to a motel in an attempt to have authorities believe that the Hillside Strangler was still on the loose and the wrong man was in prison.

Bianchi is serving his sentence at Washington State Penitentiary in Walla Walla, Washington where he was denied parole on Wednesday, August 18th, 2010 by a state board. He will be eligible to apply again in 2025.

An aside to the case:

Bianchi is also a suspect in the Alphabet Murders that took place in the Rochester, New York area in the early 1970s.

Three young girls were raped and strangled. The case got its name from the fact that each of the three girls' first and last names started with the same letters ,Carmen Colon, Wanda Walkowicz, and Michelle Maenza, and that the bodies were found in a town that started with the same letter as the girls' names, Colon in Churchville, Walkowicz in Webster and Maenza in Macedon.

Carmen Colon, 11, disappeared November 16th, 1971. She was found two days later 12 miles from where she was last seen. Although she was found in the town of Riga, the village of Churchville is the town's center of population, and the town of Chili is nearby.

Wanda Walkowicz, 11, disappeared April 2nd, 1973. She was found the next day at a rest area off State Route 104 in Webster, seven miles from Rochester.

Michelle Maenza, 11, disappeared November 26th, 1973. She was found two days later in Macedon, 15 miles from Rochester.

Although hundreds of people were questioned, the killer was never caught. One man, considered to be a "person of interest" in the case (he committed suicide six weeks after the last of the murders), was cleared in 2007 by DNA testing. In the case of Carmen Colon, her uncle was also considered a suspect until his suicide in 1991.

Kenneth Bianchi, was an ice-cream vendor in Rochester at the time, selling from sites close to the first two murder scenes. He was a Rochester native who later moved to Los Angeles, where, as we have seen, he and his cousin Angelo Buono committed the Hillside Strangler murders between 1977 and 1978. Bianchi was never charged with the Alphabet murders, and he has repeatedly tried to have investigators officially clear him from suspicion; however, there is circumstantial evidence with witnesses seeing his car at two of the murder scenes. The third girl, Michelle Maenza, had told her father that she was going out to buy an ice-cream; she disappeared between Bianchi's store and another one, close to the station where Bianchi vended ice-cream. Bianchi has denied committing the murders but remains under suspicion.

ROBERT LEROY BIEHLER

Born 5th August 1934 - sentenced to life in prison without parole. Died in prison 10th January 1993.

Robert Leroy Biehler was an American serial killer who killed four people in various neighbourhoods of Los Angeles, California, from 1966 to 1973 either to cover up previous crimes or as part of paid for contract murders. Unable to be sentenced to death due to Furman v. Georgia, Biehler was instead given four consecutive Life terms, which he served until his death in 1993.

Biehler's first recorded criminal offence dates back to February 25th, 1956, when he and two accomplices, 22-year-old Louis Evangelisti and 18-year-old Kay G. Mills, broke into the home of Paul and Marguerite Troutner in Pasadena for a robbery. After threatening to kill his wife if Troutner did not reveal where he hid his money, the trio tied them up with electric cords and gagged them with adhesive tape before stealing money and valuables amounting to $1,500. One of the trio later bought an expensive motorcycle with the loot, which led to the arrest of all three by the local authorities. For this crime, Biehler and the two men were each convicted and given a short prison term.

After his release in the late 1950s, Biehler went on to commit a variety of crimes, most notable of which was participating in an organized burglary ring that stole $10,000 from a bank in 1960. He was later caught and ordered to serve another sentence at the California Institute for men, from where he was eventually paroled in August 1966.

A few months later, on December 22nd, Biehler went to the North Hollywood home of a former crime associate, 38-year-old Julia Cook, who had an extensive criminal record for drug possession and prostitution. Fearing that she might tell the police he was part of a prostitution ring, he held her and her 15-year-old son Kenneth at gunpoint, before forcing them to kneel and shooting each twice in the head. Police later detained him and an acquaintance, Morton Molin, for parole violations and charged the pair with the murders - however, they were forced to drop the charges due to lack of evidence. As a result, Biehler was instead jailed for parole violation while Molin was later tried for unrelated offences, and despite the police best efforts, they were unable to charge him with the killings at the time.

After being paroled from prison in the early 1970s, Biehler again resumed with his criminal conduct, mainly burglaries and pimping. On October 14th, 1973, he confronted a retired paratrooper from Sunland, 28-year-old Michael Rodney Coveny at a lounge in Shadow Hills for Coveny missing the deadline for a $800 debt concerning cocaine. After driving Coveny out to supposedly meet another supplier, Biehler threatened Coveny at gunpoint with a shotgun. Despite Coveny's pleas for mercy, he was shot and killed on the spot, and after his death,

Biehler drove to the Angeles National Forest, where he buried the body in a shallow grave.

Approximately a year later, he was paid an undetermined sum of money by 34-year-old Maida Sue Ellington to kill her roommate, 33-year-old roller derby skater Carole E. Phillips, who had threatened to expose Ellington's criminal activities. Sometime during that month, Biehler, disguised as a plumber, went to the pair's shared apartment in Lake View Terrace, where he shot her four times in the head. Miraculously, Phillips survived, forcing Ellington to pay Biehler even more for a second attempt to kill her. He accepted, and on Christmas Eve, shortly after leaving a bar in North Hollywood, Biehler confronted Phillips, pressed the gun up to her face and fired two shots, one into her eye and then one into her ear. To make sure that she was dead, he fired two additional shots into the body before leaving the crime scene.

Several months after Phillips' murder, Ellington was arrested under charges of conspiracy to murder. At her trial, Ellington initially claimed that she was innocent and that an unknown person had shot and killed her friend Phillips, but evidence suggested that she was indeed the one who had paid for the hit. She was subsequently sentenced to life imprisonment and remanded to the California Institution for Women, where she was visited by Biehler. In the midst of the visitation, Biehler was arrested by officers of the LAPD and charged with fourfold murder, after they had found Coveny's body a few days prior.

The trial was marred with difficulties from the very beginning, as the prosecution asked for an extension regarding how long the convict could be detained, citing threats of harming the witnesses. The motion was granted despite the protests of Biehler's attorney, Gerald Cohen, who claimed that this act would prejudice the prospective jury. From the beginning the prosecution announced that they would seek the death penalty under special circumstances, citing charges such as contract killing, kidnapping resulting in murder and a killing with prior murders.

After accepting a plea bargain in exchange for legal immunity, Biehler's ex-wife Janet testified that she had fabricated an alibi in the 1966 murders, claiming that he had been at home with her at the time. In her testimony, she confirmed suspicions that Biehler had indeed killed Cook because she supposedly threatened to expose him to the police, and had later convinced her to lie for his benefit. Later on, one of Biehler's attorneys, Jeffrey Brodey, unsuccessfully attempted to petition for a mistrial to one of the higher courts, citing the fact that a dozen jurors had been excused from jury duty due to their views on the death penalty, but his request was promptly refused. Another attorney, Donald Wager, who later dropped out of the case, was later sentenced to 10 days in jail for contempt of court over his refusal to divulge the details of a conversation he had had with his client prior to his resignation. On his part, Biehler claimed that he was not responsible for the murders, even pinning the Coveny killing on his wife, claiming that she had accompanied the pair to the supposed meeting with the dealer and had accidentally shot Coveny after he had attempted to snatch the shotgun out of her hands.

In spite of his various claims, neither judge nor jury were swayed by Biehler's explanations, and he was subsequently convicted on all counts. The ruling came after five days of deliberations. Due to the statute at the time, Justice Harry V. Peetris was forced to sentence Biehler to four consecutive life terms with chance of parole, as the law prohibited him applying either the death penalty or life without parole. He expressed his disappointment with the verdict in court statements, but reiterated that he had to abide by the law.

In the aftermath of the verdict, Peetrus published a letter addressing the criticisms surrounding the verdict, and advocated that the citizens take action and demand judicial reform as the sentencing laws were being reviewed at the time. The later rulings did not affect Biehler's sentence, which he served at San Quentin State Prison until his death from cancer in 1993.

LAWRENCE SIGMUND BITTAKER

Born September 27th, 1940 – sentenced to death, March 24th, 1981. Died in prison December 13th, 2019 age 79.

Southern California is known as Psycho Central. The region has earned its grim reputation the hard way, producing a full ten percent of the world's identified serial killers between 1950 and 2020. Predictably, many of the killers are now celebrities, with nicknames tailor-made for the tabloids, and their cousin, 24 hour TV news.
The Night Stalker. The I-5 Killer. The Skid Row Slasher. The Hillside Strangler. The Freeway Killer. The Koreatown Slasher. The Candlelight Killer. The Southside Slayer. The Trash Bag Killer. The Sunset Slayer. The Orange Coast Killer, the list goes on.
In a predictable irony, a killer named Mack Ray Edwards helped to build the freeways, slaughtering children from 1953 to 1969, planting their bodies overnight in soil that he would pave with asphalt in the morning. By the time Edwards hanged himself on San Quentin's death row in 1971, the next generation of killers was cruising those freeways looking for their victims.
Two of the worst are now all but forgotten today. These two never had nicknames, because reporters never learned of them until they were in custody.

Lawrence Sigmund Bittaker was born in Pittsburgh, Pennsylvania, on September 27th, 1940. Mr. and Mrs. George Bittaker adopted the infant who would be known as Lawrence shortly after he was born. George's work in aircraft factories occasioned frequent moves for the family, from Pennsylvania to Florida, then to Ohio, and finally California. Something of that rootless childhood stuck with Lawrence, and he dropped out of school in 1957, after several brushes with police and juvenile authorities. Soon after dropping out of high school Bittaker was arrested in Long Beach for auto theft, hit-and-run, and evading arrest. That bust earned him a trip to the California Youth Authority, where he remained until he turned 19.

Within days of his California parole, Bittaker was picked up by FBI agents in Louisiana, charged with violating the Interstate Motor Vehicle Theft Act. He was convicted on that charge in August 1959, and was sentenced to serve 18 months at a federal reformatory in Oklahoma. His behaviour there soon earned Bittaker a transfer to the U.S. medical centre at Springfield, Missouri, where doctors released him after he had served two-thirds of his sentence.

Arrested next for a Los Angeles robbery, in December 1960, Bittaker was convicted in May 1961, and given an indeterminate sentence of one to 15 years in state prison. A 1961 psychiatric examination found him to be manipulative and "having considerable concealed hostility." Despite having a "superior intelligence," he was diagnosed as a "borderline psychotic" and "basically paranoid." The following year, a second psychiatrist noted Bittaker's "poor control of impulsive behaviour." Yet, despite this, he was paroled in late 1963, after serving just one-sixth of his possible maximum sentence.

Freedom never seemed to agree with Larry Bittaker. Two months after his conditional release, he was jailed again for parole violation and suspicion of robbery. Another parole violation sent him back to prison in October 1964. Interviewed by a psychiatrist in 1966, Bittaker confessed that stealing made him feel "important." Another diagnosis of borderline psychosis was recorded -- and authorities released him yet again, only to again see another parole violation in June 1967.

One month later, Bittaker was arrested for theft and leaving the scene of a hit-and-run accident. Convicted on those charges, he got another five-year sentence, but he was paroled after serving less than three years in April 1970. Arrested for burglary and parole violation in March 1971, he was convicted on both counts that October, receiving an additional sentence of six months to 15 years. He was freed three years later, in 1974. His next crime began as simple shoplifting, shoving a steak down the front of his pants in a supermarket. But it escalated to attempted murder in the parking lot, when Bittaker stabbed an employee who tried to stop him.

Forensic psychiatrist Dr. Robert Markman examined Bittaker before trial and warned that he was bound to escalate his criminal behaviour, moving on to more serious crimes. He was "a highly dangerous man, with no internal controls over his impulses, a man who could kill without hesitation or remorse." Bittaker later reinforced this surmise, telling a cellmate that someday he planned to be "bigger than Manson."

Prison psychiatrists agreed with Markman. A 1977 jailhouse evaluation found Bittaker "more than likely" to commit new crimes upon his release. A year later, in July 1978, another psychiatrist dubbed Bittaker "a sophisticated psychopath" whose prospects for successful parole were "guarded at best." Again the warnings were ignored, and Bittaker was released in November 1978.

But not before he had made a special friend.

Roy Lewis Norris was born in Greeley, Colorado, on February 2nd, 1948. Unlike Bittaker, Norris lived in his hometown until he was 17, when he dropped out of school and joined the Navy. He was stationed in San Diego, but in 1969 Norris spent four months in Vietnam. Norris never saw combat, but he did see drugs. Marijuana was his drug of choice, and it was widely available.

Back in Southern California by November 1969, Norris attacked a female driver in downtown San Diego. He forced his way into her car and attempted rape. Three months later Norris got arrested again. Whilst free on bail pending trial for attacking the motorist, Norris knocked on another San Diego woman's door and asked if he could use her telephone. When the woman refused, he tried to break in through a living room window and then ran around the back to the kitchen smashing a window there, he finally entered the house, but police arrived before he could harm his intended victim.

At that point, the navy had seen enough of Norris. He received an administrative discharge for "psychological problems" after he was diagnosed as having a "severe schizoid personality." Still awaiting disposition of his previous assault cases, Norris attacked a young woman in May 1970, on the campus of San Diego State College. He tackled the student from behind, clubbed her with a stone, and then slammed her head repeatedly into a concrete sidewalk. This time the charge was assault with a deadly weapon, and it was finally enough to put him in prison. He was confined to Atascadero State Hospital as a mentally disordered sex offender. He spent five years there before being released on probation. Officially he was described as someone who would bring "no further danger to others."

Norris proved the prediction wrong just three months later, in Redondo Beach. Cruising the streets on a motorcycle, he spied a 27-year-old woman walking home from a restaurant after a quarrel with her boyfriend. Norris stopped to offer her a ride, which she declined. Undeterred by the rejection, Norris leaped off his bike and attacked the woman, strangling her into semi-consciousness with her own scarf. Dazed, she did not resist as Norris dragged her behind a nearby hedge and raped her.

Police were unable to act because of her vague description of her attacker. But one month later the woman saw Norris again and recognised him. She memorized his license number and went to the police. Convicted of forcible rape, Norris was shipped to the California Men's Colony at San Louis Obispo.

. Norris also met a friend at the colony who would change his life: Lawrence Bittaker.

Years later, Norris would claim that Larry Bittaker twice saved his life at San Louis Obispo. The experience bound him to Bittaker, although the details are vague. It helped, of course, that they shared near-identical fantasies of domination, rape and torture. Next time a woman fell into his clutches, Bittaker confided, he would kill her afterwards, a sure-fire method of evading punishment. In fact, he thought, it might be fun to play a game, selecting one victim for each "teen" year, 13 through 19, and to see how long each victim could be kept alive and screaming.

Bittaker was paroled on November 15th, 1978, returning to Los Angeles, where he found work as a machinist. Norris was freed exactly two months later, on January 15th, 1979. He moved in with his mother at an L.A. trailer park, and used his navy training to find work as an electrician. Bittaker wrote to Norris in February 1979 and arranged a rendezvous at a cheap downtown hotel. Over drinks, they renewed their prison friendship and repeated their dark desires.

As a first step toward fulfilling his vision, Bittaker purchased a silver 1977 GMC cargo van. The van had its advantages – there were no side windows to worry about and there was a large sliding door on the passenger side. If their intended victims spurned the offer of a ride, Bittaker reasoned, they could "pull up real close and not have to open the doors all the way" to snatch someone from the sidewalk. He named the van "Murder Mack."

From February to June 1979 Bittaker and Norris cruised up and down the Pacific Coast Highway. They stopped at beaches, flirted with girls, and often took their photos. Norris later estimated that they picked up 20 prospects without harming one, and his estimate may have been low. Detectives later counted some 500 photos of smiling young women among Bittaker's belongings. Most were never identified.

They were just test runs, Norris later explained. The rape and murder could wait until they found the perfect isolated spot to take their victims to. Sometime in late April, cruising aimlessly, the hunters found a remote fire road in the San Gabriel Mountains, overlooking Glendora. A padlocked gate barred access, but Bittaker smashed the lock with a crow bar. It was ideal.

Now all they needed was their first victim. They found her on June 24th, 1979.

Bittaker spent the night in Murder Mack, parked outside the trailer Roy Norris shared with his mother. They spent the morning working on a bed Bittaker had constructed in the back of the van. The bed was mounted on a frame with space beneath it to conceal a body. At about 11:00 a.m. they began prowling. Bittaker described it as "a nice Sunday to cruise around the beach area, drinking beer, smoking grass and flirting with the girls. We had no set routine."

They made the rounds, driving north between Redondo Beach and Santa Monica, keeping an eye out for female hitchhikers. Sometimes they'd park the van and scout a stretch of sand on foot. It was 5:00 p.m., back in Redondo Beach, when they found a likely target. She took them both completely by surprise.

Bittaker and Norris later quarrelled over who was first to notice 16-year-old Cindy Schaeffer. Each man accused the other of pointing her out and suggesting that she be the first contestant in their "game." Ironically, she was not at the beach or wearing a swimsuit. In fact, Schaeffer was walking back to her grandmother's house, after a Christian youth meeting at St. Andrew's Presbyterian Church. Murder Mack pulled up alongside and Norris offered her a ride. Schaeffer declined and ignored the van as it trailed behind her. Then the van surged ahead and swung into a driveway, motor idling.

Norris met her on the sidewalk, smiling, repeating his offer. As Schaeffer brushed past him, Roy grabbed her and pushed her into the van. The sliding door worked perfectly, muffling her cries for help as Bittaker cranked up the radio's volume. Norris grappled with Schaeffer and then sealed her lips with duct tape. He also bound her wrists and ankles. One shoe was left behind on the sidewalk as Murder Mack sped away.

Bittaker drove to the mountain fire road and parked out of sight from the highway. The men smoked grass and questioned Schaeffer about her family, until they tired of the routine and ordered her to strip. Bittaker left the van for an hour or so, giving Norris some privacy. Then he came back to take his turn. In custody, months later, each accused the other of insisting that Schaeffer die. Norris tried to strangle Schaeffer, but he bungled the job. He left to smoke marijuana and when he returned, he said, Bittaker was choking Schaeffer, but "her body was still jerking...alive to some degree...breathing or trying to breathe." Bittaker then handed Norris a wire coat hanger and they twisted it around her neck, tightening the makeshift garrot with vice-grip pliers. Norris recalled that Schaeffer "convulsed for 15 seconds or so and that was it. She just died."

They wrapped the body in a plastic shower curtain and drove back along the fire road until they found a deep canyon. They lifted Schaeffer's body from the van and heaved her into it. Bittaker said the desert scavengers would clean up after them.

The exhausted friends agreed, it had been nearly perfect, but there was something missing. Next time, they would keep a trophy of the kill.

The pair went hunting again on Sunday, July 8th, 1979. In early afternoon they saw a likely prospect, thumbing rides along Pacific Coast Highway. But the driver of a white convertible pulled in ahead of them and plucked her from the roadside. They would follow the convertible for a while and see where the hitchhiker was dropped off.

Their patience was soon rewarded. The convertible's driver signalled for an exit ramp ahead, braking first to deposit his passenger on the slip road. She stuck a thumb out, waiting for the next ride.

Meanwhile, Norris left Murder Mack's passenger seat and threw himself under the raised bed in back. It was a change in strategy, to make the van appear less threatening.

It worked. Andrea Hall was 18 and thankful for the ride. She introduced herself to Bittaker as he pulled back into traffic, gratefully accepting his offer of a cold drink. He told her to fetch it from a cooler in the rear of the van, choosing a soda and turning back toward her seat as Norris lunged from hiding and swept her legs out from under her. Hall fought for her life, but Norris was too strong. Twisting an arm behind her back until she finally surrendered, the submission enabled Norris to bind her wrists and ankles and cover her mouth with tape.

The fire road was familiar territory now. There was no time for small talk with their second victim. They repeatedly raped her by turns. When both of them were tired, Bittaker loaded his Polaroid camera, dragged Hall from the van, and sent Norris on a beer run, down the mountain to a small roadside convenience store. When Norris returned, he found Bittaker alone, smiling over photos of Andrea Hall, her face contorted by fear.

"He told me that he told her he was going to kill her," Norris later informed police. "He wanted to see what her argument would be for staying alive. He said that she didn't put up much of an argument."

Bittaker told Norris that he had stabbed Hall twice with an ice pick, once in each ear, but he had to strangle her when she refused to die. When the murder was finished, Bittaker said he had thrown her off a cliff.

Bittaker and Norris made their third killing on Labor Day, September 3rd. Cruising through Hermosa Beach, they spotted two girls seated on the bench at a bus stop, where Pier Avenue met Pacific Coast Highway. Fifteen-year-old Jackie Gilliam and 13-year-old Leah Lamp weren't waiting for the bus, but for some reason they accepted a ride with no special destination in mind. Bittaker and Norris later told police the girls were also glad to accept Larry's offer to smoke a joint.

Lighting up, he passed the joint around and told his passengers that he was heading for the beach. Jackie and Leah challenged him moments later, as Bittaker turned away from the ocean and started driving northward, but he stalled them with excuses, claiming he merely wanted to find a safe place to park while they got high. The girls protested when Bittaker parked near a suburban tennis court. Leah started to open the door, but Norris was faster, swinging a sawed-off baseball bat against her skull.

A fierce struggle ensued. Bittaker waded in to help Norris, finally subduing the teenagers and trussing them with duct tape. Only when they were secured and silenced did he notice several tennis players watching from the nearby courts. Worried that someone might call the police, Bittaker gunned the van and sped away toward his hideout in the San Gabriel Mountains. But no one called the police.

Bittaker and Norris kept their latest hostages alive for nearly two days. They kept an audiotape of their rape and torture. Among other things, the tape captured Norris raping Jackie Gilliam, demanding that she play the role of a cousin who was the object of some of his sexual fantasies.

Tired of the game and running dangerously late for work, Bittaker repeated his trick with the ice pick, stabbing Gilliam in both ears. As with Andrea Hall, it made her scream but failed to kill her, so the rapists took turns strangling Jackie to death. Afterward, they turned on Lamp, Bittaker squeezing her throat while Norris pounded her head seven times with a sledgehammer. Once more they pitched their victims off a cliff, with the ice pick still imbedded in Jackie Gilliam's skull.

On Sunday, September 30th, they selected Shirley Sanders, an Oregon resident visiting her father in Manhattan Beach. When she declined a lift in Murder Mack, they sprayed Sanders with chemical mace and dragged her kicking from the sidewalk. Both men raped her in the van, but they were careless and she escaped. Sanders reported the assault, but she could not identify her assailants. She did not remember the license plate. Unable to pursue the matter further, she returned to Oregon.

The next month was nerve-wracking for Bittaker and Norris, worried that police might come for them at any moment. Bittaker found a new apartment in Burbank, while Norris remained with his mother. The killers began to relax as the weeks passed without any signs of police attention and went hunting again on Halloween night, deviating from their beach routine to prowl the residential streets of the Sunland and Tijunga district in the San Fernando Valley. They spotted 16-year-old Lynette Ledford hitchhiking and offered her a ride. She happily accepted--and within five minutes Norris wrestled her to Murder Mack's floor.

Bittaker chose not to waste time driving to the mountains. He reasoned they could rape and torture Ledford just as well while they drove around the suburbs of Los Angeles. Norris took the driver's seat, while Bittaker turned on the tape recorder and went to work on their captive. The tape records him slapping her, demanding, "Say something, girl!"

Bittaker parked the van and prepared for the kill. "I got a section of coat hanger," he later told police, "and wrapped it around her throat and tied it up with the pliers."

They thought it would be amusing to see what happened if they dumped their victim on someone's front lawn. They chose a yard at random in Hermosa Beach, and loaded Ledford's corpse into a bed of ivy. The corpse was discovered the next morning.

The find shocked Los Angeles, since it came only days after the arrest of "Hillside Strangler" Angelo Buono. The police said they were unaware of any other Buono victims. There were missing girls and women, of course, but who could say if they were dead? More to the point, how could police identify the killers in the latest unsolved case?

Lynette Ledford actually spoiled the fun. She was the second 16-year-old Bittaker and Norris had murdered; leaving three teenagers unaccounted for.

The hunters did not worry, though. From where they sat, it seemed as if they had all the time in the world.

Roy Norris himself was part of the problem. Despite the murder game's shortcomings, Norris enjoyed it so much that he simply couldn't keep quiet. By October 1979 he had started bragging to another friend from prison, Jimmy Dalton, emphasizing his role as a criminal mastermind. Dalton thought it all was talk until Ledford's body was found. He called his lawyer and they both went to the Los Angeles police. L.A.'s finest listened to Dalton's story and then passed him to detectives in Hermosa Beach, where Ledford's corpse had been discarded.

Hermosa Beach detective Paul Bynum headed the Ledford investigation. He had no forensic evidence to support a charge in the Ledford slaying. But Dalton's mention of a silver van rang a bell in Bynum's memory. He dispatched an officer to Oregon to interview Shirley Sanders who was attacked one month before. Photographs were taken for Sanders to examine. Leafing through the stack, she picked out Bittaker and Norris as the men who had kidnapped and raped her.

Bynum approached Deputy District Attorney Steve Kay, who had prosecuted Norris on his previous rape charge in Redondo Beach. Kay cautioned patience, even though a quick arrest would halt the murder spree they needed time to build a strong case. Police mounted surveillance on the pair. Once again, Norris was the weak link. He was seen selling marijuana on the street.

Police made their move two days before Thanksgiving 1979. They arrested Norris for parole violation on the marijuana charge, while Bittaker was jailed on suspicion of kidnapping and raping Shirley Sanders. Norris waived his right to counsel, and sparred with the interrogators for a while. Eventually he crumbled, casting himself as a reluctant accomplice to murders planned and carried out by Bittaker. After all, he owed Bittaker his life--but apparently, not his silence.

On the strength of Norris's confession, both men were charged with five counts of first-degree murder, plus additional charges of kidnapping, robbery, rape, deviant sexual assault and criminal conspiracy. Each defendant tried to blame the other. Norris now claimed that he had been high on drugs most of the time and therefore unable to resist Bittaker. But the audiotapes recorded in their van told a different story, revealing Norris as a full participant. Norris realized he would have to do more to avoid the death penalty.

In February 1980 Norris took Detective Bynum, Steve Kay and members of the Sierra Madre Search and Rescue Team on a tour of the San Gabriel murder sites. They found Leah Lamp and Jackie Gilliam, with Bittaker's ice pick still buried in Gilliam's ear, but no trace was found of Cindy Schaeffer or Andrea Hall. They were lost forever. But Norris had delivered enough evidence to clinch his plea bargain.

Reluctantly, Steve Kay agreed to waive the death penalty and grant a life sentence with parole eligibility in return for Norris's testimony against Bittaker. Before a defendant is formally sentenced, California requires a report and a sentencing recommendation from a parole officer.

Norris's officer conducted an interview and noted his "casual, unconcerned manner" as he discussed the five murders without any regret. In the officer's opinion, Norris "appears compulsive in his need and desire to inflict pain and torture upon women. The defendant himself acknowledged ...that in the commission of rape upon a woman it was not the sex that was important but the domination of the woman. In considering the defendant's total lack of remorse about the plight of the victims, he can realistically be regarded as an extreme sociopath, whose depraved, grotesque pattern of behaviour is beyond rehabilitation. The magnitude and the enormity of the defendant's heinous, nightmarish criminal behaviour is beyond the comprehension of this probation officer."

With that finding on file, Norris was sentenced to 45 years to life, with a minimum of 30 years to serve before parole. He was eligible for release in 2010 but it was refused and he died in prison on February 24th, 2020 aged 72.

For his part, Bittaker seemed to enjoy the trial proceedings. He had prepared for his trial by writing his memoirs, fittingly titled The Last Ride. Though warned repeatedly not to publish it by his attorney, Bittaker insisted on finishing the manuscript, apparently convinced that jurors would believe his assertion that Norris masterminded the operation. The gamble failed, and on February 17th, 1981, Bittaker was found guilty on five murder counts and 21 other related felonies.

California, like all other states, holds its criminal trials in stages. The first determines guilt or innocence; the second, if a defendant is convicted, determines the punishment. To support a death sentence, California prosecutors must demonstrate "special circumstances"—such as slayings deemed "especially heinous, atrocious or cruel, manifesting exceptional depravity." Bittaker's personal audiotapes were replayed for the jury, which promptly recommended death.

As with Norris another probation report was generated. Bittaker's examiner wrote that "during the years this officer has been submitting evaluations to the court, he has had occasion to interview many individuals convicted of brutal crimes, but none to the extent of the crimes for which this defendant has been convicted. During the interviews with him, although verbalizing some feeling for the teenage deaths that he has caused, there is no outward expression or emotion displayed. His total attitude was almost as if he had been able to divorce himself from the emotions felt by the major portion of society."

The report concluded that there was "little doubt that he would return to a life of crime, and possibly a life of violence" if released into society. The jury's recommended sentence clearly "would be the most permanent protection available."

The judge agreed, and Bittaker was sentenced to death on March 24th, 1981.

Death penalty sentences are neither sure nor swift. Appeal of a death sentence is automatic, regardless of the defendant's wishes. Two years elapsed before the California Supreme Court appointed Bittaker's appellate attorney, six more before the same court affirmed Bittaker's death sentence on June 28th, 1989. Bittaker was absent on October 4th, 1989, when Torrance judge John Shook set his execution for December 29th, but he had little to fear. His attorney filed yet another appeal that automatically stayed the execution. On June 11th, 1990, the California Supreme Court declined to hear the case again.

When Bittaker was not busy drafting appeals, he amused himself by filing frivolous suits against the state prison system. There were more than 40 in all by October 1995. In one case, where he claimed he had been subjected to "cruel and unusual punishment" by receipt of a broken cookie on his lunch tray, state officials paid $5,000 to have the suit dismissed. Before the state was granted summary judgment, they had to prove that Bittaker could skip his lunch and still survive by only eating breakfast and dinner.

It was all great fun and cost Bittaker nothing, since California prisoners could file their suits for free. When not pursuing nuisance litigation, Bittaker enjoyed a daily game of bridge with fellow inmates Randy Kraft, Douglas Clark and William Bonin, all three convicted serial killers with an estimated 94 victims among them. The game was left short-handed in February 1996, after Bonin was executed, but

Bittaker has other diversions. In the late 1990s, a catalogue of prison memorabilia offered his fingernail clippings for sale to murder groupies. And there was fan mail -- enough to keep him busy between card games.

Lawrence Bittaker died in San Quentin State prison on December 13th, 2019 aged 79.

ROBERT BLAKE

Born September 18th, 1933 – acquitted of murder March 16th, 2005. Found liable for his wife's death by a civil suit jury and ordered to pay $30m in compensation to her children November 18th, 2005. Died aged 89 on March 23rd, 2023.

On May 4th, 2001, the Hollywood actor, Robert Blake, took his wife Bonny Lee Bakley out for dinner at Vitello's Italian Restaurant in Studio City, California. Bakley was fatally shot in the head while sitting in Blake's vehicle, which was parked on a side street around the corner from the restaurant. Blake claimed that he had returned to the restaurant to collect a pistol which he had left inside and said that he had not been present when the shooting took place. The pistol Blake left in the restaurant was found and determined by police not to be the murder weapon. Bakley had enemies having been married 9 times and a history of exploiting older men for money using pornography.

On April 18th, 2002, Blake was arrested and charged with Bakley's murder. His longtime bodyguard, Earle Caldwell, was also arrested and charged with conspiracy in connection with the murder. A key event that gave the Los Angeles Police Department the confidence to arrest Blake came when a retired stuntman, Ronald "Duffy" Hambleton, agreed to testify against him alleging that Blake tried to hire him to kill Bakley. Another retired

Stuntman and an associate of Hambleton's, Gary McLarty, also came forward with a similar story.

On April 22nd, 2002, Blake was charged with one count of murder with special circumstances, an offence which carried a possible death penalty. He was also charged with two counts of solicitation of murder and one count of conspiracy to commit murder. Blake entered a plea of not guilty.

On March 13th, 2003, after almost a year in jail, Blake was granted bail, which was set at $1.5 million. He was then placed under house arrest while awaiting trial. On October 31st, in a major reversal for the prosecution, the judge dismissed the conspiracy charges against Blake and Caldwell during a pre-trial hearing. The junior prosecutor who handled the case, Shellie Samuels admitted that the prosecutors had no forensic evidence implicating Blake in the murder and that they could not tie him to the murder weapon.

Blake's criminal trial for murder began on December 20th, 2004, with opening statements by the prosecution and opening statements by the defence the following day. The prosecution contended that Blake intentionally murdered Bakley to free himself from a loveless marriage, while the defence claimed that Blake was an innocent victim of circumstantial and fabricated evidence. McLarty and Hambleton each testified that Blake had asked them to murder Bakley. On cross-examination, the defence brought up McLarty's mental health problems and Hambleton's criminal history. The lack of gunshot residue on Blake's hands was a key part of the defence's case that Blake was not the shooter. Blake chose not to testify himself.

On March 16th, 2005, Blake was found not guilty of murder and not guilty of one of the two counts of solicitation of murder. The other count, for solicitation to commit murder, was dropped after it was revealed that the jury was deadlocked 11–1 in favour of an acquittal. Public opinion regarding the verdict was mixed, with some feeling that Blake was guilty, though many felt that there was not enough evidence to convict him. On the night of his acquittal several fans celebrated at Blake's favourite haunt – and the scene of the crime – Vitello's.

Bakley's three children then filed a civil suit against Blake, asserting that he was responsible for their mother's death. During the trial, the girlfriend of Blake's co-defendant Earle Caldwell said she believed Blake and Caldwell were involved in the crime.

On November 18th, 2005, a jury found Blake liable for the wrongful death of his wife and ordered him to pay $30 million. On February 3rd, 2006, Blake filed for bankruptcy.

Blake's attorney, M. Gerald Schwartzbach, appealed the court's decision on February 28th, 2007and on April 26th, 2008, an appeals court upheld the civil case verdict, but cut Blake's penalty assessment to $15 million.

Blake maintained a low profile after his acquittal and filing for bankruptcy, with debts of $3 million for unpaid legal fees as well as unpaid state and federal taxes. On April 9th, 2010, the state of

California filed a tax lien against Blake for $1,110,878 in unpaid back taxes.

On July 16th, 2012, Blake was interviewed on CNN's Piers Morgan Tonight. When asked about the night of Bakley's murder, Blake became defensive and angry, stating he resented Morgan's questioning and felt he was being interrogated. Morgan responded he was only asking questions that he felt people were eager to have answered.

In September 2019, Blake started a YouTube channel titled "Robert Blake: I ain't dead yet, so stay tuned," on which he discussed his life and career.

In 2021, Blake opened up a website, "Robert Blake's Pushcart", where scripts, memorabilia, and books including his autobiography Tales of a Rascal are available to read and in the case of the latter can be ordered.

Quentin Tarantino's's novel Once Upon a Time in Hollywood, based on his film of the same name, is dedicated to Blake. Notably, Blake's later life dealing with his wife's murder mirrors Brad Pitt's's character Cliff Booth who is also accused of murdering his wife.

Blake died from heart disease in Los Angeles, on March 9th, 2023, at the age of 89.

See also CHRISTIAN BRANDO

WARREN JAMES BLAND

Born January 21st, 1937 –sentenced to death in1993. Died in prison August 30th, 2001.

The intense manhunt for Warren James Bland, 51, ended on February 9th, 1987 when a plainclothes officer acting on a tip spotted a pickup truck that fitted the description of Bland's vehicle.

The officer walked up to the truck and ended up looking eye-to-eye with Bland. The officer ordered Bland by name not to move, but Bland ran across the parking lot of Los Pancho's restaurant. When Bland refused the officer's order to stop, the officer shot him.

The bullet hit Bland in the hip and severed a major artery. He was hospitalised and recovered.

Police said local residents had reported seeing Bland -- who has a distinctive dagger tattoo on a forearm -- in the San Diego area in the recent days. Photographs of the suspect had been widely shown on television and in newspapers.

Murder charges were filed against Bland in Riverside County for the death of little Phoebe Ho, 7, who was snatched off the street on December 11th, 1986 as she walked to school near her home in South Pasadena. Her body was found eight days later in a field in Glen Avon.

Bland was also a suspect in the killing of Wendy Osborn, 14, of Placentia, whose strangled body was found on Feb. 1st, 1987 near Chino in San

Bernardino County, about 30 miles from where Phoebe's body was discovered.

Police said the two crimes had much in common: the girls were abducted while walking to school, no ransom was demanded, they were strangled, sexually assaulted and tortured with a plier-like tool and their bodies were then dumped in remote rural areas.

Bland had a record of violent attacks on women and children that dated back to the 1950s. He was on parole at the time of his arrest after being convicted of molesting an 11-year-old boy he had tortured with pliers.

Bland had been a fugitive since early January 1987 when detectives questioned him about Phoebe's death but released him when they could not produce enough physical evidence to charge him.

But after carpet fibres found in the van Bland used in his part-time painting job near the little girl's home were matched to those found on Phoebe's body, an arrest warrant was issued.

The break in the case came when an unidentified acquaintance of Bland was arrested by federal agents in Washington, D.C., and provided information linking Bland to an address in San Diego, not far from where he was captured.

Bland's attorney's raised several appeals against the lesser charges in his convictions but the appeals failed and he was sentenced to death in 1993. A ladder of appeals against the sentence continued until 2001, when Bland died in prison on August 30th aged 64.

ROBERT MAURICE BLOOM

Born 1964 – sentenced to death in 1983. Re-sentenced to life in prison in 2000.

In 1983 a jury found Bloom guilty of shooting and killing his father, Robert Bloom Sr., his stepmother, Josephine Lou Bloom, and his eight-year-old stepsister, Sandra Hughes. Robert Bloom Jr. was eighteen years old at the time of the murders.

The prosecution presented substantial evidence against Bloom. One witness testified that approximately a week before the murders Bloom asked him if he could buy a gun because he was going to kill someone. The witness agreed to obtain a gun for Bloom but never did so. Another witness testified that two days before the murders Bloom told his father on the telephone, "You are running my life now but you won't be for long."

At the time of the murders Bloom was living with his girlfriend, Christine Waller who testified that two days before the murders she observed Bloom walking in a field behind her house carrying a rifle. Waller's brother owned a .22 calibre semi-automatic rifle. The rifle was missing after the murders and was never found. The victims were shot with bullets from such a rifle.

On April 22nd, 1982, at about 4:00 a.m., David Hughes, who lived next door to Bloom Sr., heard him shout: "Robert, Robert. Come back." Hughes looked out the window and saw Bloom standing at the end of the driveway before walking off down the street. Bloom Sr. then ran down the street towards Bloom.

Another witness, Moises Gameros, testified he then saw Bloom Sr. and Bloom arguing in the street. Gameros heard Bloom Sr. say: "That's it. I'm going to call the police."

Bloom Sr. and Bloom then returned to Bloom Sr.'s house and went inside. Bloom was carrying a rifle but was not pointing it at anyone. Minutes later, Hughes heard shouting and saw Bloom Sr. Standing out in the driveway and heard him again ask Bloom to come back. Both Hughes and Gameros then heard gunfire.

Bloom Sr began screaming, grabbed his midsection, and ran to his house. Bloom followed Bloom Sr. and continued to shoot at him. Bloom Sr. eventually fell on his back in the doorway. Bloom then stood over him and shot him twice in the head.

Bloom appeared to reload the rifle before he re-entered the house. Hughes heard a woman's scream followed by two more shots. After a short pause, Hughes heard a third shot. Bloom walked out of the house, placed the rifle in a car belonging to his step-mother Josephine, and drove off.

Police officers arrived shortly after. Bloom Sr. and Josephine were dead. Sandra was still alive, but critically wounded, she had been shot in the head and had also suffered twenty-three "sharp force" stab wounds to her forehead, neck, right arm, and left back. These wounds apparently were made by scissors which were found near her body. Sandra died the next day.

Bloom was arrested within an hour after the murders. He had blood on his hands and shoes. He was not in possession of a rifle. Although the murder weapon was never found, there is no dispute that the victims were shot with a .22-calibre rifle.

Bloom initially pleaded not guilty to the three murders. Before his trial, he changed his plea to the murder of Sandra to not guilty by reason of insanity.

At trial, Bloom testified that on the morning of the murder he took the rifle and chased some "cholos", Mexican immigrants. He followed them until he was near Bloom Sr.'s house. He went inside the house and placed the rifle on a chair. Bloom Sr. and Josephine were arguing because she wanted a divorce. According to Bloom, Bloom Sr. then shot Josephine in the face and, as she was walking toward Bloom, Bloom Sr. shot her a second time.

Bloom testified he picked up the rifle, left the house, and agreed to return only after Bloom Sr. agreed to call the police. When they re-entered the house, Bloom Sr. refused to call the police, Bloom left the house, and, after Bloom Sr. made a nasty remark about Sandra, Bloom shot him. Bloom said he did not remember anything else until he was arrested.

The jury found Bloom guilty of all three counts of first degree murder. After the jury returned its verdict, Bloom withdrew his insanity plea and asked the court to let him represent himself during the penalty phase. He told the court he intended to ask the jury to return a verdict of death. The court granted Bloom's request.

During the penalty phase, the prosecution presented evidence of a prior arrest for attempted robbery and for concealing a weapon. Bloom presented no mitigating evidence. In his closing argument, he told the jurors there were no mitigating circumstances and asked them to impose the death penalty. After four hours of deliberation, the jury returned a verdict of death.

After the jury's verdict in the penalty phase, Bloom was involved in a violent jail incident. He was relieved of his self-representation status and a hearing was held to determine his competency. A jury found him to be competent. The state trial court then declined to modify the jury's verdict and upheld the death sentence.

A second trial was ordered by the appeal court in 2000 when Bloom cited miss-representation by his attorneys for allowing him to self-represent at the penalty stage. The jury again found him guilty but this time he was re-sentenced to life in prison.

In 2022 the Supreme Court overturned the convictions for killing his step-mother and step-sister ruling that his attorneys had inappropriately told jurors that he had admitted their murders when he had in fact only admitted to killing his father. He remains in jail with appeals ongoing.

RICHARD PRYDE BOGGS

Born 1933 – sentenced to life in prison February 22nd, 1992. Died in prison on March 6th, 2003.

Boggs was a Californian neurologist who was quite rich and who, for some reason, decided on murder to get his and his co-conspirator's hands on $1.5m. He lured a drunk drifter 32-year-old Ellis Henry Greene into his office in Glendale, California and disabled him with a stun gun before suffocating him with the help of co-conspirator Melvin Eugene "Gene" Hanson on April 16th, 1988.
Boggs called 911 and when paramedics arrived he falsely identified the dead Greene as Hanson after having previously forged his medical records and included Hanson's birth certificate and credit cards on Greene's body.
The officers called to the scene were initially suspicious of Boggs' story, believing it was unlikely a doctor would meet a patient in his office at 5:00 a.m. and realizing the temperature of the body when found did not correspond to the time of death given by Boggs, who as a neurosurgeon wouldn't be expected to be treating a patient for a heart complaint as Boggs had said. They refused to let Boggs sign the death certificate and cremate the body and called in the coroner. After the coroner's report ruled the death was due to myocarditis, John Hawkins, Hanson's business partner in a clothing store chain in Ohio, named Just Sweats, was called in to identify the body, which he

did. Unknown to the authorities, Hawkins was also in cahoots with Boggs and Hanson for a share in the money.

The case was officially closed, and the body was quickly cremated at the behest of Hawkins who collected the $1 million life insurance policy he had taken out on Hanson, cleaned out his bank accounts, shared it with the other two, and promptly disappeared. Hanson also went into hiding, adopting an identity as Wolfgang Von Snowden

Meanwhile, Farmers Insurance, the company that had paid out the insurance policy, obtained Melvin Hanson's driver's license to compare to the picture of the body taken in the morgue. They didn't match. The insurance company were checking for possible insurance fraud, and what they found led them to hire a private investigator to look into the case. At the same time, Columbus Dispatch Newspaper reporters Robin Yocum and Catherine Candisky also began to look into the case, as well as the California Department of Insurance Fraud Division (CDI) and Glendale Police Department. Mike Jones, the lead investigator assigned at CDI, recognized that Hanson's driver's license photo did not match the coroner's morgue photo or the thumbprint of the deceased at Boggs's office, and with CDI investigator Kathy Scholz, they reviewed missing person reports in the LA area.

After Investigator Scholz located the missing person report of Ellis Greene, CDI investigators identified Greene as the dead man, and a second coroner's report based on photographs and the original finding ruled Greene had been murdered. Hanson was arrested while arriving at DFW Airport from Acapulco, Mexico after being detained by an alert U.S. Customs officer who suspected Hanson was a drug courier because he was carrying a large amount of U.S. currency and had scars from plastic surgery. Hanson was referred to the U.S. Customs Office of Enforcement, where agents began an interrogation and discovered numerous inconsistencies in Hanson's story and paperwork.

In Hanson's knapsack, the Customs agents found $14,000 of undeclared cash, several stolen or forged identification cards including the California state driver's license of Ellis Greene, and a Dade County library book, How To Create a New Identity. The Customs agents contacted the FBI in Columbus, and after confirming an outstanding arrest warrant, placed Hanson under arrest. Boggs was then arrested the same week at his office.

Hawkins managed to leave the United States despite a flurry of media exposure. His case was profiled on America's Most Wanted and The Oprah Winfrey Show, and he was reported as seen around the world before he was captured off Sardinia by Italian police in 1991.

Boggs and Hanson were both convicted of Greene's murder and multiple counts of fraud and were sentenced to life imprisonment plus nine years without parole. Hawkins was convicted of conspiracy to murder and fraud and was sentenced to 34 years to life. Hawkins received a lighter sentence as he had not been involved in the actual murder, he was paroled in 2010.

Yocum and Candisky published the book Insured for Murder detailing the case. The story was also featured in two of the TruTV series: The Forensic Files episode titled "Mistaken for Dead" and the fourth episode of Murder by the Book, which guest-starred Jonathan Kellerman. Also, the crime was featured in the episode "Doctor of Death" in Blood, Lies and Alibis. In 1992, Edwin Chen, an investigative reporter for the Los Angeles Times, wrote a book titled Cheating Death, which provides an in-depth review of the murder.

Unsolved Mysteries and America's Most Wanted profiled the case when Hawkins was still a fugitive of justice. It was through The Oprah Winfrey Show, profiling John Walsh's America's Most Wanted episodes, that an international viewer provided the critical lead for law enforcement to apprehend John Hawkins in Italy. Vanity Fair also published an exposé on the case in 1992.

Richard Boggs died of a heart attack at the age of 69 on March 6th, 2003 while serving his sentence at Corcoran State Prison. At the time of his death, Boggs had been HIV positive for over ten years, and had also been diagnosed with terminal pancreatic cancer.

WILLIAM GEORGE BONIN

Born January 8th, 1947 – executed by lethal injection February 23rd, 1996.

Between December 1972 and June 1980, authorities in seven Southern California counties recorded the violent deaths of at least 44 young men and boys, attributing their murders to an unknown "Freeway Killer."

Of eleven victims slaughtered prior to 1976, most were known or suspected homosexuals, their deaths lending credence to the notion that the murderer himself was gay. While strangulation was the favoured mode of death, some victims had been stabbed with knives or ice picks, and their bodies bore the marks of sadistic torture.

Homicide investigators noted different hands at work in several of the murders, but they finally agreed that 21 were almost certainly connected. All were young males and all had been sodomised. Sixteen others would be solved in 1983, with the arrest of "Scorecard Killer" Randy Kraft.

The first "definite" connected victim was 14-year-old Thomas Lundgren, abducted from Reseda on May 28th, 1979, and discarded the same day, near Malibu.

Mark Shelton, 17, was next, reported missing from Westminster on August 4th, his body recovered a week later at Cajon Pass.

The day after Shelton's disappearance, 17-year-old Marcus Grabs was kidnapped in Newport Beach, his violated corpse discovered at Agoura on August 6th.

Donald Hyden, 15, was also found in Agoura, on August 27th -- the same day he disappeared from Hollywood.

On September 7th, 17-year-old David Murillo vanished from La Mirada, his body found in Ventura five days later.

The remains of Robert Wirostek were found off Interstate 10, between Banning and Palm Springs, on September 27th, but eleven months would pass before he was identified.

Another "John Doe" was discovered in Kern County, on November 30th, with 18-year-old Frank Fox murdered at Long Beach two days later.

The killer's last victim for 1979 was another unidentified male, aged 15 to 20, his violated body found on December 13th.

The New Year got off to a bad start in Southern California, with 16-year-old Michael McDonald abducted from Ontario on January 1st, 1980 and found dead two days later in San Bernadino County.

Charles Miranda, 14, disappeared from Los Angeles on February 3rd, his body discarded in Hollywood later that day.

On February 5th, 12-year-old James McCabe was kidnapped in Huntington Beach, his body recovered three days later in Garden Grove.

Ronald Gatlin, 18, disappeared from Van Nuys on March 14th, found dead the next day in Duarte.

Fifteen-year-old Russell Pugh was reported missing from Huntington Beach March 21st, his body found the next day at the Lower San Juan Campground, along with the corpse of 14-year-old victim Glen Barker.

Three days later, police found 15-year-old Harry Turner slain in Los Angeles proper.

The killer claimed two victims on April 10th, 1980, abducting 16-year-old Steven Wood from Bellflower, and returning to snatch 18-year-old Lawrence Sharp from Long Beach hours later. Wood's body was found April 11th, at Long Beach, but Sharp's remained missing until May 18th, when his remains were discovered in Westminster.

Meanwhile, on April 29th, 19-year-old Daren Kendrick was reported missing in Stanton, his body recovered from Carson on May 10th, with traces of chloral hydrate ("knockout drops") in his system.

On May 19th, 14-year-old Sean King vanished without a trace in South Gate; he has never been found.

Eighteen-year-old Stephen Wells was the last to die, he was kidnapped in Los Angeles June 2nd, his body discovered the next day at Huntington Beach.

Police got a lead on June 10th, when 18-year-old William Ray Pugh was brought in on another charge and confessed "inside" knowledge of the murder series. Pugh identified the killer as William George Bonin, a 32-year-old Vietnam veteran and truck driver residing in Downey. A glance at his record revealed Bonin had a 1969 conviction, in

Torrance, on counts of kidnapping, sodomy, child molestation and forcible oral copulation.

Those charges stemmed from four separate attacks, between November 1968 and January 1969, with Bonin diagnosed as a mentally disordered sex offender and committed to Atascadero State Hospital. He was released in May 1974, on the recommendation of psychiatrists who found him "no longer dangerous." Two years later, he was back in prison, convicted of kidnapping and raping a 14-year-old boy. Bonin had been paroled in October 1978, seven months before the death of Thomas Lundgren.

Officers established round-the-clock surveillance on Bonin. On the night of June 11th, 1980, he was arrested while sodomizing a young man in his van and booked on suspicion of murder and various sex charges. He was held in remand in lieu of $250,000 bond, Bonin was still in jail when police picked up his friend 22-year-old Vernon Butts on July 25th, charging him as an accomplice in six of the Bonin "freeway" murders.

Between July 26th and 29th, Bonin was formally charged with 14 counts of murder, eleven counts of robbery, plus one count each of sodomy and mayhem. Vernon Butts faced six counts of murder and three counts of robbery, he quickly began "singing" to the police, naming more alleged accomplices in the murder ring. James Michael Munro, 19, was arrested in Michigan on July 31st, returned to California for trial on charges of killing Stephen Wells.

Three weeks later, on August 22nd, 19-year-old Gregory M. Miley was arrested in Texas, waiving extradition on charges of murdering Charles Miranda and James McCabe, plus two counts of robbery and one count of sodomy.

Orange County raised the ante on October 29th, 1980, charging Vernon Butts with the murders of Mark Shelton, Robert Wirostek, and Darin Kendrick, plus 17 other felony counts including conspiracy, kidnapping, robbery, sodomy, oral copulation and sex perversion. Greg Miley was also charged with another Orange County murder, plus seven related felony counts. By December 8th, suspect Eric Marten Wijnaendts, a 20-year-old Dutch immigrant, had been added to the roster, charged with complicity in the murder of Harry Turner.

Under California law, a murder committed under "special circumstances" that is, accompanied by robbery, torture, or rape, may be punished by death. In December 1980, Bonin's accomplices began cracking, pleading guilty on various felony charges and drawing life sentences in return for their promise of testimony against Bonin. They spelled out details of the torture suffered by assorted "freeway" victims, and the glee with which Bonin inflicted pain. As one remarked, "he loved the sound of screams."

On January 11th 1981, after telling police of Bonin's "hypnotic" control, Vernon Butts hanged himself in his cell, finally successful with his fifth suicide attempt since his arrest.

With the new testimony in hand, Orange County indicted Bonin on eight more counts of murder, with 25 related counts of robbery and sexual assault. William Bonin's trial on twelve counts of murder opened November 4th, 1981, in Los Angeles.

Greg Miley and James Munro testified for the prosecution, describing how Bonin, following his arrest, had urged them to "start going around grabbing anyone off the street and killing them," in a bid to convince authorities that the "Freeway Killer" was still at large and they had arrested the wrong man.

On January 5th, 1982, after eight days of deliberation, jurors convicted Bonin on ten counts of murder and ten of robbery. He was acquitted in the deaths of Thomas Lundgren and Sean King. Two weeks later, he was formally sentenced to death. He was given the death sentence in two trials, one at Los Angeles County on March 12th, 1982 and the other in Orange County August 26th, 1983. He was the first person to be executed by lethal injection in California in San Quentin State Prison on February 23rd, 1996 age 49. He was cremated with his ashes scattered into the Pacific Ocean.

One aside of this was that three weeks after the execution, authorities discovered that his mother had openly exploited an administrative error on her son's social security disability payments – which Bonin had begun receiving for a mental disability in 1972 and which should have terminated upon his 1982 imprisonment – to maintain payments on her Downey home. This administrative error totalling approximately $79,424 was only discovered after a funeral director notified the Social Security

Administration of Bonin's death. Alice Benton subsequently agreed to pay restitution for receiving these payments in March 1996.

As for his 'helpers'...

Munro was sentenced to a term of fifteen years to life for the second degree murder of Wells on April 6th, 1981. He has repeatedly appealed his sentence, claiming that he had not known Bonin had been the Freeway Killer until after Wells' murder, and that he had been tricked into accepting a plea bargain whereby he pleaded guilty to this second degree murder charge. He has also written to successive governors, requesting he be executed rather than spend the remainder of his life behind bars for what he claims is "a crime I didn't commit". Munro has repeatedly been denied parole and is incarcerated at Mule Creek State Prison. He is next available for parole in 2029.

Miley was sentenced to a term of 25 years to life for the first-degree murder of Charles Miranda on February 5th, 1982. He was informed he would need to serve a minimum of sixteen years and eight months before he would be considered for parole. He was later sentenced to a concurrent term of 25 years to life for the abduction and murder of James Macabe. On May 25th 2016, Miley died of injuries he had sustained two days previously when he had been attacked by another inmate in an exercise yard at Mule Creek State Prison. At the time of his death, his next scheduled parole hearing was to be held in 2019.

Pugh was sentenced to six years in prison for the voluntary manslaughter of Harry Turner on May 17th, 1982. Pugh had initially been charged with the first-degree murder of Turner, in addition to companion charges of robbery and sodomy; however, after five days of deliberation, the jury found Pugh guilty of the reduced charge of manslaughter and innocent of robbery and sodomy. He served less than four years of his sentence, and was released from prison in late 1985.

WILLIAM RAY BONNER

Born March 28th, 1948 – Sentenced to life in prison on December 17th, 1973.

According to police files Bonner had been arrested six times since 1966 in connection with narcotics, assault and grand theft auto. In the most serious case he was sentenced to three years on probation for assaulting a police officer.

He was an unemployed service station attendant who, at the age of 25 years, went on a shooting spree through the South Side area of Los Angeles, California on April 22nd, 1973 that left a total of seven people dead and nine others wounded and ended with his arrest after he had been injured in a shootout with police.

The shooting began at Bonner's home at approximately 2:35 p.m. after he had got into an argument with Otha Leavitt, a friend of his mother, who had paid them a short visit to make a phone call. Enraged he went outside and, with a handgun, fired a shot each at 16-year-old Anthony Thomas and 17-year-old Carolyn Cleveland, who had accompanied Mrs. Leavitt and were waiting in her car. Leaving the two teenagers severely wounded Bonner returned inside and killed Otha Leavitt with a shot to her head and then hijacking her Plymouth Valiant, which Thomas and Cleveland had managed to run away from.

Armed with his handgun and a 20-gauge shotgun Bonner drove to a gas station about 1.5 miles from his home, where he had been employed previously as a service station attendant. Arriving there at about 2:43 p.m. he approached the occupants of a Chevrolet Impala, 18-year-old Vicky Wells and her 13-year-old sister Aileen, both known to him since their early childhood. He shot Vicky in the back with his shotgun, critically wounding her and killed Aileen, also by a shot in the back, as she was running towards the service area.

Bonner then drove to another gas station, where he had worked until a week previously. When he arrived there at 2:45 p.m. carrying his shotgun he entered the service bay area where he called out for his friend and former colleague, Raleigh Henderson, who had helped him get the job there. When Henderson turned around Bonner shot him once in the stomach and then fired again when Henderson exclaimed "What have I done?"

Pointing at the body on the floor Bonner asked service station attendant James Morrow: "Do you know if anyone wants some of that?" He approached a female customer, fired a shot in the air and then left to drive to the home of Jevie Thompson, with whose son, Vernon, he had an argument the night before. Bonner arrived there about 5 minutes later and killed Jevie Thompson with a shotgun blast in the stomach, and critically wounded his wife, Eddie Mae, as well as his 15-year-old son Alfred.

Bonner's next stop was Smitty's Drive-In Liquors, where he appeared at 3:14 p.m. Believing he had been short-changed there some time ago, he killed the shop owner, Smitty Sneed with a shot to the stomach, and wounded a customer, 58-year-old Duly Oscar Bennett, in the shoulder, before heading towards Liquorama Liquors, where he shot and critically wounded 23-year-old employee Robert L. Smith with a shot in the stomach, and hit 28-year-old Roosevelt D. Jenkins, another employee, in the leg.

A couple of minutes later Bonner barged into the house of his former girlfriend, 22-year-old Diane Lore Andrea, who had taken the side of Vernon Thompson during the argument the day before, and had broken up their relationship afterwards. He shot her in the neck with his shotgun, severing her jugular vein and spinal cord. She died instantly.

By now the police were after him. Bonner eluded them until 3:25 p.m. when he was spotted in his car by two patrolling police officers, blocking their way out of an alley. Bonner pointed his shotgun at them and repeatedly pulled the trigger, but when it failed to shoot he threw it away and sped off, while the police officers fired four shots at him and initiated a pursuit. Bonner crashed his Plymouth into the rear of the car of 45-year-old Mary Felton, who had stopped at a traffic light. He jumped out of his own vehicle and into the back seat of hers threatening her and her two daughters with his pistol ordering her to drive.

The scene was observed by security guard Versell Bennett who then took up pursuit in his car and eventually managed to force them to stop. Bennett then left his vehicle armed with his shotgun and opened fire at Bonner, who returned fire. When police finally caught up with Bonner, a shootout ensued in which he was hit five times in his legs and lower body. Though, some officers apparently mistakenly aimed their fire at Bennett first, mistaking him for the gunman. He was hit twice in the head and shoulders and died from these wounds four days later. Mrs. Felton also suffered minor injuries in the shoulder. At 3:29 p.m. Bonner was taken into custody and brought to Los Angeles County USC Medical Centre for treatment.

His victims were:

Diane Lore Andrea, 22, Bonner's girlfriend

Versell Bennett, 58, security guard, shot by police

Raleigh "Butch" Henderson, 33, friend of Bonner

Otha Leavitt, 53, friend of Bonner's mother

Smitty B. Sneed, 58, owner of Smitty's Drive-In Liquors

Jevie D. Thompson, 57

Aileen Wells, 13

Preliminary hearings for the case opened in July and on August 21st 1973 Bonner was formally charged with seven counts of murder, eight counts of assault with deadly weapon and three counts of kidnapping, whereupon he pleaded innocent and innocent by reason of insanity.

On November 13th Bonner changed his mind and pleaded guilty to one count each of first degree murder, second degree murder and assault with a deadly weapon and a month later, on December 17th, he was sentenced to life imprisonment.

As far as can be established he is still an inmate at California State Prison in Solano now age 76.

BENJAMIN HERBERT BOYLE

Born July 22nd 1943 – executed by lethal injection in Texas on April 21st, 1997.

    Gail Lenore Smith, age 20, had been working as a waitress at a topless bar in Fort Worth, Texas. She had no car and so when she decided it was time to see her mother in Lake Meredith, 300 miles away she had her friends drop her at a truck stop just outside Fort Worth, telling them she was going to hitch a ride and for them to take note of licence plate of the truck she took. Gail stuck her thumb out, waiting for a ride. It didn't take long and they saw her board a cherry-red Peterbilt tractor-trailer.
    On October 14th, 1985, police in Amarillo got a call from an excited trucker, who had stopped along the highway, north of town, to answer nature's call. Nearby in the brush, he found a woman's naked, lifeless body, bound in silver duct tape, with a man's tie knotted tight around her throat. An autopsy later discovered evidence of beating prior to death.
    A fingerprint comparison identified the victim as Gail Smith. One of the friends that had seen her off when she departed from Ft. Worth, although not taking note of the registration numer of the vehicle, remembered her first lift as a big, red semi-trailer Peterbilt, with its trailer bearing the legend JEWETT SCOTT Truck Line Inc. Detectives traced the firm to Mangum, Oklahoma two days later, and an examination of the schedules on file revealed that Herbert Boyle had been the only driver in the area.

He was due in Diboll, Texas where the police met him and with his permission searched his truck.

Boyle readily identified a snapshot of the victim, claiming he had dropped her off, alive, in Wichita Falls, near the Texas-Oklahoma border. If she died near Amarillo, someone else must be responsible.

A search of Boyle's belongings netted a roll of silver duct tape, several sheets and blankets. Fibres from the truck carpet were dispatched to Washington, D.C., where FBI analysis described them as identical with fibres found on Gail Smith's body. Boyle's wife recalled that she had seen some bloody sheets inside the truck, a short time earlier. Stray hairs recovered from the corpse was also matched to Boyle, and fingerprints, recovered from the duct tape used to bind Gail Smith, completed the array of damning evidence.

A background check on Boyle revealed that he was forty-two years old, had completed three years military service during August 1963, thereafter moving on to Colorado, where he lived and ran an auto body shop from 1969 to February 1980.

Boyle was next employed at a Las Vegas body shop, returning to his native Oklahoma in November 1981. He had been driving long-haul trucks since then, on routes that took him all over the country.

Working a variety of jobs had not prevented Boyle from stalking female victims in his leisure time. He had attempted to abduct a 28-year-old in Colorado Springs, November 20th, 1979, but she produced a knife and stabbed him several times in self-defence. Boyle's guilty plea to an attempted kidnap charge had earned him five years on probation.

At the time of his arrest in Texas, Boyle was also being sought for rape, in Canyon City, Colorado, where the victim had identified his photograph. A review of Boyle's extensive travels linked him with a second homicide, near Truckee, California, where a "Jane Doe" victim was discovered on June 21st, 1985. Her naked body had been stuffed inside a cardboard box, her hands and feet bound up with bandages and several kinds of tape. A wad of bedding had been left beside the corpse, and FBI reports said fibres taken from the body matched a blanket found inside Boyle's Oklahoma residence.

Boyle went to trial for Gail Smith's murder in October 1986. It took a jury three short hours to convict him on October 29th. The judge passed a sentence of death which was carried out by lethal injection on April 21st, 1997 after eleven years of appeals were rejected.

WILLIAM RICHARD BRADFORD

Born 1946 – sentenced to death in 1988. Died in prison March 13th, 2008.

In July 1984, while out on bail and awaiting trial for rape, Bradford met Shari Miller, a barmaid at a Los Angeles strip club called "The Meet Market". Bradford told her that he was a professional photographer and offered to help her build a modelling portfolio. He took her to a remote campsite in the deserts north of Los Angeles which was the site of the alleged rape for which Bradford was awaiting trial, there he photographed her in a variety of modelling poses, and then strangled her. After killing her, Bradford sliced off her tattoos and removed her blouse before he took her body to a Hollywood parking lot and dumped the corpse in an adjoining alley. When the body was found, there was no identification on it, leading Shari Miller to be labelled "Jane Doe #60".

Shortly thereafter, Bradford convinced his 15-year-old neighbour Tracey Campbell that she could be a model and took her out to the same desert campsite, where he photographed and strangled her. Bradford left the body there, covering the face with Shari Miller's blouse.

Bradford came under suspicion when investigators learned that he had been the last person to see Tracey Campbell alive. This, coupled with his pending rape trial, compelled police to obtain a search warrant for his apartment where they found the photos of Shari Miller and Tracey Campbell along with an assortment of 54 other photos of unidentified women. Police recognized the photos of Miller as their "Jane Doe #60" and arrested Bradford on suspicion of murder. Using a rock formation visible in one of the photos of Miller, police were able to locate the camp site in the desert where the murders had occurred. Upon searching the site, police found Campbell's decomposed body behind the rock formation. Shortly thereafter, Bradford pleaded no contest to the rape charge he was awaiting trial for and was sentenced to eight years in prison.

Bradford was put on trial for the murder in 1988 opting to act as his own counsel. During the phase of the trial in which Bradford acted as his own attorney, he offered no evidence or arguments as to his innocence. The prosecution identified Bradford as a serial killer during the course of the trial, but offered no information on murders aside from those of Miller and Campbell. In his closing statement, Bradford implied that he had murdered several other women in addition to Campbell and Miller saying, "Think of how many you don't even know about."

The jury found Bradford guilty of both murders and he was sentenced to death.

Ten years later in 1998, Bradford dropped all of his appeals, claiming that life in San Quentin had become unbearable. Having had no legal representation for the past 10 years, Bradford then hired a lawyer to help speed the process of his execution and began writing poems about life in San

Quentin. His poetry attracted attention from the press, who dubbed him "Death Row Poet".

Five days before his scheduled execution, Bradford said that he had changed his mind, professing his innocence and declaring that he wanted the execution process to be halted. His attorneys started the appeals process again.

In 2006 Los Angeles police suddenly voiced new interest in the Bradford case, releasing a data sheet depicting headshots taken from the photos in Bradford's apartment. Why they waited 10 years to do so has not been explained? Detectives claimed that they believed the women could all be Bradford's victims. Since releasing those photos, at least one woman, "#28", has been identified as Donnalee Campbell Duhamel, a woman whose decapitated corpse was found in a canyon in Malibu in 1978. It has been determined that Duhamel met Bradford in a Culver City bar, "The Frigate", a few days before her body was found. This adds credence to Bradford's statement of 'Think how many you don't know about' that he made at his trial.

Investigators have also revealed that several of the women have since been identified as Bradford's ex-wives, though no indication has been given whether they are alive or dead, or if dead whether Bradford is suspected of murdering them.

William Richard Bradford died of natural causes in Vacaville prison medical facility on March 13th, 2008 age 61.

ROGER HOAN BRADY

Born 1966 – sentenced to life in prison in Oregon in 1996. Sentenced to death in California on March 16th 1999.

On December 27th, 1993, Officer Martin Ganz, 27, pulled over a vehicle outside a mall in what was described as a routine traffic stop. When the officer approached the car, the driver, Roger Brady, began firing shots with a semi-automatic weapon.

When Ganz attempted to find cover behind his patrol car, Brady left his vehicle and chased him while still firing. Ganz's 13-year-old nephew, Don Ganz, was on a school holiday ride-along with his uncle, and Brady pointed his weapon at the boy; thankfully, the gun jammed, meaning he fled the scene without harming the youngster.

Ganz had been struck with three bullets; he had been wearing a bulletproof vest, but two of the bullets had hit him above the vest.

Several bystanders came to his aid, and young Don Ganz called for help on the police radio. Martin Ganz was taken to hospital but died later. Ganz's service revolver was found lying on the ground beside him; unfortunately, he had been unable to return fire.

Don Ganz, along with another witness, Jennifer La Fond, who had been driving past at the time, gave the investigators a description of the killer and his vehicle.

A month later, an anonymous tipster told the police that the killer had been Roger Brady. Unfortunately, neither Don Ganz nor La Fond could pick Brady out of a selection of photographs.

The case had stalled until August 1994 when officers from Oregon began investigating Roger Brady for a murder committed in their state. He was suspected of shooting a 55-year-old nurse, Catalina Correa, 55, during a robbery at a Beavertown, Oregon store. The nurse had been in the store and followed Brady in her car when he fled the scene. He had noticed her following, pulled over and shot her.

By this stage, Brady was living with his parents in Washington State, and when officers went to the home, they noticed that his car matched the description from the Ganz case.

A further search of Brady's property revealed a firearm that matched the one used to kill Officer Ganz. Finally, witness Jennifer La Fond was able to pick him out of a line-up, which led to him being charged with Ganz's murder.

Brady was first convicted and sentenced to life in prison for the murder in Oregon before he was sentenced to death in California for killing Officer Martin Ganz.

Roger Brady remains on death row at San Quentin at the time of writing. In 2019, Governor Newson ordered a moratorium on California's death penalty whilst he remains in office. He has called the death penalty and "abject failure."

CHRISTIAN BRANDO
(son of the actor Marlon Brando)

Born May 11th, 1958 – sentenced to 10 years for manslaughter February 21st 1991. Died January 26th, 2008.

On May 16th, 1990, Christian Brando fatally shot Dag Drollet, the boyfriend of his half-sister Cheyenne in the living room of his father's house in Beverly Hills, California. Drollet was in a four-year relationship with Cheyenne, who was 8 months pregnant at the time.
A few days before the incident, Drollet had flown in from Tahiti to Los Angeles to visit Cheyenne. Cheyenne was visiting her father along with her mother, and both were staying at Marlon Brando's residence. Marlon Brando had known the Drollet family for years; however, Christian Brando only met Dag Drollet for the first time several hours before shooting him dead.
On the evening of the killing, Brando and Cheyenne had dinner at Musso and Frank Grill, where Cheyenne told Brando that Drollet had been physically abusive toward her. Later, around 11 p.m. that night, Brando, who admitted to being drunk at the time, confronted Drollet at the Brando home about the abuse and shot him dead. Brando claimed that he did not intend to kill just to scare him. Drollet and Cheyenne was staying in separate rooms. Christian Brando claimed that he and Drollet were fighting over the gun when it accidentally went off.

Brando was initially charged with murder; however, prosecutors were unable to proceed with a murder charge because of the absence of Cheyenne, who was a crucial witness to their case. Marlon Brando had Cheyenne admitted into a psychiatric hospital in Tahiti. After several attempts to get her to return to California and testify, a judge eventually quashed all efforts by the prosecution to subpoena her. Without Cheyenne's testimony, prosecutors felt they could no longer prove that Drollet's death was premeditated; therefore, Christian was not charged with first-degree murder and was presented with a plea deal. When his father pleaded for a reduced sentence for his son, he took the stand in the Santa Monica courthouse and said, "I think that perhaps I failed as a father." After heavily publicized pre-trial proceedings, Brando pleaded guilty to manslaughter and spent five years in prison.

Cheyenne attempted suicide twice during the trial. Then, in 1995, a year before Christian was released from prison, she succeeded by hanging herself at her mother's house in Tahiti at the age of 25 after losing custody of her son.

Brando died of pneumonia on January 26th, 2008, at Hollywood Presbyterian Medical Centre at the age of 49. He had been admitted on January 11th, 2008

Christian Brando was buried on February 17th, 2008, at the Kalama Oddfellows Cemetery in Kalama, Washington.

An interesting aside:

Actor Robert Blake and his defence attorneys claimed that Christian Brando was involved in the 2001 murder of Blake's 44-year-old wife Bonny Lee Bakley.(see under ROBERT BLAKE) Blake was ultimately charged with his wife's murder and although acquitted in the criminal trial, he was found liable for her death in the civil case brought by her children.

Testimony introduced during the criminal pre-trial hearings and the subsequent civil trial attempted to implicate Christian Brando in the murder, suggesting that he had the same motive as Blake to have Bonny Lee Bakley killed. Bakley had become pregnant and claimed to both Brando and Blake that they were the father. A DNA test subsequently determined that Robert Blake, not Christian Brando, was the biological father.

According to trial testimony, just days before her death Bakley continued to claim Brando was the father of her child. Dianne Mattson testified in court that Brando became enraged, and at one point stated "somebody should put a bullet in that bitch's head". In a tape-recorded conversation between Brando and Bakley, Brando stated, "You're lucky. You know, I mean, not on my behalf, but you're lucky someone ain't out there to put a bullet in your head."

According to pre-trial testimony and corroboration, Christian Brando was in Washington State on the night Bakley was shot dead. Other pre-trial testimony alleged that associates of Brando were involved in the murder. One of those allegedly involved was the prosecution's star witness: Duffy Hambleton, a stunt man. Hambleton claimed that Blake tried to hire him to kill Bakley. Hambleton claimed he refused the offer. Blake, however, testified that he hired Hambleton for personal security to protect himself and Bakley from a stalker. Criminal pre-trial and civil trial testimony claimed that Hambleton was an associate of Christian Brando and that he arranged the murder of Bakley to curry favour with Brando. The judge in the criminal case prevented the defence from presenting that view during the trial.

Brando was called as a witness in Blake's civil trial but refused to testify, invoking his Fifth Amendment constitutional rights. Brando's behaviour in court got him a contempt of court charge and conviction.

SPENCER RAWLINS BRASURE

Born 1968 – sentenced to death on August 25th, 1998. Died in prison age 49 on November 14th, 2019.

What this victim endured is unbelievable. This is taken from the prosecution evidence.

In September 1996, Spencer Brasure and his girlfriend Sonia Rodriguez were living with Billy Davis at a house in Hawthorne owned by Davis's father. Brasure, Davis, Rodriguez and another woman, Sandra Johnson, regularly used methamphetamine together and sold the drug to one another. In outline, the prosecution evidence showed that in early September, with Johnson's help, Brasure and Davis kidnapped Guest, with whom they were all acquainted; that Brasure and Davis then tortured Guest for some time at Davis's home; and that the two men (and perhaps another, Matt Ormsby) eventually took Guest to an isolated recreation area, where they put him under a bush, doused him with gasoline and set him alight.

Sandra Johnson pleaded guilty to conspiracy to kidnap and agreed to testify truthfully in proceedings involving Guest's death in exchange for a grant of probation with a jail sentence not to exceed one year.

Johnson testified that in August 1996, she, Davis and Brasure discussed their grievances against Guest. Johnson was annoyed because Guest, who had expressed unwanted romantic feelings for her, had been following her around and paging her often, and on one occasion had thrown an ice pick at her. He also acted paranoid and accused her of conspiring to get him hurt. Davis was also angry at Guest for stealing items from Davis's house after staying with him and for hitting him on one occasion without provocation. Brasure was angry because some of the items Guest took were his property. They agreed Guest should be beaten up, and Brasure said he and Davis would do it if Johnson would bring Guest to them.

A few days later, Johnson discussed this proposal with Scott Crosby, who was also angry at Guest for thefts and fights Guest was involved in while staying with him. Sometime later still, when Crosby discovered where Guest was then staying, he and Johnson formulated a plan to pick up Guest (on the pretext they needed him to broker a drug deal) and deliver him to Brasure. Brasure and Davis also having agreed, they executed the plan: Johnson and Crosby persuaded Guest to accompany them, and with Johnson driving and Guest riding in the backseat of Johnson's two-door car they went to a fast-food restaurant parking lot a few miles from Davis's house. Johnson telephoned Brasure, and he and Davis soon arrived at the parking lot in Brasure's pickup truck. Brasure took Crosby's place in the front passenger seat of Johnson's car and, at gunpoint, ordered Guest, in the backseat, to turn around. Ignoring Guest's repeated plea of, "Can't we just work this out?" Brasure bound Guest's wrists with a plastic zip tie and directed Johnson to drive them to Davis's house.

Johnson left them at Davis's house, then drove to Crosby's and, eventually, to the home where she was staying. Later, she received a page to call Sonia Rodriguez. When Johnson called her, Rodriguez asked Johnson to come and take her out of the house because "these guys are crazy." Johnson drove to Davis's house and honked the horn for Rodriguez, but then fell asleep in the car. After about 45 minutes, Davis came out to her car and told Johnson to come inside the house.

Following Davis into the house and down the hallway to the back room (referred to as the "red room" for its carpet colour), Johnson twice heard a buzzing, crackling sound, followed by a moan or whimper. Guided into the red room by Davis, she smelled burning skin and saw Guest lying across a chair, his hands and feet tied together behind him and his mouth covered with duct tape. Brasure was standing in front of him, holding a wire or rod attached to a car battery, which was strapped to a large dolly.

Brasure touched the wire or rod to Guest's skin. Guest jerked and cried, and Johnson smelled his skin burn. Brasure told her to bend down and look Guest in the eye. She saw there was a bump on his forehead, his nose was bloody, and he looked scared and hurt. There were 10 to 12 red spots on his body where he had been burned with the rod. Brasure laughingly asked Johnson if Guest looked like a bitch. Afraid, Johnson answered that he did, she then went into a smaller side room to see Rodriguez. Asked how long this had been going on, Rodriguez said a couple of hours. While talking to her, Johnson heard the buzzing sound several more times, followed by Guest moaning. She also heard the voices of Brasure, Davis and Matt Ormsby.

From the small side room, Johnson heard Brasure laugh and tell Davis and Ormsby to get trash bags and a trash can. She then heard the sound of bags being opened, thudding and a person whimpering. After she heard Brasure's truck start up and drive away, she and Rodriguez emerged from the small room. The red room was empty of people; the chair Guest had been lying on, as well as the dolly and battery, were also gone. Johnson took Rodriguez to a donut shop for about a half-hour then dropped her back at Davis's house.

After these events, Johnson went to Davis's house less often. On one occasion, Brasure told her he had put broken glass in Guest's mouth, duct-taped it shut and hit him in the face.

Nestor Largaespada testified he was drinking with Matt Ormsby outside a house near Davis's on the evening of September 7th, 1996, when Brasure shouted for Ormsby to come over to Davis's. Ormsby did so, and sometime later Largaespada followed him. Inside the back part of Davis's house, Ormsby led him to the red room. Largaespada saw a man wearing a Halloween mask seated with his hands crossed in front of him. Brasure, standing next to him, said something like "This is what we do with white trash." Largaespada, afraid, left and told no one what he had seen.

Joey March, Richard Lago, Ricardo Rivera and James Luna all testified to incriminatory statements Brasure had made after Guest's death. Although Matt Ormsby had made a statement to the prosecution's investigator and given grand jury testimony corroborating Johnson's and Largaespada's testimony in many respects, and recounting incriminatory admissions by Brasure, when on the witness stand he recanted most of these statements, saying he had made them up or based them on things he had heard on the street or from the police.

March listened in on a telephone conversation between Brasure and Davis, who was staying with March sometime after Guest's death. Brasure told Davis that if he went down for Guest's death, he would not go down alone. Davis responded in kind, and the two then reviewed what they had done together. Brasure said that after taking Guest from the fast-food restaurant parking lot at gunpoint, they took him to Davis's house and tied him up in the homemade "electric chair." He offered Guest a hit of methamphetamine, then shoved the glass pipe into Guest's mouth. Both he and Davis, Brasure noted, burned Guest with a torch. They also used Krazy Glue to glue Guest's eyes shut. Later, Brasure recounted, they took him in a van to a spot near Gorman, dumped him on the ground — causing his eyes to pop open and show his expression of pain — and doused him with gasoline. Brasure complained to Davis that because "none of you guys had a lighter," he had to use a flare from the van to set Guest alight. After providing this information to law enforcement officers, March received sentencing benefits in two of his own convictions.

Lago testified Brasure told him he had made an electric chair, used it over the course of several days on a man, then taken the victim to "the desert" in Ventura County and set him on fire. Brasure was laughing and "getting kicks" out of this story as he told it. Rivera testified Brasure told him he had used a car battery, transformer and jumper cables (which belonged to Rivera) to inflict pain on Guest ("the short dude with the Boston accent"), then taken the victim, whom Brasure referred to as "white trash," to the desert. Luna testified Brasure told him he had made an electric chair and had electrocuted and killed a man "who had gotten out of line."

Guest's body was found on September 13th, 1996, at a campground in the Hungry Valley State Vehicular Recreation Area (Hungry Valley SVRA) near Gorman in Ventura County. The body was underneath a partly burned juniper bush. Guest had third and fourth degree burns across his body. In some areas, including the face, his flesh was darkly charred and split from burning. His eyes were collapsed and decomposed, his nose flattened, and his mouth charred and mummified. Guest's body was identified by dental records and a distinctive tattoo. The flesh of his legs had been eaten and gnawed by animals. The medical examiner was unable to assign a cause of death; though there was soot in Guest's airway, the presence of live maggots made it impossible to say the soot had entered by inhalation. From the size of the maggots on Guest's body, the medical examiner estimated Guest had been in the juniper bush for a week or two. A magnesium plate, similar to those used by Davis's father in his printing business, was found against Guest's face. An X-ray showed a staple in his head, and there was a small fragment of glass in his mouth. Found at the scene were a flare, a flare cap, pieces of melted zip ties and duct tape, staples, a large trash can and liner, and a partly burned folding chair. Blood matched to Guest's by DNA analysis was on the trash can liner, human tissue was on the zip ties, and blood that could not be tested was on the magnesium plate and trash can.

The prosecution presented evidence that while in jail on murder charges Brasure wrote several letters to his friend Noreen Donaldson. In one, Brasure asked Donaldson to give a copy of a "rat list" to another person, continuing, "Ricardo Rivera, James Luna, Joey March, Richard Lago, Scott Crosby are main rats that need to be killed ASAP before my next court date, July 16th, 1997."

A Ventura County fire investigation specialist testified that magnesium, once ignited, burns at 5,400 degrees Fahrenheit and is very difficult to extinguish, but that a magnesium plate strapped to the head of a person and resting against the ground would be difficult to ignite with gasoline.

In a second letter to Donaldson Brasure said he hoped she was "helping me out with spreading the Joey March and Billy story and taking care of the rats." In a third, he instructed her to "type a letter to Lago stating that we (Hells Angeles) have located his son Steve. He'd better not testify in court on our family friend Spencer .... We are watching and there is no escape."

Donaldson testified she received several letters apparently signed by Brasure asking that Billy Davis, Richard Lago, Sandra Johnson, James Luna and Joey March be killed. She showed some of them to Brasure's brother, Chad Brasure. She also tried to hand deliver a letter from Brasure to Nestor Largaespada, but Largaespada refused to accept it having heard on the street that there was a rat list and believing he was on it. Richard Lago testified he received telephonic threats against his life and that of his son if he testified. A small explosive device was also thrown into his driveway by people directed by Chad Brasure. Sandra Johnson testified that when she appeared in the same courtroom as Brasure, she heard him tell another person that she, Johnson, was a "rat" who was trying to get him convicted of murder.

In May 1997, a superior court judge, with Brasure present in court, ordered that he not be allowed to send letters from jail except to his attorneys. In September and October 1997, Brasure nonetheless sent letters to Billy Davis and another person.

Earlier, Rangers at the Hungry Valley SVRA saw smoke and had found a burning van on September 6th, 1996, outside a campground (a different one than where Guest's body was later found). Automobile and plumbing parts were scattered around, and Brasure's palm print was on the driver's side mirror.

James Luna testified that in September 1996, he had recently been terminated from a plumbing company job but still had keys to the van he had been using and to the company parking lot. He told Brasure about a valuable new engine recently installed in the van, and the two formed a plan to steal the van and sell the engine. They took the van from the plumbing company premises, and Brasure drove it to near Davis's house. Brasure told Luna he would take it to the desert and "chop" it up and would give Luna some of the profits. Two days later, however, Brasure told Luna the engine had blown on the way to the desert, so he had burned the van to prevent its recognition.

Sonia Rodriguez testified that she, Brasure and Davis took the plumbing van to a campground near Gorman in September. The men worked on the van for a long time but were unable to get the engine out, so they left it there and drove home in Brasure's truck. The van caught fire as they were leaving she said.

Brasure was charged in count 1 with murdering Guest with special circumstances of murder while engaged in kidnapping and intentional murder involving the infliction of torture; in count 2 with kidnapping Guest; in count 3 with torturing Guest; in count 4 with arson of Guest's property ; in count 5 with conspiracy to commit grand theft automobile; in count 6 with attempted grand theft of the plumbing van engine; in count 7 with arson of the plumbing van; in count 8 with conspiracy to kidnap Guest; in counts 9 through 13 with threatening Richard Lago,

James Luna, Joey March, Richard (Ricardo) Rivera and Scott Crosby; and in count 14 with disobeying a court order, a misdemeanour.

The jury convicted on all counts except count 13, on which it acquitted, and found the special circumstance allegations true. After the penalty phase trial, the jury returned a verdict of death on August 25th, 1998. The trial court denied Brasure's motion for new trial and his automatic motion for modification of penalty and sentenced him to death on count 1. Execution of sentence on counts 2, 3, 4 and 8 was stayed. On the remaining felony counts, the court sentenced Brasure to an aggregate determinate prison term of two years eight months.

Spencer Brasure died in alone in his cell on death row at San Quentin State prison on November 14th, 2019 age 51

THOMAS EUGENE BRAUN

Born 1949 – sentenced to death, later commuted to life in prison. Died in prison February 9th 2010 age 61.

A native of rural Washington State, born in 1949, Thomas Braun lost his mother in early childhood as the result of a clumsy, illegal abortion. Left in the care of their alcoholic father, Braun and his younger sister were frequently locked in a truck while the old man made his rounds of the local taverns.

On August 17th, 1967, Braun, age 18, left his job as a gas station attendant in Ritzville, Washington, and picked up his best friend, slow-witted Leonard Maine, on his way out of town. The 18-year-olds had two pistols, a car, and no clear destination in mind. In Seattle, on August 18th, the boys stopped at a rooming house, asked about lodgings, and then pulled their guns on the landlady, fleeing in panic when she began screaming.

The next afternoon, outside Redmond, they pulled over 22-year-old Deanna Buse, pretending that something was wrong with a tyre on her car. Forcing the young woman into his vehicle at gunpoint, Braun drove on to Echo Lake with Maine following in Buse's sedan. Arriving at their destination, Braun marched his captive into the woods, forced her to strip, and then shot her five times. They then dumped their old car in Seattle and keeping the new one they drove south into Oregon.

On August 21st, Samuel Ledgerwood saw them changing a flat tyre and stopped to offer help, getting two shots in the head for his trouble. Leaving his corpse where it lay, the boys torched Buse's car and drove off in Ledgerwood's vehicle, bound for California.

Timothy Luce and Susan Bartolomie were residents of Ukiah, California. On the evening of August 21st, 1967, shortly before 6 p.m., they left Ukiah in a car and drove to a wrecking yard in Hopland to buy a spare part. During the return trip something went wrong with their car. They pulled over and started walking back toward Ukiah. They were given a ride by Braun and Maine who were driving south but turned around and drove back to pick them up. Braun and Maine were driving Samuel Ledgerwood's 1967 light green Buick sedan. Susan later testified that Maine was driving the car when they were picked up. After travelling a short distance they turned off the highway and threatened Tim and Susan with guns being pointed at them. Susan saw two pistols. While Maine stayed in the car with her, Braun left with Tim and a single shot was heard by Susan. After the shot, Braun came back to the car and Susan heard the pair talking about a wallet and about $6.

Sometime before 7 p.m. the same day, Tim's body was found on a small roadway adjacent to a vineyard south of Ukiah. As later determined, Tim's death was caused by a single gunshot wound in the nape of the neck at the base of the skull.

Shortly after Tim's murder, Braun and Maine resumed driving south, taking Susan with them. During this journey, they stopped three times — at a service station, a restaurant and a motel. Before reaching the motel, Braun and Maine talked about wanting money from Susan's parents, but she told them that her parents had no money. Arriving at the motel, Susan was taken to a cabin where first Braun, then Maine, raped her.

Sometime later they got back in the car and resumed driving. At about 10 or 11 p.m. they reached another motel on Highway 99, north of Turlock, where Braun registered. After a couple of hours' stay, they left that motel, too. Susan was shot sometime after that by Braun while she was outside the car. The evidence indicates that she was shot shortly before 5 a.m. on August 22nd, 1967, and her body was thrown into a ditch from which she crawled back up to the roadway where she was discovered by a Mr. and Mrs. Mease at about 6 a.m. Before the arrival of the authorities, Susan spoke to Mrs. Mease giving a recount of the shootings and a description of Braun and Maine and their vehicle. Acting upon this information passed on by Mrs. Mease the police arrested the killers in the Jamestown Hotel, Jamestown, California, at about 9:15 a.m.

A search of the room occupied by Maine found a plastic carrying case which contained a blanket, a .22 calibre Ruger automatic, and a .22 calibre Colt single-action pistol. Both pistols were fully loaded. In the pocket of a pair of jeans the officers found a wallet, some change and a number of .22 calibre hollow-point bullets. In the pocket of a pair of jeans found in Braun's room the officers found a car key, two wallets and a number of .22 calibre hollow-point bullets. During the search of the Buick, which took place after it had been towed to the Sonora police station, the officers found two suitcases and a .35 calibre Remington rifle. One of the suitcases contained seven boxes of .22 calibre cartridges and a box of .35 calibre Remington cartridges. A fingerprint examiner who processed the vehicle found prints which he identified as those of Tim, Susan, Braun and Maine. A criminalist testified that, in his opinion, a cartridge casing found by Tim's body and four cartridge casings found near Susan on the highway were all fired from the Ruger .22 calibre automatic pistol found in Maine's room. The same criminalist testified that, in examining a pair of tennis shoes found in Braun's room, he discovered stains of human blood on the right shoe. These stains were of blood group A, which was Susan's blood type. Tim's blood type was O, as was the blood type of both Braun and Maine.

Both were sent to trial and convicted of first degree murder. Braun was sentenced to death later reduced to life in prison and died in San Quentin prison from cancer in February 2010 age 61. Maine escaped with life in prison but also died there from natural causes.

Susan Bartolomie was paralyzed and could only communicate by blinking. She died on March 17th, 2001 basically from the wounds she received in 1967.

VINCENT BROTHERS

Born May 31st, 1962 – sentenced to death September 27th, 2007.

On Sunday July 6th, 2003, Joanie Harper, her three children and her mother, Earnestine Harper, attended a Sunday morning church service. It was the first time at church for six-week-old Marshall Harper. After the service they went to dine at the Black Angus before going home. Once home they lay down to take a nap prior to returning to the church for the evening service. Joanie and her children were in the rear bedroom while her mother was in another bedroom at the other end of the house.

An intruder, armed with a .22-calibre pistol, entered the house through the backyard and quietly moved to the rear bedroom.

Two days later on Tuesday morning family friend, Kelsey Spann, decided to check on her friend Joanie Harper and her family as she had not heard from her in several days, which was unusual, and feared something was wrong. She went to a side door and inserted the key given to her by Joanie into the lock. Something was blocking the door keeping her from pushing it open so she walked around to the back of the house and tested the sliding glass door. It was unlocked which was very unusual. Kelsey entered the house and walked through to Joanie's bedroom.

A call was placed to 911 at 7 am. When the police arrived they witnessed the horrific scene that Kelsey Spann had stumbled upon:

Joanie Harper was found face down on the bed. She had been shot three times in the head and twice in the arm. She had also been stabbed seven times.

Marshall Harper, the six-week old was found next to his mother under a pillow. He had been shot in the back.

Marques Harper, the four-year-old was found on the bed. He had a gunshot to the right side of his head and his eyes were open. The fingertips of one of his hands had been bitten to the bone. It was surmised that he had seen the killer and been so frightened he had stuck his fingers in his mouth.

Lyndsey Harper, the two-year-old was found at the foot of her mother's bed. She had been shot in the back.

Ernestine Harper was found in the hallway. She had been shot twice in the face. The pistol she held when she confronted the intruder was found lying next to her body.

Almost immediately after the murders were discovered, suspicion fell on Vincent E. Brothers, the estranged husband of Joanie Harper. It took nine months before he was caught and charged with five counts of first-degree murder.

Vincent Brothers was well-known and well-liked in the Bakersfield, CA community. He was respected as a mentor and a Christian family man. Brothers has a bachelor's degree from Norfolk State University and a master's degree in education from

California State University, Bakersfield. He began his career as a substitute teacher in 1987 and eventually became the vice-principal of Fremont Elementary School in 1995.

His trial began on February 22nd, 2007. Brothers pleaded not guilty and claimed that he was in Ohio visiting his brother at the time of the murders. A brother he had not seen in ten years.

According to the prosecution Brothers was an admitted adulterer who never loved his family and used murder as a means to rid himself of the financial burden they placed on him. The prosecution claimed that on July 2nd, 2003 he flew to Ohio to visit his brother in order to establish an alibi. When he touched down in Ohio he rented a Dodge Neon from Dollar Rent-A-Car. Detectives seized the rental car and alleged that the company records proved that while the car was in his possession, Brothers put more than 5,400 miles on the clock. More than enough mileage for him to have driven to Bakersfield, murdered his family and driven back to Ohio. Prosecutors contended that Brother's drove approximately 4,500 miles in three days.

The radiator and air filter were seized by the police and taken to the Bohart Museum of Entomology for testing. Prof. Lynn Kimsey from the University of California took the stand and testified that she found several insect species in the car parts that were found only in the west and that the types of insects found indicated that the car had only been driven at night.

The prosecution introduced video evidence that proved that Vincent's brother, Melvin, used Vincent's credit card at Wal-mart. Melvin also admitted to forging his brother's signature and that he had no knowledge of his brother's whereabouts between July 4th and 7th. Evidence showed that a call was placed to Melvin Brother's cell phone in Ohio around 4 pm on the day of the murder from the Harper residence.

The defence claimed that the extra marital affairs were being used to discredit his character and were not relevant. They claimed that cell phone records placed Brother's in Ohio at the time of the murders and that he had also been involved in a minor traffic accident when a boy on a bike darted out in the street and ran into Brother's car. Columbus police tracked down the man who was actually involved in the traffic accident with the boy on the bike and he testified in court. It was not one of the Brothers. Also there was no video evidence of Brother's in over 100 gas stations and mini marts between Ohio and California. Plus, the murder weapon was never found. Brother's took the stand in his on defence and claimed that he had also spent time driving around with his other brother, Troy, which was why Melvin did not know where he was from the 4th through the 7th of July.

Troy Brother's was subpoenaed to testify for the defence but he disappeared. A $100,000 arrest warrant was issued.

On May 15th, 2007, the jury found Vincent E. Brothers guilty of five counts of first-degree murder and on September 27th, 2007 he was sentenced to death and, at the time of writing, sits on death row in San Quentin State prison.

ALBERT GREENWOOD BROWN

Born August 18th, 1954 – sentenced to death February 19th, 1982.

On an early morning in 1976, Albert Brown broke into a home in Riverside and hid in a closet until all of the residents had left. Then, when a 14-year-old girl returned from her paper round to go to school, he choked her unconscious and brutally raped her in her mother's bedroom.

Brown pleaded guilty to charges of First Degree with Force on May 4th, 1978, and was sentenced to state prison. He was paroled on June 14th, 1980, and found work cleaning and preparing new cars for sale at Rubidoux Motors in Riverside County.

On the morning of October 28th, 1980, Brown abducted 15-year-old Susan Louise Jordan while she was on her way to Arlington High School in Riverside. He had been posing as a jogger on the school route and after dragging her to an orange grove Brown brutally raped and sodomized her before he strangled her to death with one of her shoelaces. He also took her identification cards and school books. Susan's mother, Angelina Jordan, who had coincidentally left her car to be serviced at Brown's workplace, Rubidoux Motors, went to the school to search for Susan after her younger sister, Karen, and younger brother, James, returned home without her and said she hadn't attended school at all that day.

After finding the family's number in a phone book, Brown called Angelina Jordan from a payphone at around 7:30 p.m. to tell her where he left her daughter's body. According to court documents, he said, "Hello, Mrs. Jordan, Susie isn't home from school yet, is she? You will never see your daughter again. You can find her body on the corner of Victoria and Gibson." Susan's body was found after Brown repeatedly made calls to the Riverside Police Department and the Jordan residence each time giving a different location. One of Brown's subsequent calls was recorded by a police officer.

Brown was arrested on November 6th, 1980, after three witnesses came forward to identify him and his Pontiac Trans Am with a Rubidoux Motors trade paper plate seen near the site of the murder. Susan's identification cards were found in a phone booth at a nearby Texaco service station.

During a search of Brown's home on November 7th, police found Susan's books, a newspaper article about the case, and a Riverside telephone directory in which the page opposite the listing for the Jordan family was folded as a marker. Brown was discovered to have been late to work on the day she disappeared. A jogging suit stained with blood and sperm was found in his locker at the employee coffee shop. Brown's shoes were matched to footprints from the crime scene.

On February 4th, 1982, a Riverside County jury convicted Brown of first-degree murder with the special circumstances of first-degree kidnapping and first-degree rape, oral copulation, and first-degree sodomy. During sentencing hearings, his defence attorney argued that Brown was remorseful and presented evidence of psychiatric problems, including sexual dysfunction. Brown claimed that his aunt had physically abused him as a child and that he was regularly beaten by his mother. His mother denied abusing Brown but claimed that he was out buying milk at the time of the murder. The surviving victim of the 1976 rape case testified against him. The jury deliberated for less than three hours on February 19th and sentenced Brown to death. On March 2nd, 1982, he was placed on death row at San Quentin State Prison in San Quentin California.

In 1985, Brown's sentence was overturned by the California Supreme Court and then reinstated by the US Supreme Court in 1987. Since then he has come close to being executed several times but remains on death row in San Quentin State Prison at the time of writing.

BARRY AUSTIN BROWN

Born 1953 – sentenced to three life-in-prison terms 1974.

Barry Brown is a convicted triple murderer who killed a store clerk in Santa Cruz in June 1974 and two other people in San Mateo County in July of that year and has been denied parole by, the Santa Cruz District Attorney's Office basically because he has always refused to engage in substance abuse treatment and self-help programming while in prison. Brown has declined to do that over the last 40 years.

At the last parole hearing, Santa Cruz Assistant District Attorney Kristina Oven argued that Brown had no insight into his murder spree, remorse or credibility for the truth. She said in a statement asking that parole be denied again in 2015.

"Until Mr. Brown can tell our community why he began to murder in 1974, why he committed three murders and why he murdered these specific three victims, he is as dangerous today as he was in 1974,"

Prosecutors at the 1974 trial said Brown walked into a 7-Eleven at 218 Cardiff Place in Santa Cruz on June 25th, 1974 and shot and killed store clerk Richard Pipes, 29, three times in the head for no specific reason. Brown then killed his mother's best friend, Lois McNamara, on July 12th, 1974, and a hitchhiker, Stephen Russell, on July 17th, 1974, shooting both victims in San Mateo County.

Brown pleaded guilty to the three murders the same year, but then recanted in 1996 to say his then-girlfriend shot all three victims. He was found guilty of three murders and received three life sentences.

In an earlier parole hearing, prosecutors said he claimed he was asleep or waiting in the car when she shot all three victims and claimed his actions at each murder scene were all "a blur".

He has been in prison 50 years and until he accepts treatment he will remain there denied parole. He is now 74.

JOHN RONALD BROWN

Born July 14th, 1922 – sentenced to 15 years in 1999. Died in prison May 16th, 2010.

The son of a physician, Dr.John Brown was born in 1922. He did well in school, graduating from high school by the age of 16. When drafted by the US Army during World WarII, he scored exceptionally highly on the Army General Classification Test, which resulted in the Army sending him to medical school.

Brown graduated from the University of Utah School of Medecine in 1947, and worked as a general practitioner for almost two decades. However, after almost losing a patient during a thyroidectomy, he decided to undertake formal surgical training.

By the early 1970s, Brown was in the vanguard of gender affirming surgery carrying out operations on transgender patients at a small clinic he set up in San Francisco. He would later claim to have performed 600 such surgeries during the course of his career.

At the time, only a small minority of patients met the exceptionally strict criteria for gender-affirming surgery. The program at John Hopkins Gender Identity Clinic, for example, only approved surgery for 24 out of the first 2000 people who approached them with the request for it. Brown, by contrast, freely admitted that he was willing to operate on anybody who would pay him. His lack of a formal surgical qualification made it necessary for him to carry out gender-affirming procedures in his office on an out-patient basis, rather than in a fully equipped surgical theatre with a recovery ward. He also operated on patients in motel rooms, and his own garage.

In 1977, following the death of one patient and a lawsuit from another, Brown's medical license was revoked by the California Board of Medical Quality Assurance for "gross negligence, incompetence and practicing unprofessional medicine in a manner which involved moral turpitude". He was also charged with allowing potential patients to work as unqualified, medical assistants as payment for their own subsequent surgery, failing to hospitalize a patient who had developed a life-threatening infection and making false claims on medical insurance forms. Brown continued to practice medicine outside of California, but was successively barred from practicing in Hawaii, Alaska and the island of Saint Lucia.

During the 1980s Brown began soliciting and advertising surgical services in the United States, whilst performing the actual surgical procedures across the border in Mexico. In 1986, an article in the magazine Forum reported on his procedure for surgically increasing penis length. The Forum article and an Inside Edition television documentary made several years later ("The Worst Doctor in America") both portrayed Brown as an incompetent and inept surgeon. While some of his patients were satisfied with their surgical results and praised Brown, he gained an overall poor reputation and the nickname "Butcher Brown" amongst the transgender community. Despite this, desperate individuals continued to seek him out.

In 1990, Brown spent 19 months in prison for practicing medicine without a license. The charge came after Brown operated on a thirty-year-old transgender woman from Orange County, California. After leaving prison, Brown worked as a taxi driver for a year before re-establishing himself once again in medical practice.

On May 9th, 1998, Brown performed a leg amputation on Philip Bondy, a 79-year-old, retired satellite engineer from New York, in Tijuana, Mexico. Bondy was one of the rare individuals suffering from Body integrity identity disorder – a desire to have a healthy limb amputated. Very few reputable surgeons are willing to treat this disorder by carrying out such an amputation due to its direct violation of the Hippocratic Oath.

The morning after the surgery, Bondy was found dead in a National City, California hotel room, by Dr. Gregg M. Furth, a New York child psychologist and fellow BIID sufferer who had travelled with Bondy to Mexico after being denied apotemnophilic surgery in the UK. Though they both wanted their legs amputated, Furth had backed out of having surgery with Brown at the last moment after seeing an assistant of Brown's carrying a large, obviously non-surgical, knife. An autopsy showed Bondy had died of gas gangrene. A police search of Brown's home – a ground floor unit in a San Ysidro apartment building – revealed blood-soaked towels, sheets and mattresses, as well as anaesthetizing drugs, surgical instruments and hundreds of tubes of super glue. Police also discovered video tapes of Brown's operations.

Brown was prosecuted in California for second-degree murder – an unusually severe charge in medical cases. A surgeon, who was a witness for the prosecution, testified that Brown had not left a large enough skin flap to properly cover the bone and remaining stump of Phillip Bondy's leg. The flap was stretched too tightly to allow adequate blood flow and the tissue in the flap died, allowing an infection of clostridium perfringens and producing gangrene. To make the murder charges stick, the prosecution had to establish that Brown had a history of incompetence and recklessness. A number of transgender women gave testimony of their experiences of Brown's treatment and subsequent medical history. However, he continued to have some supporters amongst former patients, even after his arrest.

Brown was convicted by unanimous decision and sentenced to fifteen years to life in prison in 1999.

By spring 2010, John Ronald Brown's health had deteriorated greatly and he came down with numerous health problems, including a severe bout of pneumonia. Treatment for his pneumonia eventually proved useless, his body eventually rejecting antibiotic medication. While arrangements to move Brown to a rest home in San Diego were being made, he died on the evening of 16th May 2010, at age 87.

ANGELO BUONO

Born October 5th 1954 – died in prison of a heart attack on September 21st, 2002.
See KENNETH BIANCHI

DAVID BURKE

Born May 18th, 1952 – died December 7th, 1987 in suicide air crash with 43 other people.

David Augustus Burke was an employee of USAir, now merged with American Airlines since 2015, who had been on unpaid leave following an investigation into his theft of $69 from an airline fund. In a hearing on December 7th, 1987 he was dismissed from his job by his supervisor, Raymond Frank Thomson, even after he pleaded for leniency. As he left his office, he was told sarcastically by Thompson to have a nice day, for which he replied, "I intend on having a very good day."

Burke then purchased a ticket on PSA Flight 1771, a daily flight from Los Angeles, California to San Francisco that Ray Thomson, his supervisor, took daily as Thomson lived in San Francisco and worked at Los Angeles International Airport. Using his USAir credentials, Burke was able to bypass security armed with a loaded .44 Magnum pistol. After he got onto the plane at Los Angeles International Airport, he wrote a note on an air-sickness bag. The note read:

Hi Ray. I think it's sort of ironical that we ended up like this. I asked for some leniency for my family. Remember? Well, I got none and you'll get none.

As the plane was cruising at 22,000 feet, Burke left his seat and headed to the lavatory, dropping the note on Thomson's lap. As he exited the lavatory a few moments later, Burke took out his handgun and shot Thomson, as the cockpit voice recorder sounds later confirmed. He then headed for the cockpit door. The recorder then picked up the voice of a female, presumed to be a flight attendant, who told the cockpit crew, "We have a problem." The captain replied, "What kind of problem?" Burke then appeared at the cockpit door and announced, "I'm the problem," simultaneously firing two more shots that probably killed the pilots.

Several seconds later, the cockpit recorder picked up increasing windscreen noise as the airplane pitched down and began to accelerate. This may have been deliberate on the part of Burke, or may have been the result of the dead pilots slumping down onto the control columns. At this point, Burke turned the gun on himself. As the plane descended through 13,000 feet, at a speed of Mach 1.2, it broke apart and crashed in a farmer's field in the Santa Lucia Mountains near the coastal town of Cayucos, California.

Forty-three people, including Burke, were killed in the shootings and plane crash, making David Burke the worst African-American mass murderer in US history.

Previously, Burke had worked for an airline in Rochester, New York, where he was a suspect in a drug-smuggling ring that was bringing cocaine from Jamaica to Rochester via the airline. He was never officially charged.

It was determined several days later by the FBI, after the discovery of both the handgun containing six spent bullet casings and the note written on the air-sickness bag in the wreckage, that Burke was the person responsible for the crash. In addition to that evidence uncovered at the crash site, other factors surfaced: Burke's co-worker admitted to having lent him the gun, and Burke had also left a farewell message on his girlfriend's telephone answering machine.

Strict new federal laws were passed after the crash, including a law that required "immediate seizure of all airline employee credentials" upon termination from an airline position, and another policy that was put into place where all members of any airline flight crew, including the captain, were to be subjected to the same security measures as are the passengers.

JAMES BUTLER Jr.

Born December 18th, 1972 – sentenced to 29 years 4 months in prison for manslaughter on April 5th, 2006.

James Butler Jr. is an American light heavyweight boxer, and former USBA Super Middleweight champion. He had a career record of 20-5-0, with 12 wins coming by way of knockout. He was nicknamed 'The Harlem Hammer.'

Butler's infamy began with his actions after a nationally-televised bout on November 23rd, 2001 at the Roseland Ballroom in Manhattan, New York. After losing by unanimous decision to Richard "The Alien" Grant, Butler had his gloves removed and went to Grant's side of the ring for an expected exchange of congratulations. Suddenly, Butler hit the unsuspecting Grant with a right hook to the jaw. Grant went down and dripped blood from his mouth onto the mat. Butler was arrested and charged with aggravated assault.

On October 12th, 2004, boxing writer Sam Kellerman, brother of boxing analyst Max Kellerman, was murdered in his apartment. His body was not found until October 17th when the apartment was set on fire. Butler, whose last bout was a split-decision loss on August 10th, 2004, was considered a potential suspect as he and Kellerman had been friends for ten years and he was, at that time, staying in Kellerman's apartment. After interrogation he was arrested on October 27th.

On October 29th, Butler pleaded not guilty to murder and arson. He was held on $1.25 million bail. Prosecutors claimed that Butler, the only suspect in the case, repeatedly struck Kellerman in the head with a hammer, then torched Kellerman's Hollywood apartment in an attempted cover-up.

On July 8th, 2005, a Los Angeles judge ruled that there was sufficient evidence for Butler to stand trial on the charges of murder and arson.

On March 27th, 2006, Butler pleaded guilty to voluntary manslaughter and arson in the 2004 death of Sam Kellerman. On April 5th, Butler was sentenced to 29 years, four months in prison by Superior Court Judge Michael Pastor.

Butler was also ordered pay $17,853 in funeral expenses to Kellerman's family, $10,000 to the state's victim restitution fund and $11,882 to the owner of the victim's apartment, which was left torched and blood-soaked after the killing.

RAYMOND OSCAR BUTLER

Born 1975 – sentenced to death on July 29th, 1996.

Raymond Butler would seem to be very lucky or very astute. On March 25th 1994 he shot dead two Japanese students as he carjacked their vehicle in a supermarket car park for which he was tried and sentenced to death in 1996.

Whilst awaiting execution in prison in 1995 prior to being sentenced for the carjacking he killed Tyrone Fleming, 23, a fellow inmate with a self-made knife. Why he killed him is unknown.

Prison authorities testified that Butler was a violent prisoner and had to be kept isolated away from other prisoners after several aggressive attacks. Butler received a second death penalty for the murder of Fleming in 1997.

Butler decided he would represent himself at trial and during his appeals. He seems to have done a good job as although the Supreme Court affirmed the sentence for the carjacking murders the prison murder is still at the appeal stage. 25 years on.

RICARDO SILVIO CAPUTO

Born 1949 – sentenced to 25 years in prison in 1995. Died in prison October 1997 age 48.

Ricardo Caputo was an Argentine American serial killer active during the 1970s who was known as the "Lady Killer." Caputo was born in 1949 in Mendoza, Argentina. In 1970, he moved to the United States and settled in New York City.

Though he could not definitively be linked to any murders after 1977, he remained a fugitive throughout the 1980s, and finally surrendered to police in 1994.

Incarcerated at Attica State Prison in New York, Caputo had a fatal heart attack in October 1997, at the age of 48.

He met Natalie Brown, of 19, Floer Hill, New York who was a teller at the Marine Midland Bank branch where he cashed his pay checks and they began dating. On July 31st, 1971, Ms. Brown was stabbed to death and soon after Mr. Caputo was arrested. Four months later he was found incompetent to stand trial and was sent to Matteawan State Hospital, part of the state prison at Fishkill. He was then declared mentally incompetent to stand trial at the time and moved to Manhattan Psychiatric Centre on Wards Island in 1974 from where he escaped the same year.

He murdered Judith Becker, 26, in Yonkers, New York in 1974. Judith was a psychologist who had treated Caputo whilst he was in the Manhattan Psychiatric Centre.

He then went on to murder Barbara Ann Taylor, 28, in San Francisco in 1975. Next he killed Laura Gomez in Mexico City in 1977.

He was suspected of the murders of:

Devon Green, 23, Los Angeles in 1981 – Caputo became a suspect in Green's death when a former co-worker of hers spotted him on a crime show and identified Caputo as having worked at a Los Angeles restaurant where Green was a chef. Already imprisoned when this information came to light in 1994, Caputo was neither charged with nor did he admit to her murder.

Jacqueline Bernard, 64, New York killed in 1983. Caputo was suspected of her murder but never charged due to lack of evidence.

Caputo died of a heart attack in prison on October 1st 1997, aged 48.

DEWAYNE MICHAEL CAREY

Born 1961 – sentenced to death December 16th, 1996. Died of COVID July 4th, 2020 on death row in San Quentin Prison.

On April 19th, 1995, Billy Campbell found his wife, Ernestine, 51, dead in the hallway of their home in Harbor City in Southern California. Ernestine's body was in an upright position at the bottom of the staircase; her hands were tied to the handrail. Ernestine had been stabbed to death, and many items of property had been stolen from the home.

On the morning of the murder, Dewayne Carey was seen leaving the Campbell home, and was later connected to property stolen from the Campbell's. After his arrest, Carey confessed to killing Ernestine Campbell.

At 9:00 a.m. on April 19th, 1995, the day of Ernestine Campbell's murder, Bertram Ashe, who lived two houses away from Billy and Ernestine Campbell, was taking a walk in the neighbourhood when he heard the front door to the Campbell residence open and close. He watched Carey walk from the Campbells' porch toward the sidewalk. Carey greeted Ashe and continued toward the house next door, where he lived with his aunt and uncle, Naomi and Herbert Baker, and their daughter Pamela.

That morning Ernestine Campbell attended a class at Los Angeles Harbor College from 9:00 a.m. until about 9:50 a.m. Around 10:30 a.m., Robert Lee Vaughn, a family friend, arrived at the Campbell residence to do maintenance work. When Vaughn knocked on the door, he heard Ernestine call out from inside, asking him to return in 30 minutes. Just before 11:00 a.m. Vaughn saw Carey come out of the Bakers' garage and walk to his yellow Ford pickup truck, which was parked on the street. Carey started his truck and then, leaving the engine running, asked Vaughn for a ride to the gas station, explaining that he did not have enough gas to drive there himself. After a second knock on the Campbells' door went unanswered, Vaughn agreed to drive Carey to the gas station. Vaughn mentioned to defendant that Ernestine Campbell had not answered the door. At Carey's suggestion Vaughn telephoned the Campbell residence from a phone booth at the gas station; no one answered. Sometime after 11:00 a.m., Jack Shaw, who lived across the street from the Campbell's, was in his driveway working on his car when he heard a scream; he was unsure from where it came and did not respond. Several minutes later, Shaw saw a yellow Ford pickup truck drive past his house; the driver waved as he drove past Shaw.

After visiting the gas station, Vaughn returned to the Campbell residence. Vaughn knocked on both the front and side doors, but received no response. A few minutes later, he walked to Billy Campbell's office nearby and told him that the latter's wife had not responded at the house. Billy Campbell telephoned home, but no one answered.

Campbell and Vaughn then drove to the Campbell residence, where Campbell discovered his wife's body tied to the banister of the interior staircase. Campbell called 911, and he told a paramedic, "I think my wife has fallen on a knife and killed herself." Vaughn testified that when he entered the hallway he saw Ernestine Campbell's body sitting upright on the staircase with her hands tied to the handrail. After calling 911, Billy Campbell retrieved a small steak knife from the kitchen and cut his wife's body down from the handrail. At about 11:40 a.m., Los Angeles County Sheriff's Deputy Robert Stevens arrived at the Campbell home. Stevens searched the home and saw that the screen on the kitchen window had been partially removed. He also found blood on the stairs and on the blade of a kitchen knife that lay near Ernestine Campbell's feet. A severed electrical cord was tied to the banister and a second, smaller knife lay at the top of the stairs. When Los Angeles County Fire Department paramedics Brian Dallas Jones and Derrick Ho responded to the scene at 11:42 a.m., Ernestine's body lay on the floor at the bottom of a stairway. In a vain effort to resuscitate her, Jones cut open Ernestine's shirt, revealing stab wounds to her chest and neck. Ho saw a large kitchen knife next to Ernestine's left hand and a second knife lying at the top of the stairs.

About 2:05 p.m., Los Angeles County Sheriff's Homicide Detective Byron Wisberger arrived at the Campbell residence. He saw a large butcher knife on the first step of the stairs, a cut electrical cord attached to the stairway handrail, and a second, smaller knife on one of the upper stairs. He also saw a single earring and a bracelet on the stairs. On the kitchen counter was an open purse, its contents scattered about the stove. In an upstairs bedroom Wisberger found two other purses, their apparent contents strewn about the bed. All the doors were locked, except for a closed but unlocked sliding door leading to the patio. The kitchen window was also closed but unlocked, and its glass was smudged with handprints; the window screen was hanging loosely.

Los Angeles County Deputy Medical Examiner Solomon Riley testified that Ernestine Campbell died as a result of multiple stab wounds. Seven of the wounds were to the left side of her chest, penetrating the heart and left lung. To the right side of the neck were two stab wounds, one of which was an inch deep and penetrated the thyroid gland. There were abrasions on the bridge of the nose and between the upper lip and nose. There was also bruising under the skin of the right wrist. Blood leaks from the victim's eyes indicated a lack of blood supply to the brain, which could have resulted from suffocation or strangulation.

Carey's friend Robert Leach testified that Carey arrived at his house around 11:30 a.m. or noon on April 19th, 1995. He was in good spirits and was better dressed than usual. Carey asked Leach to help him remove some items from his truck, including a .12-gauge shotgun and a large Sparkletts water bottle containing change and paper money. They counted the money from the bottle, which totalled about $1,200. The two men then had dinner, after which Carey left Leach's house. Carey left behind the items from his truck, saying he would return the next day.

Detective Wisberger testified that, in an interview conducted about 8:45 p.m. on April 19th, 1995, Carey mentioned getting a ride to the gas station with Vaughn and thereafter leaving home around 11:00 a.m. to visit his friend Leach. Carey denied any knowledge of Ernestine Campbell's murder. After the interview, Wisberger saw a full gasoline can in Carey's truck. That same evening between 11:00 and 11:30 p.m., Carey telephoned Leach and said the police had questioned him for two hours about a neighbour who had been killed earlier that day. After telling Leach that he had given the detectives Leach's name, address, and telephone number, Carey asked Leach not to tell the police about the money or the gun that Leach had earlier helped remove from his truck. The next day, Leach took the gun and some of the coins to his friend Christopher Floyd's house and stored the items in Floyd's garage. Leach told Floyd that the gun belonged to Carey. After leaving Floyd's house, Leach encountered Carey on a nearby street. When Leach inquired about the money and the gun, Carey assured Leach they were "legit."

Several days after the murder, Leach and two female companions exchanged some $780 worth of coins from the Sparkletts water bottle for paper currency. Carey then picked up the money from Leach and gave him about $100. On April 21st, 1995, Carey went to the house of his former girlfriend Michele Leathers to visit their young daughter. According to Leathers, Carey gave his daughter approximately twelve $2 bills and he gave her half-sister one or two. Carey told Leathers that he got the money "legally." Leathers recalled that Carey appeared calm during the visit. Carey's cousin Pamela Baker testified that, on April 22nd, 1995, Carey attended a family barbeque. Baker was surprised that Carey had bought meat for the barbeque because he usually did not have any money, but she did not ask where he had got the money from.

Carey's female friend Peggy Moseley testified that in the latter part of April, Carey took her to a park where he gave her a small bottle of cologne, a watch, a diamond pendant, and three $100 bills. A few days later, Carey gave Moseley five silver dollars and some loose change. Moseley described Carey as being "his normal self" during this period.

On May 2nd, 1995, the police interviewed Leach, and he told them about concealing the shotgun and the money in the Sparkletts water bottle. He said that Carey had assured him the property was "legit." Leach gave the detectives a bag of dimes and other property belonging to Billy Campbell and his murdered wife Ernestine, and took the detectives to Floyd's house, where they recovered the shotgun.

About 2:30 a.m. on May 3rd, 1995, Carey appeared at Peggy Moseley's house "ranting and raving." According to Moseley, Carey was very emotional and asked her to come outside to talk. She did so while her fiancé, Edward Moseley, who was worried by Carey's manner, called the police. Carey said something had happened. According to Peggy Moseley, he was "babbling" but saying "nothing in particular." Peggy Moseley got into Carey's car to talk to him and he started driving. He drove to a hotel and got a room where they spent the night. Throughout the night, Carey repeatedly said he wanted to "go away" with Moseley. The next morning, he was not as agitated and they spent the day driving around. Carey did not mention the murder.

Detective Wisberger testified that on May 4th, 1995, he saw Carey's truck parked across the street from the home of Kenneth Reedus, Carey's cousin. Wisberger and his partner Detective Isaac Aguilar then spoke to Reedus. During their conversation, Reedus received a telephone call from Carey. Aguilar spoke to Carey on the phone and they agreed to meet at the Baker residence at 8:00 p.m. The detectives waited until 9:15 p.m., but Carey did not arrive. Leach testified that approximately two weeks after the murder, Carey showed him a gold bracelet with diamonds; he would not tell Leach where the bracelet came from.

After receiving information that Carey might be in Tustin, Orange County, Detective Wisberger contacted Tustin Police Officer Kenneth Maddox and asked him to be on the lookout for Carey. On May 7th, 1995, Maddox found Carey and Peggy Moseley at a motel in Tustin. He arrested Carey and transported him and Moseley to the Tustin Police Department. There, police officers contacted Edward Moseley and told him to bring them Peggy Moseley's purse. Found in the purse were jewellery and other items belonging to the Campbells. That afternoon, Detectives Wisberger and Aguilar began interviewing

Carey. After being advised of his rights Carey denied any knowledge of, or involvement in, the murder. He claimed that at the time of the murder he had been at home watching the O.J. Simpson trial on television. Wisberger knew there had been no coverage of the Simpson trial that day because of extensive coverage of the Oklahoma City bombing, which occurred the same day as Ernestine Campbell's murder. When Carey was told that a witness had seen him outside the Campbell residence, he said that Leach had committed the burglary and murder, and that he, Carey, had acted only as a lookout. Upon further questioning, Carey said, "Okay, Robert Leach had nothing to do with this."

Carey explained, both in an unrecorded statement and in a later recorded version, that the night before the murder he formulated a plan to burglarize the Campbell home to obtain money for his friend Peggy Moseley. On the day of the murder, he approached the front door of the Campbells' home and rang the doorbell to see if anybody was home. Nobody answered the door. He then entered through the kitchen window and placed several items, including coins and jewellery, into a pillowcase. Carey said he was upstairs when Ernestine Campbell came home; he walked down the stairs, armed with a shotgun he had found in the house. He and Ernestine Campbell spoke for about 10 or 15 minutes. She urged him to leave and said she would not tell Carey's uncle or the police. He did not believe her, however, and proceeded to tie her to the stair railing with an electrical cord. He then used a small knife to stab her several times in the neck and chest. These initial wounds were not fatal, and at one point Ernestine Campbell screamed. Carey discarded the smaller knife in the kitchen sink and retrieved a larger knife with which he stabbed Ernestine three or four more times in the chest until he thought she was dead. He left the knife in her chest, and continued burglarizing the home. Carey then threw the stolen property over the wall separating the Campbells' home from that of the Bakers, with whom he lived, and hid it in the Bakers' garage. After leaving the Bakers' home, Carey noticed that Vaughn, the Campbells' friend, was still in the neighbourhood. He did not want Vaughn to discover Ernestine Campbell's body right away, so he asked Vaughn to take him to the gas station. After returning from the gas station, he retrieved the stolen property that he had hidden in the Bakers' garage and drove to his friend Leach's house. Later that day, he gave some of the property to Peggy Moseley and hid the pillowcase filled with jewellery behind some bushes in an alley behind his mother's house.

Detective Aguilar later recovered the pillowcase from the alley. The Campbells' daughter, Helene Campbell, testified that various items of property had been taken from her parents' home, including jewellery, a shotgun, and a five-gallon Sparkletts water bottle containing coins and bills. She identified various photographic exhibits of items recovered by police as depicting property belonging to her family.

Los Angeles County Deputy Sheriff Lauren Hernandez, a forensic identification specialist, testified that two fingerprints lifted from a white cardboard jewellery box taken as evidence matched Carey's thumbprints.

On May 8th, 1995, the day after his arrest, Carey called his former girlfriend Michele Leathers from jail. She asked him how he could have killed an innocent lady. He replied, "Yes, but that's not here or there." On June 27th, 1995, defendant called his cousin Pamela Baker from jail. When Baker asked him why he had killed Ernestine Campbell, defendant said he needed quick money to fund Peggy Moseley's illegal drug use.

At trial in 1996 Carey was found guilty of first degree murder and sentenced to death on December 16th, 1996. Evidence was presented that showed he had previously been convicted of voluntary manslaughter having originally been charged with murder but negotiated the lesser charge with a guilty plea and had served 13 years. He also had three incidents of criminal violence on his record with two being stabbings whilst in prison.

Dewayne Michael Carey died of COVID complications, aged 59, on July 4th, 2020 in San Quentin Prison whilst on death row.

DAVID JOSEPH CARPENTER

Born May 6th, 1930 – sentenced to death July 6th, 1984. Still on death row at the time of writing aged 94.

In 1961, when he was thirty-three years old, David Carpenter, the future "Trailside Killer" brutally attacked a woman with a hammer, earning fourteen years in prison. Back in circulation by the latter part of 1970, he drew another seven years on two counts of kidnapping and robbery. Before his transfer to the penitentiary he joined four other inmates in escaping from the Calaveras County jail. Recaptured by the FBI, he did his time and was paroled in 1977.

He found a job in San Francisco, close to his home at 36 Sussex Street, working for a photo print shop, and seemed to be "going straight." In fact, his brief hiatus was the calm before a lethal storm. The terror began with Edda Kane, age 44, whose naked, violated body was discovered on a hiking trail in Mount Tamalpais State Park, near San Francisco, on August 20th, 1979.

Edda was murdered execution-style, shot through the head while kneeling. Then on March 7th, 1980, Barbara Swartz, age 23, went hiking in the park. Her body was recovered one day later on a narrow, dirt trail. She had been stabbed repeatedly in the chest while kneeling in the dirt. Next, Anne Alderson went jogging on the fringes of the park on October 15th, 1980, and did not return.

The 26-year-old was found next afternoon; three bullets in the head had snuffed her life while she was kneeling at her killer's feet. On November 27th, Shauna May, age 25, did not show up to keep a lover's rendezvous in the parking lot at Point Reyes Park, a few miles north of San Francisco. Two days later, searchers found her body in a shallow grave. Beside her body lay the decomposing corpse of a New Yorker, 22-year-old Diana O'Connell, who had disappeared while hiking in the park a full month earlier. Both women had been killed by gunshots to the head.

Just hours before the corpses at Point Reyes were unearthed on November 29th two other victims were discovered in the park. They were identified as Richard Stowers, 19, and Cynthia Moreland, 18, they had been missing since September, when they had told friends of their plans for hiking in the area. Again, both victims had been murdered execution-style.

As panic gripped the Northern California camping areas, the media indulged in speculation linking the sadistic "Trailside Killer" with the "Zodiac," another serial assassin -- still at large today -- responsible for seven murders in the latter 1960s.

Homicide detectives had not linked the Zodiac with any documented crimes since 1969, and now the press began to speculate these killings were his return, perhaps from serving time in prison or a sanatorium. Unlike the Zodiac, however, the elusive "Trailside Killer" felt no need to taunt police with mocking letters. He was satisfied to let his actions speak for themselves.

On March 29th, 1981, the killer struck again, this time in Henry Cowle State Park, near Santa Cruz. He ambushed hikers Stephen Haertle and Ellen Hansen, brandishing a .38 and announcing to Ellen that he intended to rape her. When she warned him off, the gunman opened fire on them both, killing her outright and leaving young Haertle for dead.

Haertle survived wounds that ripped his neck, a hand, and one eye, and crawled for help. He was able to offer homicide detectives a description of the killer's crooked, yellow teeth. Upon release of the description, other hikers told police that they had seen a man resembling the gunman in a red, late model foreign car. Despite the new, important leads, police had reason for concern. From all appearances, publicity had caused their man to change his hunting ground and weapon. All the other gunshot victims had been murdered with a .45 not a .38, and if the original pistol was destroyed or lost, a major portion of their case might well go up in smoke.

On May 1st, 1981, a resident of San Jose informed detectives that his girlfriend, Heather Scaggs, was missing. She had last been seen en route to buy a car from fellow print shop worker David Carpenter, who lived in San Francisco.

Carpenter, she said, had made a special point of asking Scaggs to come alone when she came to get the car. Police went to question Carpenter, immediately noticing his strong resemblance to composite sketches of the Trailside Killer. In his driveway sat a small, red, foreign car.

A background check revealed his felony arrests, and Stephen Haertle picked out his mug shot as a likeness of the Santa Cruz assailant in a photo line-up. Carpenter was taken into custody on May 14th, and ten days later, the remains of Heather Scaggs were found by hikers in Big Basin Redwood State Park, north of San Francisco. She had been executed with the pistol used on Stephen Haertle and his girlfriend, Ellen Hansen, back in March. Despite a search of Carpenter's belongings, homicide investigators still had not recovered any weapons.

Finally, they got a break, discovering a witness who remembered selling Carpenter a .45 -- illegal in itself for a convicted felon to own -- and although they never found the gun, at least a link, of sorts, had been established to the early homicides. A short time later, testimony from a suspect thief facing trial for robbery revealed that Carpenter had sold the thief a .38 revolver back in June. The weapon was recovered, and its barrel markings matched the bullets fired at Ellen Hansen, Heather Scaggs, and Stephen Haertle. As detectives worked to build their case, they linked their suspect, David Carpenter, with another unsolved homicide.

On June 4th, 1980, Anna Menjivas had been discovered, dead, in Mount Tamalpais State Park. Her murder had not been connected with the "Trailside" slayings at the time, but now investigators learned she was a long-time friend of David

Carpenter, who often let him drive her home from work.

The link appeared too strong to be mere coincidence, and Anna's name was added to the murder chain, making ten in all. Media publicity before his trial led Carpenter's defence attorneys to request a change of venue. When his trial convened in April 1984, he faced a jury in Los Angeles, but relocation did not change the damning evidence of guilt.

Convicted of the Scaggs and Hansen murders on July 6th, 1984, Carpenter was sentenced to die in the gas chamber at San Quentin. Judge Dion Morrow, in pronouncing sentence, told the court, "The defendant's entire life has been a continuous expression of violence and force almost beyond exception. I must conclude with the prosecution that if ever there was a case appropriate for the death penalty, this is it."

Then, nearly 4 years later, on May 10th, 1988, a San Diego jury convicted Carpenter of first degree murder in the slayings of Richard Stowers, Cynthia Moreland, Shauna May, Diana O'Connell, and Anne Alderson.

Carpenter was also pronounced guilty of raping two of the women and attempting to rape a third.

In December 2009, San Francisco police re-examined evidence from the October 21st, 1979 murder of Mary Frances Bennett. Bennett, 23 years old at the time of her murder, had been jogging at Lands End, San Francisco when she was attacked and stabbed to death. A DNA sample obtained from the evidence was matched to Carpenter through state Department of Justice files. In February 2010, San Francisco police confirmed the match with a recently obtained sample taken from Carpenter.

At the time of writing David Joseph Carpenter still sits on death row in San Quentin State Prison aged 94, the oldest inmate on California's death row.

JAMES CLIFFORD CARSON

Born 1950 – sentenced to 75 years to life in prison in 1984.

In 1977, James Carson was in Phoenix, Arizona, when his first wife noticed severe behavioural changes of a violent and spiritual nature in his personality and left with their daughter, Jennifer. Carson soon began a relationship with Susan Barnes, a divorcée with two teenage sons. They married, and became involved in drugs and mysticism. Carson took the name "Michael Bear", telling his daughter in a letter that God had given him the new name "Michael"; Susan became known as "Suzan Bear."

By 1980, after spending a year in Europe, the Carsons/Bears returned to the U.S. and moved into the Haight-Ashbury area of San Fransisco, California where they continued their involvement with drugs and the counter culture. By this time, Michael's former wife had become so afraid that he would harm her and try to abduct their child that she had taken to hide herself and their daughter from him. She went so far as to move numerous times and cut off contact with all their mutual acquaintances.

In March 1981 23-year-old Karen Barnes, no relation to Suzan, an aspiring actress from Georgia who was the Carsons' roommate in San Francisco, was found dead in their shared apartment. She had been stabbed thirteen times and her skull crushed before being wrapped in a blanket and hidden in the basement. The Carsons became the prime suspects. However, the family disappeared before the body was found. Later after being arrested the Carsons confessed to killing Karen after Suzan had decided Karen was a witch.

The Carsons had fled to a mountain hideout near Grants Pass. Oregon, where they remained until spring 1982 living in abandoned buildings. They then moved to Alderpoint, California, where they lived and worked on a marijuana farm. According to other workers on the farm, the Carsons were anarchists who advocated a people's revolution and predicted that a nuclear apocalypse would soon occur.

In May 1982, Michael shot and killed Clark Stephens, a co-worker on the farm with whom he had a dispute over a drug debt. He then attempted to dispose of the body by burning it and burying it under chicken fertilizer in the local woods. Two weeks later, Stephens was reported missing to the Humbolt County Sheriff, leading to a search and the discovery of his burnt remains.

The Carsons, who by this point had fled, were again considered suspects. Upon searching their abandoned belongings, detectives found a manifesto they had written which called for the assassination of then-President Ronald Regan. However, due to their continual movement from one place to the next, the authorities had difficulty tracking them down.

In November 1982, Michael was picked up by police in los Angeles after an acquaintance saw him hitchhiking. However, through a police error, Carson was quickly freed and vanished before Humboldt County detectives had a chance to question him. He left evidence behind, including a mug shot, address information, and a gun left in a police car.

The following January, 1983, the Carsons were hitchhiking near Bakersfield and were given a ride by 30-year-old Jon Charles Hellyar, who was driving to Santa Rosa. Suzan decided that Hellyar was a witch and had to be killed. While he was driving on U.S. Route 101 in Sonoma County, an argument and physical fight broke out between Hellyar and the Carsons, resulting in the car coming to a stop on River Road. The fight escalated outside the vehicle, where Suzan stabbed Hellyar while he and Michael struggled over a gun. Michael gained control of the gun and killed Hellyar in view of passing motorists, one of whom contacted police. A high-speed chase ensued as the Carsons attempted to flee in Hellyar's car which crashed and they were both taken into custody.

The Carsons initially confessed to the murders of Hellyar, Stephens, and Barnes but just before the trial, they withdrew their confessions and entered pleas of not guilty. They claimed the three killings were in self-defence to lift spells put upon them by the three victims who were all witches. They proclaimed themselves to be Muslim assassins waging a Holy war against witches and infidels. The prosecution claimed this was a ruse for them to be termed insane and escape the death penalty.

On June 12th, 1984, the Carsons were convicted first of Barnes' murder and sentenced to 25 years in prison then later, they were convicted of the murders of Stephens and Hellyar, for which they received sentences of 50 years to life and 75 years to life, respectively. In 1989, the First District Court of Appeal affirmed their third conviction as it had previously done on the other two.

Rumour was rife that the Carsons were responsible for up to twelve other murders in Europe and the US but no supporting evidence has surfaced.

As of this date Michael is incarcerated at Mule Creek State Prison, and Suzan is incarcerated at Central California Women's Facility.

DEAN PHILLIP CARTER

Born August 30th, 1955 – sentenced to death in 1985.

In the early evening of Sunday, April 1st, 1984, Dean Carter entered the Rocking Horse Bar and Grill located in Lafayette, California. The bartender, Nicole Didion, testified that business was slow that evening when Carter sat down at the bar, ordered a drink, and introduced himself to her as "Phil." He wore casual pants, which she believed were jeans, and a sweatshirt. He told Didion that he worked as a cameraman. Cocktail waitress Margo Fulton observed Carter sitting at the bar, and joined in the conversation with Didion.

Approximately one-half hour later, Tok Kim entered the bar, sat down a few bar stools apart from Carter and ordered a glass of white wine. She left the bar soon after, only to return a few minutes later declaring that she had been unable to start her Honda automobile. Carter offered to help her and left with her. After a few minutes, Carter returned to the bar and asked whether anyone had "jumper cables." A restaurant employee obtained cables and the car was started. Carter then returned to the bar to gather his belongings and remarked to a cocktail waitress that he was getting a ride to the local BART station. Approximately 9:00 p.m. the same evening, Carter and Kim walked into Jim Sutton's Lafayette Shell gasoline station and reported car trouble. David Hogan, an employee at the station, assisted the couple in towing the disabled vehicle to the station. Because the alternator apparently was malfunctioning, the vehicle was left at the station overnight for repairs.

The next day, April 2nd, Kim and Carter returned to the Shell station. Hogan noticed that Carter's neck bore a "big red mark – like a hickey on his neck," he said to Carter, "Well, looks like you had fun last night." Carter replied: "I don't even know what I'm doing here, I don't even know her."

At approximately 11:00 p.m. on Tuesday, April 10th Kim's neighbour, Connie Santos, heard Kim arguing with someone. Santos knew the voice of Kim's boyfriend, Ray Blevins, and testified that the person with whom Kim was arguing "was not Blevins, definitely, but instead belonged to someone younger." Santos could not discern the precise words spoken, but recalled that the persons arguing sounded "really angry." Santos thought that perhaps she should call the police, but instead she went to bed, pulling the bed covers over her head in an effort to block out the noise.

On Thursday, April 12th, Kim failed to arrive at her job at the Concord Macy's department store. Her manager at Macy's, Ingrid Maleska-King, telephoned Kim's apartment manager, William Elson, to request that he check whether she was at her apartment. Elson, who had observed Carter standing near Kim's apartment mailbox earlier that same week, did not find Kim at her apartment. He also observed that Kim's vehicle was not in its designated parking space or anywhere to be seen. When Kim did not appear for work again on Friday, April 13th, Maleska-King again contacted Elson and asked him to recheck whether Kim was at her apartment. As Elson approached the apartment on this second occasion, he said he "felt instinctively that she was in there because of the bad odour that I smelled." Elson found Kim's lifeless body sprawled upon the floor of her bedroom.

Oakland Police Detective Raymond Conner investigated Kim's death, arriving at her apartment on the morning of April 13th. Beneath Kim's neck, he discovered a curtain tie approximately 18 to 24 inches in length. Kim's body had decomposed to an extent that it precluded a determination of a cause of death. The pathologist who performed the autopsy, Thomas Rogers, testified that the tie found beneath Kim's neck could have been used to fatally strangle her. On cross-examination, Rogers acknowledged that in view of the body's advanced state of decomposition, he could not eliminate the possibility that Kim might have died from natural causes.

Susan Knoll and her sister, Sandra Pender, grew up in Wisconsin. Knoll's best friend was Bonnie Guthrie. In 1972, Pender relocated to San Diego, and in 1979 Knoll journeyed west to live with her. Guthrie also relocated to the Los Angeles area at some point and resumed her close friendship with Knoll. In March 1984, Knoll moved into a Culver City apartment with Jillette Mills. Knoll and Mills were both 25 years of age.

On April 10th, 1984, Knoll appeared at work at Mitsubishi Bank, according to Annette Cheng,

Knoll's colleague. On April 11th, Knoll was absent from work, and Cheng received a telephone call from a male who declined to identify himself. The caller informed Cheng that Knoll was "just involved in a traffic accident and she have some minor injury and would like to go to hospital for the check-up, but she asked me to call the bank to let the bank know that she won't be in today." Cheng asked the caller if he was a friend of Knoll's, and the caller replied: "No, I just happened to be in the accident scene and she asked me to call for her." When Cheng asked for the caller's name, he hung up the telephone. Cheng never saw Knoll alive again. On cross-examination, Cheng acknowledged that when she spoke to the caller, she believed he was a Black man with a southern accent.

For a few days prior to April 10th, 1984, Jillette Mills's brother, Jeff, tried without success to contact Jillette. On April 11th, 1984, Jeff and his friend, Christopher Thurman, began searching for her. Jeff and Christopher travelled to Jillette's Culver City apartment, to her place of employment at Laird Studios, and to a local community college where she had attended classes, but were unable to locate Jillette or her car, a distinctive white Datsun 280 ZX that bore the license plate "PHANTM Z." Jeff and Christopher then returned to the apartment building, scaled a security fence, and approached the apartment. Jillette's apartment door was unlocked. After searching much of the apartment without success, Jeff and Christopher found a framed piece of artwork leaning against the doors of a bedroom closet. Opening the closet doors, Christopher noticed "feet on the floor" and advised Jeff that "we have a problem." The fully-clothed bodies of Susan and Jillette were lying on the floor of the closet, one stacked upon the other. Jeff called the police, and Christopher went outside to await their arrival. While Christopher waited by the curb, he leaned on the left front fender of a blue Honda that investigators subsequently determined belonged to Tok Kim. Inside the vehicle, investigators later recovered a pair of sunglasses identified at trial by David Hogan, the Lafayette gasoline station attendant, as matching the pair he observed resting atop Carter's head.

Police investigators examined Jillette's apartment for fingerprints and other physical evidence. Two wine glasses found in the kitchen appeared to have been wiped clean to eliminate any traces of fingerprints. A latent palm print was retrieved from the bathroom sink. Martin Collins, a latent print investigator employed by the California Department of Justice, testified that the latent print matched Carter's right palm print with "100 percent" certainty.

In addition to its personalized license plate, Jillette Mills's white Datsun was easily identifiable by a black, front-fender car cover emblazoned with the vehicle model "280 ZX," black engine cover vents, dual-coloured pinstripes, a tinted-glass "T-top" roof, black "sports slats" that covered much of the rear window, a black rear stabilizer, and dual-coloured wheel rims shod with Goodyear Eagle GT tires.

Dr. Lakshmanan Sathyavagiswaran, the Chief of Forensic Medicine at the Los Angeles County Medical Examiner's Office, testified that Jillette Mills died of asphyxia due to ligature strangulation. He added that "considerable force" had to have been "continuously applied" for approximately two minutes or more in order to cause death. Jillette also suffered "blunt force type trauma" to her head, and injury to her genital area consistent with "traumatic sexual assault" including "penile penetration and ejaculation."

Sam Le, a Los Angeles County criminalist, testified that a white nightgown found in the apartment contained seminal fluid consistent with Carter's PGM type and that of 15.8 percent of the population. Seminal fluid recovered from Mills's vaginal area "was of an insufficient quantity for typing."

Dr. Sathyavagiswaran further testified that Susan Knoll died of asphyxia due to manual strangulation, the result of "considerable compression force."

Susan also suffered blunt force injuries and haemorrhages consistent with having struggled against her assailant. Dr. Sathyavagiswaran stated: "When Miss Knoll was strangulated and was asphyxiated, this was probably a terminal event." Seminal fluid recovered from Knoll's vaginal area was of an insufficient quantity for typing. Each victim had been dead for a minimum of 15 hours prior to the time the autopsies were performed upon their bodies.

In the early afternoon of April 11th, 1984, Bonnie Guthrie, then 34 years of age, and a friend, Geula Vehab, purchased fruit together in Santa Monica. The two parted company at approximately 1:20 p.m. Between 3:00 p.m. and 4:00 p.m., Matty Spiro, the manager of the apartment building in which Guthrie resided, entered her West Los Angeles apartment, accompanied by Manny Gleberman, to repair a leaky bathroom faucet. As Gleberman worked on the faucet, Spiro observed Guthrie lying on her stomach on the bedroom floor: "So I said to Manny, the plumber, 'Look at that, Manny. She's sleeping on the floor.' I said, 'I better close the door and let her sleep.' "

The next morning, April 12th, Spiro noticed that Guthrie's automobile was still in the garage. Wondering why Guthrie apparently had not gone to work, he returned to Guthrie's apartment and knocked on the door. Upon entering the open apartment, Spiro noticed Guthrie lying in the same position as he previously had observed. He then notified the police.

Dr. Sathyavagiswaran testified that Guthrie died of ligature strangulation. He added that Guthrie's body bore the signs of having suffered blunt force injury as well as genital abrasions consistent with traumatic sexual assault. Vaginal area samples revealed the presence of spermatozoa.

Two days later, on April 14th, Adolph Romero, a commercial fisherman, noticed a white Datsun 280 ZX parked in front of a San Diego shipyard. Approximately 50 feet from the vehicle,

Romero retrieved Guthrie's wallet from beneath some bushes. When Guthrie could not be reached, the wallet was turned in to the local police.

On or about April 12th, 1984, Janette Cullins, who was 24 years of age, died by strangulation. Janette originally had encountered Carter in a San Diego bar in February 1984, and saw him socially the following month. Lee Ann Johnson, who resided across the street from Janette's apartment, reported that during April 1984 she observed a distinctive looking vehicle arrive and depart from the area on several occasions. At trial, Johnson testified that the vehicle, a white Datsun 280 ZX, resembled the one owned by Jillette Mills. One night that April, Johnson observed the vehicle parked across the street, its engine running for 10 or 15 minutes, "and then all of a sudden I heard the car start and take off, and it sort of screeched and made a u-turn and came up past my house to the corner and didn't stop for the stop sign and went through the stop sign." Johnson never saw the vehicle again.

Approximately at midday on April 13th, Janette Cullins's previous room-mate, Nancy McEachern, drove to Cullins's apartment because they had planned to conduct a yard sale on the following day, a Saturday, and McEachern wanted to drop off some items to sell. As she was parking her vehicle in front of the apartment, Carter drove up in a white Datsun 280 ZX. He asked McEachern whether Cullins was home. McEachern replied, "Her car is not here. She hasn't answered a phone call." Which had been made by McEachern earlier that morning. Carter left, and McEachern entered the apartment. Inside, the drapes were drawn and the Venetian blinds were closed, causing the apartment to appear dark, which McEachern testified was "unusual" for that time of day because "We had the habit of opening everything up and making it real bright first thing in the morning." McEachern left a note for Cullins on the dining table and left the apartment. McEachern returned the next day to discover Janette's body lying in the bedroom closet. The cause of her death was asphyxiation due to strangulation.

Records of Great American Bank revealed that on April 13th, 1984, a withdrawal from Janette Cullins's account in the amount of $60 was made from an automatic teller machine (ATM) located at the bank's Point Loma Branch. A four-minute videotape of the transaction, introduced into evidence and shown to the jury, depicted a man wearing a black jacket.

Approximately 10:50 p.m. on April 17th, 1984, Arizona Highway Patrolman Robert Dapser was completing a traffic stop on Interstate 40 in northern Arizona, when he received a call from a truck driver on the citizen's band radio located in his patrol vehicle. The caller advised that "an erratic vehicle had been driving in his location, passed by him twice and nearly cut him off both times," and he identified the California license plate on the car as "PHANTOM 2." The subject vehicle, a Datsun 280 ZX, drove by as Officer Dapser was receiving this information.

Officer Dapser pursued the vehicle, which he observed "swerving across the centre line of the highway." He activated the emergency lights on his patrol vehicle and initiated a traffic stop. After illuminating the Datsun with a spotlight, Dapser approached the car and requested that the driver produce identification. Carter, the lone occupant of the vehicle, produced an expired driver's license issued by the State of Alaska. Dapser asked for the vehicle registration documents. Carter searched the centre console and glove box and then stated, "I can't find it, she must not have it in here." Dapser thought he observed a burnt marijuana cigarette in the centre console of the Datsun and, having witnessed the vehicle's erratic movement, decided to take Carter into custody. He advised Carter of his rights and placed him in the patrol vehicle.

Officer Dapser returned to the Datsun to search for the burnt marijuana cigarette. He noticed beer bottles, one of which was empty, located on the passenger side floorboard. While searching for the marijuana cigarette, Dapser observed a bank identification card located in the crevice between the driver's seat and the centre console. The name on the card was that of Janette Cullins.

Believing that the truck driver who originally noticed the Datsun had misidentified the license plate, Dapser transmitted a message over his police radio, advising that the license plate was not "PHANTOM 2," but "PHANTM Z." Within several minutes, a dispatcher instructed Dapser to detain the vehicle and all occupants at the request of California law enforcement officials. Dapser discontinued his search of the Datsun and arranged for it to be towed to a locked police storage area. Officer Dapser administered a breathalyser test to Carter, which revealed that his blood-alcohol content was .078 percent approximately 80 to 90 minutes after the traffic stop. Carter was transported to the Yavapai County jail in Prescott, Arizona.

On April 18th, 1984, Officer Dapser released the contents of Jillette Mills's Datsun 280 ZX, as well as certain personal property confiscated from Carter's person, to West Los Angeles and Culver City police detectives. The detectives inventoried the personal property and other objects recovered from the vehicle, which included the following items introduced into evidence at Carter's later trial: an American Tourister suitcase containing a plastic jar filled with pennies and labelled "black bean soy sauce," a Korean-made, wood-handled kitchen knife, yellow rubber gloves, and a gold chain – all identified as having belonged to Kim; a sweatshirt depicting a location in Alaska; an Alpha Beta supermarket CASHEX card identified as having belonged to Susan Knoll; towels, athletic wear, and photographic equipment identified as having belonged to Jillette Mills; three hand-woven sweaters identified as having belonged to Bonnie Guthrie; a "Member's Only" jacket, which contained a butcher knife, a knee-high nylon sock, a business card from Jim's Lafayette Shell gasoline station; a key ring identified as having belonged to Janette Cullins; and a piece of paper with the words "SHY LAS" – the access code to Cullins's Great American Bank (originally San Diego Federal Savings and Loan) account; and a number of items emblazoned with the names of Las Vegas casinos. A pair of jeans recovered from the Datsun contained a yellow half sock and a blue bandana.

Carter was sentenced to death for the murders in 1985 and is also suspected of 30 more throughout the western United States. He used to spend much of his time on death row in San Quentin Prison writing columns for his website 'deadmantalking.com' but seems to have been quiet since 2022.

STEVEN DAVID CATLIN

Born 1944 – sentenced to death 1990.

Steven Catlin's first marriage was stormy and violent, and his use of drugs added to the domestic problems. In 1966, he married a second wife without divorcing the first, using a pseudonym on the marriage license.

A few months after the second marriage, he was arrested for stealing a credit card at the gas station where he worked. The judge sentenced him to serve time in the state prison at Chino, where he spent the next three years.

When he was released, Catlin divorced his first wife and remarried his second, this time using his real name, but the relationship was stormy and doomed. The couple separated after ten months, and Catlin married a third time, divorcing eight months later. A fourth wife, Joyce, was next, but she would prove less fortunate than her predecessor in escaping from a dead-end marriage.

Catlin's fascination with cars led to a job with the pit crew of racer Glendon Emery, based in Fresno, California. Infatuated with Emery's stepdaughter, Catlin began to court her while still married to fourth wife Joyce.

In April 1976, Joyce Catlin was admitted to Bakersfield's Mercy Hospital with a severe "flu"; she seemed to improve, then took a sudden turn for the worse and died of "pneumonia" in May 1977. Also, in the same month, Catlin married his fifth wife,

Glenna Kaye, and moved to Fresno, finding employment at a local garage.

Quick promotions placed him in charge of 40 employees, but Catlin had expensive tastes, and cash was always short. On October 28th, 1980, his adoptive father died suddenly, and the fluid in his lungs was attributed to cancer. Once again, the body was swiftly cremated on orders from Catlin.

In 1981, Catlin's employers at the Fresno garage noticed missing auto parts. A subsequent background check turned up his criminal record, and he was forced to resign, though no charges were filed. Financially, the strain began to mount. On February 17th, 1984, Glenna Kaye Catlin suddenly fell ill while visiting Las Vegas with her mother. Returning to Fresno, she was hospitalized with fluid in her lungs. Physicians were still trying to diagnose her illness when she died on March 14th.

Catlin, meanwhile, had received $57,000 from life insurance payments on the deaths of his previous wife and acquired another fiancée, encountered on a visit to the hospital. Back in Bakersfield, his third ex-wife had followed the series of deaths in Catlin's life, and she approached the local sheriff with suspicions. Joyce Catlin had been cremated, but the hospital retained some of her tissue samples, which were submitted for analysis in November 1984.

A few days later, on December 8th, Catlin's mother, Martha, collapsed and died from a "stroke," shortly after a visit by Catlin and his new fiancée. Catlin had ordered that his mother's body be cremated, but the process was postponed until an autopsy could be performed.

Analysis of tissue samples from his mother and his two late wives revealed that all had suffered poisoning from paraquat, a highly toxic herbicide used as a weed killer. A bottle of paraquat, complete with Catlin's fingerprints, was found in his garage.

On December 23rd, 1985, Catlin was charged in Kern County with the 1976 murder of Joyce Catlin, his fourth wife, and the 1984 murder of Martha Catlin, his mother.

Shortly after marrying his sixth and final wife Catlin was indicted for the murder of his fifth wife, Glenna Kaye Catlin. Owing to negative pre-trial publicity Catlin's trial for this murder was held in Monterey County before the Kern County trial. In April 1986, Catlin was convicted of Glenna Kaye's murder, and the jury fixed a penalty of life imprisonment without the possibility of parole.

On June 1st, 1990, a Kern County jury returned a guilty verdict on the murder counts of Joyce and Martha Catlin. The jury agreed with the prosecution's allegations of special circumstances being, murder for financial gain, murder by poison, and multiple murders. On June 6th, 1990, the jury fixed Catlin's penalty at death. The fact that Catlin had already been convicted for Glenna Kaye's murder was not introduced until after the verdict.

Steven Catlin is sat on death row in San Quentin Prison at this time, age 80.

BILLY LEE CHADD

Born 1954 – sentenced to death May 12th, 1979. Overturned and re-sentenced to life in prison without parole.

Billy Lee Chadd was born in San Diego in 1954. His mother and stepfather were both alcoholics. At an early age, his friends taught him how to steal, and he got away with multiple car thefts.

In July 1970, Chadd, age 16, was arrested for rape. He was found guilty and sentenced to two years in juvenile based on the victim's testimony and a partial footprint found in her driveway. He escaped from the California Youth Authority twice.

After his second escape, he knocked on the door of a house and told the lady who answered that his car had broken down and requested to use her phone. The woman refused, explaining that her husband was at work, and she never let strangers into her house while she was alone. When Chadd heard that she was home alone, he decided to break into her home through the front door using a brick. Once inside, he found the woman in her bathroom taking a shower and grabbed her by the hair, dragging her into her bedroom. There, he pushed the victim onto her bed threatening her at knifepoint. After pulling his own pants down, he froze, dropping his knife. A few seconds later, he picked it up and told her to stay on the bed, and left the house.

A short time later, when he was captured, he was transferred to CYA's Youth Training School, where he attempted suicide by hanging himself. He was subsequently sent to Atascadero State Hospital, where he later claimed in a self-penned autobiography to have had his first homosexual experience. He also first used drugs there.

On the evening of July 27th, 1974, Chadd broke into a residence in Linda Vista, intending to burglarize it. However, after noticing the home's occupant, 30-year-old Patricia Franklin, in her bathtub, he became sexually aroused. He proceeded to bind Franklin's hands and feet with a curtain cord, blindfolded her with a towel, and forced her into her bedroom. There, he raped her multiple times vaginally, anally, and orally. During the ordeal, Chadd nearly bit off one of her nipples. He later strangled Franklin and stabbed her 15 times with a steak knife, killing her. Afterwards, he ransacked the home before leaving. Franklin's body was discovered by her room-mate. Investigators found one fingerprint at the crime scene, but were unable to connect it to Chadd, the case went cold.

On August 7th, 1975, Chadd, then 21, met Delmar Bright, a 29-year-old busboy working for a hotel in Las Vegas. Chadd stated that Bright offered him $20 and a six-pack of beer in exchange for Chadd posing nude for photos. Chadd agreed, and the two went to Bright's apartment. Once they arrived, Bright asked Chadd to tie him up with extension cords. He obliged, telling Bright to lie on his stomach, after which he tied the man's hands together. He then retrieved another cord and wrapped it around his neck in a slip knot. Chadd asked Bright for one reason not to kill him. Bright thought he was joking until Chadd showed him his knife. Chadd proceeded to cut the victim's throat and strangled him to death. Afterwards, he masturbated before cleaning the apartment in an attempt to get rid of forensic evidence. Then, he left and hailed a taxi.

On February 15th, 1978, Chadd raped and murdered Linda Hewitt at the house where she was babysitting in National City after seeing her at a local store and following her. He bound Hewitt, who was with her 9-month-old son, with a cord, and raped her. At one point, he picked up her son by the hair, threatening to harm him if Hewitt did not sexually satisfy him. He then stabbed her several times, the fatal wound being to her throat. One hour later, shortly after noon, the two kids she was babysitting returned home and discovered her body. They alerted their neighbour, who called the police. The Police investigation noted Hewitt was last seen alive at a drugstore. The store's clerk witnessed a man with her, who he described a short, clean shaven with short hair in his early 20s who had a medium-build. He also wore a t-shirt and jeans.

Chadd, joined the Marine Corps, and in 1978 was working as an orderly attendant, tasked with collecting background information on Marine patients, at the Balboa Hospital in San Diego. While on the job, he noticed a wife and daughter visiting their father, a patient with a terminal illness. After sifting through medical records, he found their address. On the night of March 31st, 1978, Chadd, armed with a bowie knife, broke into their Chula Vista home by cutting through a screen window. Once inside, he made his way to the wife's bedroom and demanded that the woman take off her clothes. He proceeded to tie her up with a cord and over the course of three hours he raped the victim twice as her family slept upstairs. He eventually allowed her to dress, and left the knife on the dresser. The woman lunged for the knife and screamed for her family. The first to enter the room was her 17-year-old daughter. Chadd had already wrestled his knife away from the woman, and ordered the daughter to bring the rest of the family into the bedroom. After the woman's mother, father, and three youngest children went into the bedroom, Chadd ordered them to sit on the bed, and ordered the 17-year-old girl to tie them up. Afterwards, he forced the girl into the living room, where he raped her. He later cut lamp cords and returned to the bedroom to bind the feet of the family members. He then raped the girl a second time. At approximately 5 a.m., Chadd forced the mother and daughter into his car parked at the front of the house. Planning to kill them, he drove to a secluded dirt road near Route 94. However, the road became muddy due to rain, making him unable to drive along it. Because of this, he let the victims go.

He became a suspect after his two rape victims recalled seeing their attacker, who they recognized as a marine, at Balboa Hospital before they were attacked. Chadd had once approached the mother and asked her to fill in her name and address for a benefits form. Chadd was arrested in Lafayette,

Louisiana. Fingerprints subsequently connected him to the murders of Franklin and Hewitt. When detectives presented the evidence to him, he confessed to their murders plus Bright's murder – who authorities previously charged serial killer Wayne Donald Horton with – and a fourth murder of a male hitchhiker in June 1974. Chadd claimed to have bludgeoned the hitchhiker to death with a rock in Ellsworth, Kansas, before throwing him and his dog into a nearby creek. Although Chadd was able to identify the creek on a map, a search of the area yielded no results, and police were unable to find any matching homicides or missing person reports to tie into Chadd's confession.

While imprisoned, he wrote, "Dark Secrets," a 57-page autobiography detailing his life and crimes. Intending to publish it and make a profit from it. The manuscript was instead taken and used as evidence in his murder trial. In 1979, Chadd changed his plea from innocent to guilty, and was sentenced to death for Hewitt's murder and received a life sentence for Franklin's murder, as the death penalty was deemed unconstitutional at the time of that crime. Although Chadd had originally been adamant about receiving the death penalty, he decided that he wanted to live after being convicted. The California Supreme court ordered a retrial because Chadd changed his plea against his lawyer's wishes, and the court deemed that defendants cannot plead guilty to capital crimes if their lawyers object. After receiving a life sentence in Nevada for murdering Delmar Bright, he again pleaded guilty to Franklin and Hewitt's murders in exchange for the prosecution not to seeking a death sentence. In all he received three sentences of life in prison for the murders and an additional 13 years for the Chula Vista rapes and kidnappings. At the present time he is now imprisoned at Mule Creek State Prison age 70, having avoided death row by his guilty pleas.

RICHARD TRENTON CHASE

Born May 23rd 1950 - sentenced to death May 8th 1979, committed suicide December 26th, 1980.

In the history of serial killers the murders of Richard Trenton Chase—also known as "The Vampire of Sacramento"—have to be near the top of the list of most twisted, disturbed and horrific crimes ever committed by one human being. I don't usually offer a warning but this story involves descriptions of child and animal abuse, along with grisly details about murder and other assaults. It may disturb some readers.

Richard Chase's family and the legal and mental health systems missed many opportunities to manage his clearly troubling and escalating violent tendencies and get him the treatment he needed, which may have prevented his 1977–1978 crime spree resulting in the deaths of six people and countless animals.

Richard Trenton Chase was born on May 23rd, 1950 in Sacramento, California. He was a disturbed child from a very young age. He exhibited early signs of troubling patterns, sometimes called the Macdonald Triad, a theory that connects abnormal childhood behaviour of cruelty to animals, arson or fire-setting, and enuresis or "bedwetting" to later serial criminal acts.

Chase's home life was chaotic. Between the ages of 12 and 13, family issues worsened—they experienced financial problems, losing their house, and Richard's parents fought constantly. His mother Beatrice was evaluated by two psychiatrists, later accusing her husband of poisoning her.

His father Richard Sr. was an alcoholic disciplinarian; Richard's younger sister Pamela recalled her brother being shaken and thrown into a wall by their father, along with repeated verbal abuse.

At 13, Richard, for some unknown reason, began believing he was a member of the James-Younger Gang, the notorious outlaw group of murderers and robbers in the late 1800s. His obsession included hanging a poster of the gang with his own face pasted onto it.

Between the ages of 14 and 21, Chase was a mediocre to poor student while in high school and college. His serious drug problems escalated during this time, including getting arrested for marijuana possession. During this period, he saw a psychiatrist who believed Chase was mentally ill, but there is no evidence that he received any treatment.

In 1971, Chase moved into an apartment with friends, but his odd behaviour—boarding up the doors of his bedroom and closet, and heavy drug use—caused his roommates to request that he leave. When he refused, his friends moved out and unable to pay the rent Richard was forced to move back into his parents' home.

Throughout his teen years and young adulthood, Richard Chase tried to have a normal dating life, but his few relationships ended in sexual frustration as he struggled with impotence no doubt exacerbated by drug use, mental illness, and past physical and emotional abuse.

As he became more unhinged, Chase began to believe that he didn't have enough blood in his body, which led to him ingesting the blood of animals to "replenish" his own blood supply. He also believed that eating animals he captured and drinking their blood prevented his heart from "shrinking."

On top of these paranoid ideas, he also believed that someone had stolen his pulmonary artery and that his blood flow had stopped.

There is a long list of bizarre beliefs and increasingly dangerous and alarming actions that ultimately led to Richard Chase's murder spree. A timeline of events reflect not only a wildly troubled individual slowly declining into a total mental collapse, but the complete lack of accountability of those medical 'experts' around him who did almost nothing to prevent Richard Chase's horrifying crimes.

At a party in 1973, Chase fondled a girl and the police were called. As he was being escorted out, a gun fell from his belt and he was sent to jail and bailed out by his father.

Chase tried living with his grandmother in Los Angeles, but she eventually sent him back to his parents because of his 'inhuman' behaviour.

Throughout 1973, he continued to complain of non-existent ailments, like head injuries and stomach aches, and maintained his claims of a missing pulmonary artery, a "shrinking heart," and made-up imagined blood flow problems. A neurologist stated that Richard Chase was suffering from "a psychiatric disturbance of major proportions," and admitted Chase to the psychiatric ward of a local hospital. His mother removed him from the facility without giving any reason.

During 1975 Chase is in and out of hospitals and mental institutions. The staff in one such facility began referring to Chase as "Dracula."

In 1976 Chase was hospitalized again, this time committed as a "schizophrenic suffering from somatic delusions." He had injected himself with rabbit's blood and given himself blood poisoning.

Richard escaped from another hospital after medical staff refused to release him because he was considered a "danger to others." He was caught and sent to an extended care mental hospital, where staff found dead birds outside Chase's window. Chase was eventually released from the hospital with a diagnosis of "paranoid schizophrenia."

On one occasion in 1977, Chase's mother Beatrice was greeted at her front door by her son offering her a dead cat. He proceeded to cut up the animal and smear its blood on himself. His mother went inside the house and didn't report the incident.

Beatrice later helped her son plan and pay for an extended trip out of state. In August, Bureau of Indian Affairs officers in Nevada came upon Chase's car stuck in the sand on reservation land; inside they found a bucket of cow's blood, a cow liver, and two guns. Chase was located nearby, naked and screaming, with cow's blood covering his entire body claiming the blood had leaked out of his own flesh.

He was arrested but released, with the U.S. Attorney's Office opting not to prosecute.

Chase continued to purchase and capture animals for use in his blood rituals. He also bought a .22 calibre semi-automatic pistol, a weapon he shot into a woman's Sacramento house but no one was harmed, and a gun he later used for much deadlier purposes.

In 1977, Richard Chase was again found covered in cow's blood on the Pyramid Lake reservation in Nevada.

Even when reviewing just these few incidents taken from a much deeper timeline of alarming behaviours, it doesn't take long to notice a pattern of family and authority figures failing to understand the severity of Chase's illness and find him the correct doctors.

His mother Beatrice, who reportedly experienced severe mental problems as well, supported her son throughout his troubles while simultaneously ignoring the severity and urgency of Chase's downward mental spiral and his truly disturbing actions and behaviours. Beatrice Chase died in 1990.

Left unchecked by his parents, the courts, law enforcement, and medical personnel, despite the obvious warning signs, it was inevitable that Richard Chase's crimes would go to the next level. But no one was prepared for how grisly and deranged those crimes would be.

On December 29th, 1977, Ambrose Griffin, a 51-year-old engineer, was carrying groceries into his

Sacramento home when he was shot dead by a drive-by gunman. Griffin would be Richard Chase's first known human victim.

Chase wasn't caught, but the police investigation turned up a 12-year-old boy who reported being shot at by a man in a car who looked like Chase. It was also revealed through forensic analysis of the bullets in the Griffin murder that the same gun had been used to fire into the woman's home two days earlier, just a few blocks away from the Griffins.

Throughout January of 1978, Chase was witnessed in the area acting strangely, trespassing on people's property, and making those he encountered uneasy, as he was clearly not in his right mind.

Nancy Holden was approached in a grocery store by a dishevelled man who recognized her. She was startled to learn it was "Rick Chase" from high school. She couldn't believe the clean-cut, pleasant boy she remembered had transformed into the malnourished, grimy, agitated tramp who made her feel very uncomfortable. Chase followed her out to her car but she managed to lock the doors and drive away.

Dawn Larson, one of Chase's neighbours, reported being asked for a cigarette by Chase. She gave him one, but then he physically restrained her until she gave him the entire pack before he let her go.

A few weeks later, Jeanne Layton reported Chase appearing at her patio door. When he found it locked, he went to some windows that were also locked. He returned to the door and stared at Jeanne for some time, then casually lit a cigarette and left.

Chase then entered the home of Robert and Barbara Edwards, who arrived home from grocery shopping to hear a noise inside their house. Suddenly, Chase came running around the corner towards them but managed to evade Robert who tried to stop him. The couple found their house ransacked; Chase had urinated and defecated on their infant son's baby clothes and bed.

Chase then entered the home of David and Teresa Wallin. David was at work, but Teresa, three months pregnant, was home and just taking out the trash when suddenly, Richard Chase was in the house.

He shot her three times, killing her instantly. Chase then raped her corpse and disembowelled and disfigured her body with a knife. In the process, he had spread her blood all over his hands and face while drinking it from a discarded yogurt container. He took some of her body parts with him when he left.

Several days later, Richard Chase came upon an unlocked front door at the home of 38-year-old Evelyn Miroth. She was in the bath, but her 51-year-old friend Dan Meredith was watching Evelyn's six-year-old son Jason and her 22-month-old nephew David. Dan went to the front hallway when Chase entered the home and was shot in the head by Chase, killing him instantly.

Taking Meredith's keys and wallet from his body, he followed young Jason into his mother's bedroom, shooting him twice before also shooting his toddler cousin David.

Chase entered the bathroom and shot Evelyn in the head. A scene similar to the Teresa Wallin murder then occurred, with Chase sodomizing her body while consuming her blood.

A young girl neighbour knocked on the door for a pre-arranged play-date with Jason, startling Chase, who fled in Dan Meredith's car with some of Evelyn's internal organs and the body of 22-month-old David, leaving behind a bullet hole in the baby's pillow in his crib.

Despite a long trail of clues, investigators didn't connect Chase to the murders.

After the Teresa Wallin murder, FBI investigators Russ Vorpagel and Robert Ressler were brought in to help assess the case. Their profile of the killer was eerily accurate, making the determination that the killer would be a tall, skinny loner with a history of mental issues and a lack of hygiene.

The profile characterized him as a "disorganized" killer due to the messiness of his actions—he appeared to give little thought to what evidence he left behind or the consequences of his actions. They also believed he would likely continue killing until he was stopped.

Five days after the Wallin murder and one day after the multiple murders, Nancy Holden, Chase's old high school friend, heard about the FBI profile and contacted authorities with information about her encounter with Chase at the grocery store. Police investigators ran a background check on Chase and alarm bells rang immediately—they found Chase's history of mental illness, weapons charges, drug busts, Nevada arrest, and his registration of a .22 semi-automatic pistol.

Law enforcement immediately went to Chase's apartment, where he was apprehended while trying to leave, wearing a bloodstained parka and shoes, with Dan Meredith's wallet in his pocket and pictures of Evelyn Miroth's family. He was also carrying a bloody box with bloodstained contents: wallpaper pieces and rags, along with his .22.

After Chase was taken into custody, a search of his apartment proved to be one of the most sickening crime scenes ever investigated. Most contents of the kitchen—food, dishes, glasses, a blender, etc.—were covered in blood. The refrigerator was filled with human remains, including bone fragments, brain tissue, and other body parts. Pictures of human organs were found, along with pet collars and a newspaper with "pets for sale" ads circled.

Perhaps most chilling was a calendar with the previous murder dates circled and the word "Today" written on each; the same word appeared 44 times on future dates.

As lead prosecutor Ronald Tochterman was putting together his death penalty arguments in the case of California v. Richard Trenton Chase, a janitor at a church found a box with the remains of a male baby inside. It was young David, who had been taken from the Miroth's home after the killings. All of Chase's victims were now accounted for.

The Vampire of Sacramento trial began on January 2nd, 1979 with Richard Chase charged with six counts of murder. Chase's defence team thought their only hope for a defence strategy was to plead "not guilty by reason of insanity," bolstered by the fact that he hadn't planned his crimes.

A venue change was approved by the judge due to the notoriety of the case in Sacramento. The trial was moved 120 miles south to Santa Clara County.

Chase was examined by a dozen psychiatrists. He told the doctors that he was scared that his victims might come back from the dead seeking vengeance and that he thought the blood he drank was therapeutic.

Although the details of the horrible crimes were compelling in the prosecutor's larger narrative, the most viable evidence was the .22 that Chase used in all the murders and Dan Meredith's wallet found in his pocket.

Chase took the stand in his own defence, likely a strategy to bolster his insanity plea. He looked terrible, with hollow, dim eyes and an unsettlingly thin gaunt frame of 107 pounds, and his testimony reinforced that he was deeply unhinged.

But it wasn't enough to convince a jury that he should continue living. On May 8th, 1978, the jury deliberated for five hours and came back with verdicts of first-degree murder on all six counts. They also determined that Chase was legally sane and that he should be given the death sentence. The judge agreed and sentenced him to die in the gas chamber.

Other inmates at San Quentin were uncomfortable around Chase and they conspired to provoke him to kill himself.

Their strategy worked—Chase began stockpiling his prescribed antidepressant Sinequan tablets, and on December 26th, 1980, he was found in his cell, sprawled upside-down and hanging partway off his bunk, dead of "toxic ingestion" from a deliberate suicidal overdose.

JUAN CHAVEZ

Born 1966 – sentenced to life in prison without parole June 22nd, 1999. Committed suicide in prison September 9th, 1999.

In 1992, Juan Chavez was convicted on multiple counts of kidnapping and robbery in unrelated cases and was sentenced to life imprisonment.

Elsewhere, cold case investigators re-examined the unrelated case of four murders from 1989 and came to the conclusion that an unidentified serial killer was targeting gay middle-aged men. After a further examination, they started re-investigating the murder of Alfred Rowswell. In 1994, the fingerprint that was found on Rowswell's car was entered into a database and it corresponded with an inmate currently in a Washington prison.

Investigators travelled to the prison and spoke with the inmate, who declared that a man named Juan Chavez had given him the car and requested to abandon it as far as he could travel in it. After learning that, Chavez became the prime suspect in Rowswell's case.

After an interview with high-profile investigators, Chavez confessed to killing Rowswell. After a further examination, cold case authorities tied him to the murder of four men in two months, Ruben Panis, 57, Donald Kleeman, 46, Michael Kates, 46, and Leo Hildebrand, 52, as he was identified as the man seen looting one of the victims ATM's on camera after the killing. When asked why he did it, he claimed he wanted to clear California of gays because he wanted to bring an end to the sexually transmitted virus HIV, which causes AIDS.

Chavez pleaded guilty to killing Roswell, and later to the killing of the four other men in 1989. He received a total of five life sentences on June 21st, 1999. On September 9th of that year, Chavez hung himself in his cell at Folsom State Prison.

WILLIAM JENNINGS CHOYCE

Born 1954 –sentenced to death December 5th, 2008.

William Jennings Choyce was born on December 19th, 1953, in Alameda County, California. He grew up in Oakland, married Alice Swafford, and had a daughter named Crystal Choyce. His wife Alice later alleged William Choyce had a penchant for strip clubs and sex workers from the initial days of their dating and continued maintaining such relationships throughout the marriage. She also contended that Choyce was disturbed, citing incidents where he made her watch porn, including rape videos, and asked her to wear clothes and lipstick akin to strippers and sex workers.

After dating for four years, the couple had tied the knot even after Alice had allegedly caught Choyce with a sex worker in bed after returning home early from work. She claimed that Choyce returned one night and stated he had been robbed and needed a gun for protection. Since then, he used to go out every night, armed, and did not return home most nights. In 1985, he called Alice from the police station after being arrested for soliciting a prostitute.

Alice and daughter Crystal later alleged Choyce's behaviour started getting darker and twisted, and he started abusing and harassing them both at home. His behaviour became so erratic that he stopped bathing and washing, watching porn throughout the day. Unknown to them, Choyce had committed several rapes and was not getting enough of a thrill from just the rape, so he escalated to murder.

Choyce's first victim was Victoria Bell, and Oakland police found her body on April 3rd, 1988. Police reports stated that he picked her up while driving through the shady Oakland streets before bundling her into his van and taking her to a secluded location. She was raped, her hands and feet were bound together, and she was shot execution-style before he dumped the body in a sexually explicit pose. His crime streak continued, and he again came to the notice of law enforcement when a young woman claimed she had been abducted and raped at gunpoint and named him. However, he evaded justice by asserting the sex had been consensual.

Choyce committed his next two murders in quick succession, with Gwendolyn Lee's body being found in San Joaquin County on July 2nd, 1997, and Lawanda Beck's body being found in Stockton on August 11th, 1997.

Like Victoria Bell, both women were sex workers and were shot execution-style after being abducted and raped. He humiliated Gwendolyn's dead body by bounding her hands and ankles and leaving her naked from her waist down, while Lawanda was discovered wholly nude.

The investigators noted the similarities between the three murders, but Choyce continued to be free until two women positively identified him as their rapist. He was convicted of the two rapes in 2002 and was sentenced to 11 years in prison.

With the advancement of forensic science, law enforcement officials decided to re-open the murders of Gwendolyn and Lawanda and run DNA analyses. They took a DNA sample from Choyce and ran it against the DNA samples retrieved from both crime scenes. When it matched, the detectives further established that the bullets used to kill the two women were fired from the gun belonging to him.

The officers also linked Choyce to Victoria's murder back in 1988. While in jail, he was charged in 2005 with kidnapping, raping, and fatally shooting Gwendolyn and Lawanda and the murder of Victoria. On July 17th, 2008, his murder trial began, and he was convicted of all charges on August 11th, 2008. On September 18th, 2008, the jury recommended the death penalty, and he was sentenced to death on December 15th, 2008.

William Choyce's defence rested on his childhood trauma while growing up with an abusive mother but, as a valid argument, it was dismissed by the judge. In December 2008, the 54-year-old was the 678th inmate to await execution in California. He tried to appeal his sentence, but his death sentence was affirmed each time. William Choyce, now 70, remains on death row and is incarcerated at the San Quentin State Prison.

THOR NIS CHRISTIANSEN

Born December 28th, 1957 – Sentenced to life in prison June 1980. Stabbed to death in Folsom State Prison March 30th, 1981 by an unidentified assailant.

Thor Christiansen was born in Denmark, and emigrated to Inglewood with his parents and on to Solvang when he was five years old.

His father, Nis, ran a restaurant in Solvang, which was noted for its Danish atmosphere. Thor had a high IQ and was a good student until his junior year of high school, when he began using marijuana, drinking, and neglecting his schoolwork.

He moved out of his parent's house, dropped out of high school, and began working as a gas station attendant; he also became overweight at 275 lbs.

Then he moved to Oregon, lost weight, and moved back to Santa Barbara County and completed his high school diploma at a junior college. He moved into an apartment in Goleta with 20 year old Kathy Soliz, whom he met while she was hitchhiking. Soliz characterized him as "very, very nice" and "not capable of murder." While he was living with her he committed the Los Angeles murder and attempted murder.

His first three murders in late 1976 and early 1977 were of young women of similar appearance from Isla Vista, California, and led to large demonstrations opposed to violence to women, and in favour of better transportation for the young people residing in Isla Vista.

His fourth murder in 1979 was of a young African-American woman from Los Angeles. A fifth intended victim escaped with a bullet in her head, and later identified him after recognising him in a Los Angeles bar.

His victims:

Jacqueline Anne Rook, Nov. 20th, 1976, aged 21 (Isla Vista, originally from Del Mar)

Mary Ann Sarris, Dec. 6th, 1976, aged 19 (Isla Vista, originally from Santa Rosa)

Patricia Marie Laney, Jan. 18th, 1977, aged 21 (Isla Vista, originally from Huntington Beach)

Laura Sue Benjamin, May 26th, 1979, aged 22 (body found, Los Angeles County)

Christiansen would get his victims into his car when he came on them hitchhiking. He would then shoot them in the head with a 0.22 calibre pistol, and rape them. The fifth intended victim, Lydia Preston, aged 24 of Baldwin Park was shot in the head by Christiansen in his vehicle on April 18th, 1979, but managed to run away severely injured and later identify him.

Victims, Rook, Sarris, and Laney all disappeared without any communication from their killer; all were reported missing. Laney's body was found two days after her disappearance on an isolated road in the Santa Ynez Mountains northwest of Isla Vista near Rancho del Cielo; Rook's body was found the next day near Laney's body. Sarris' body was found on May 22nd, 1977 near Los Alamos. Benjamin's body was found in a culvert near Angeles Forest Highway and Big Tujunga Road in the San Gabriel Mountains north of Los Angeles; she was reported to have been working as a prostitute.

Lydia Preston, 24, saw Christiansen again on July 11th, 1979 in the Bottom Line Bar in Hollywood, and reported her sighting to the police, who promptly arrested him. Because of Christiansen's address in Goleta, California and the similarity of Preston's experience to forensic evidence in the Rook, Saris, and Laney cases, Christiansen became a main suspect in all the Isla Vista murders.

After his arrest and back checking their files, Santa Barbara County law enforcement realized they had investigated him as a suspect in 1977, and had noted his possession of a 0.22 calibre pistol when he was arrested for drunk driving.

Christiansen was charged on July 27th, 1979 with three counts of first degree murder and tried in early 1980 in Santa Monica for the murder of Laura Benjamin; he initially pleaded insanity, but he withdrew the plea. He then pleaded guilty in June, 1980 in Santa Barbara to the Isla Vista murders, and was sentenced to life in prison. At that time, California did not have the death penalty.

Christiansen was stabbed to death in Folsom State Prison on March 30th, 1981; the perpetrator was not identified. Psychiatrists had predicted that he was likely to be killed in prison, as he was white, young, blond, and his last victim was an African-American.

DOUGLAS DANIEL CLARK

Born March 10th 1948 – died of natural causes in prison on October 11th, 2023.

Douglas Daniel Clark was an American serial killer and necrophile. Clark and his accomplice, Carol Mary Bundy, were collectively known as the Sunset Strip Killers and were responsible for the deaths of at least seven individuals although they are considered suspects in the deaths of several other women and young girls. Clark was charged with six murders in Los Angeles, California, and was convicted in 1983. Clark's victims were typically young prostitutes or teenage runaways and his victims were decapitated and their severed heads kept as mementos. He would also perform sex acts on the corpses.

Doug Clark was born on March 10th, 1948, and was the third son of five children of an international Naval Intelligence officer. His family moved frequently during Clark's childhood due to his father's job, and he later claimed to have lived in 37 countries including India, Switzerland, and the Marshall Islands. In 1958, his father left the Navy for a civilian position as an engineer with the Transport Company of Texas, but the family still moved around. Clark was sent to the exclusive International School of Geneva and later attended Culver Military Academy while his father continued to work abroad.

As a teenager, Clark reportedly recorded his sexual escapades with girls at school without their knowledge and began developing dark sexual fantasies of rape, murder, mutilation and necrophilia.

When he graduated in 1967, Clark enlisted in the U.S. Air Force and was stationed in Colorado and Ohio. Clark was eventually discharged from the Air Force and he drifted around for the next decade, often working as a mechanic. He moved to Los Angeles and was employed as a steam plant operator for the Los Angeles Department of Water and Power, working at the Valley Generating Station before abruptly quitting for no reason. Subsequently, Clark became a boiler operator at the Jergens soap factory in Burbank but was fired due to a high rate of absences and violent threats he had made against his co-workers.

During this time, Clark also spent the majority of his spare time in local bars and nightclubs searching for lonely, older women whom he could seduce out of their money. One of the bars he frequented in the area was Little Nashville, where he met 36-year-old Carol Bundy on Christmas Day 1979. Bundy was a vocational nurse and a mother of two who had left her abusive husband in January 1979. Clark moved into her home the same night as he met her.

Bundy and Clark developed an intense sadomasochistic relationship, and Clark frequently brought sex workers back to the couple's apartment to have threesomes. Then, when Clark took an interest in an 11-year-old neighbour, Bundy helped lure the girl into posing for pornographic photographs. Clark quickly escalated from paedophilia to murder, talking about how much he would like to kill a girl during sex. He persuaded Bundy to purchase two pistols for him to use, reportedly seeking to fulfil his fantasy of killing a woman during sex and feeling her vaginal contractions as she died. During 1980, Bundy and Clark are believed to have claimed the lives of at least seven persons, but both perpetrators also admitted culpability in the homicides of other additional women.

The partial remains of two victims were found in Los Angeles County, California on January 26th, 1980, at around 1:00 p.m. in a river bed north of Magic Mountain Parkway, west of the Old Road and south of the Valencia Sewage Treatment Plant. Both had been shot to death and are known as the Valencia Jane Does.

On June 30th, 1980, a group of snake hunters off the Golden State Freeway near Sylmar, in the San Fernando Valley, discovered a woman's mummified corpse. She was identified as 17-year-old Sacramento runaway Marnette Carrie Comer. Last seen alive on June 1st, the young prostitute had been dead at least three weeks when she was found.

On June 11th, 1980, stepsisters Gina Narano, 15, and Cynthia Leigh "Cindy" Chandler, 16, vanished from Huntington Beach, while trying to meet with friends. They were found the following morning, beside the Ventura Freeway near Griffith Park, in Los Angeles; each had been shot in the side of the head. Clark later came home and told Bundy about the two teenagers whom he had murdered after picking them up on the Sunset Strip. He had ordered them to perform fellatio on him and then shot them both in the head before taking them to an empty garage and raping their dead bodies. An uneasy Bundy phoned the police, admitting to having some knowledge of the murders but refused to provide any clues as to Clark's identity. Clark told Bundy that if either of them were apprehended, he would take the blame in the hope that she would be allowed to go free.

On June 24th, 1980, Clark killed two sex workers, 24-year-old Karen Lee Jones, and 20-year-old Exxie LaFaye Wilson. Jones was found that day behind a Burbank, California steakhouse, murdered by a single gunshot to the head. Later police were summoned to Studio City, where the headless body of Wilson had been found by pedestrians. Clark had lured Jones and Wilson into his car, shot them, and dumped their bodies in plain sight but not before removing Wilson's head. Clark took the head back home and stored it in the refrigerator.

Upon seeing it, Bundy put make-up on it before Clark used it again for another "bout of necrophilia." She later recalled, "We had a lot of fun with her. I was making her up like a Bardie with makeup." On June 27th, the couple put the freshly cleaned head in an ornate wooden box and dumped it in a Hollywood alleyway.

On August 5th, 1980, Bundy attended a country music performance by 45-year-old John

Robert Murray, her former apartment manager and lover. After the performance, Bundy conversed with Murray and drunkenly talked about what she and Clark were doing. Murray was alarmed and implied that he might tell the police. Bundy then went with Murray into his van to have sex. Once they were inside, she shot, stabbed and decapitated him. Bundy left various clues behind in the van, including shell casings. Two days later, Bundy confessed to her co-workers that she had killed Murray. They called the police, and she gave a full confession to them about her and Clark's crimes. Murray's head was never found.

Clark is believed to have murdered an unidentified female who was discovered on August 26th, 1980, in Newhall, California, near a pair of water towers by a maintenance worker inspecting the source of a foul smell. The remains had been somewhat disarticulated; the female had been killed by a single .25 bullet to one of the temporal bones of her skull and was found wearing only a red sweatshirt. Her face was reconstructed by the National Centre for Missing and Exploited Children in efforts to identify her, as her remains were unrecognizable due to skeletonization. Bundy informed police that Clark had stated this particular victim was a prostitute from Hollywood. She elaborated that he had shot the female in the back of the head during a sexual act while inside his vehicle. After her death, she was disposed of in Newhall, after she was raped post-mortem. She is known as the Newhall Jane Doe, or as Jane Doe 18.

Another unidentified female was allegedly killed by Clark after a sexual encounter, based on statements made by Bundy that he had dumped her body in Tuna Canyon as they drove past the area in late July 1980. She had been shot in the left side of her forehead, and her clothing had been removed and placed around her hips. The woman was not explicitly described as a prostitute. The woman's partially mummified skeleton was found by a passer-by at the base of a hill on August 28th, 1980, in a mountainous area in Malibu, California. Clark denied involvement, providing an alibi that placed him hundreds of miles from the scene on the day this victim was killed. The jury, however, decided that he was, indeed, responsible. She is known as the Malibu Jane Doe, or Jane Doe 99.

"Cathy," also known as Jane Doe 28, was a female whose remains were recovered on March 2nd, 1981, in Green Valley. Only the skull, mandible, a femur, along with some ribs and vertebrae were recovered. She had been shot in the head. She was allegedly a sex worker who had been killed in late July 1980 while engaged in a sexual act. Clark claimed Bundy was the shooter and that she had instructed him to drive to the location in Green Valley, where she stripped the body naked and disposed of it. Clark also declared that Bundy fondled the victim's body along the way. During the trial phase of their prosecution, documents regarding this victim were misplaced, and evidence was ruled "irrelevant." Neither Clark nor Bundy was charged for the murder although it is generally believed they both were responsible.

Clark and Bundy were arrested and jailed on August 11th, 1980. After the pair were arrested, the murder weapons were found hidden at Clark's workplace. Bundy was charged with two murders: Murray and "Cathy" whose killing she confessed to having been present at. Clark was charged with six murders. At his trial, he acted as his own defence counsel and tried to blame Bundy for everything, claiming he had been manipulated. The jury did not believe him, and he was sentenced to death in 1983. Clark remained on California's death row until his death from natural causes in 2023. Bundy made a plea bargain and in return for her testimony was sentenced to fifty-two-years-to-life imprisonment. Bundy died in prison from heart failure on December 9th, 2003, at the age of 61.

HERBERT JAMES CODDINGTON

Born 1959 – sentenced to death January 20th, 1989.

On May 16th, 1987, Herbert James Coddington lured Alecia Thoma, 14, and Monica Berge, 12, to a mobile home in South Lake Tahoe, California. Coddington had told them they would be used as actresses for an anti-drug film, but it was a ruse. He killed their two chaperones and sexually assaulted both the girls. After Coddington was arrested, police discovered he was also responsible for the murder of Sheila Jo Keister, a 12-year-old, who had been murdered in 1981.
Using the alias, Mark Bloomfield, a film producer, Coddington called various modelling agencies and requested young female models to act in an anti-drug film.
On May 13th, 1987, Coddington called the Avalon Agency and asked about female models for an anti-drug film he was shooting at Lake Tahoe.
Coddington had also contacted a woman named Candice Smith. Candice was familiar with Coddington from her croupier work; he often played blackjack at a table where she was a dealer. Coddington called Candice at 3:00 a.m. and introduced himself as John Parrot. He explained he was calling from a company stationed in Atlanta, Georgia, who was looking for a woman to be in a beer commercial. According to court documents, during the call, Coddington mentioned Candice's

daughter. Candice declined the offer and hung up. At 9:00 a.m. Coddington called back and told Candice that the call was legitimate and offered to put his partner on the phone, Candice was not fooled and believed it was the same person. Coddington then asked Candice to lunch; she hung up.

On May 14th, 1987, Coddington contacted the Barbizon Modelling School and Agency and told the person who answered the phone his name was Mark Bloomfield, and he was with a communications company in Georgia. The following day Coddington went in person to the agency and had a business card that said the word "Parrot" on it for Parrot Communications. The owner of the modelling agency believed that he "was nervous and in disguise" and refused to give him any models.

On the same day, Maybelle "Mabs" Martin, 69, owner of Showcase Models took Coddington on as a client and set up an audition for him at her modelling agency. Coddington showed up to the audition, using the Mark Bloomfield alias, wearing a dark pinstripe suit with glasses. Alecia Thoma and Monica Berge, along with several other young females, auditioned for what they believed was an anti-drug commercial. The girls would read lines from cue cards as an audition.

The following day, on May 15th, 1987, Coddington had another audition set up at the Barbizon Modelling School. Later in the evening, he auditioned another model from the prior agency, Showcase Models, Jennifer. Jennifer was older and already driving. She had driven herself to the audition and once, speaking with Coddington about the part, wanted to drive herself to the location of where the commercial would be filmed. Coddington had told her he wanted to drive to Tahoe with everyone and had arranged for Jennifer to meet him at the Golden Nugget. Later that night, Coddington called Jennifer and told her that his photographer decided she was too old. He would also call Monica and Alecia to tell them they were chosen for the parts and would receive $50 an hour.

On May 16th, 1987, Mabs told her son she was driving with the girls and a friend, Dottie Walsh, 67, as chaperones. Mabs picked up the girls, picked up Dottie, and then drove to the Golden Nugget to meet Coddington. Coddington took the group of 4 to the trailer in South Lake Tahoe, California.

Upon arriving at the trailer, Coddington instructed Alecia and Monica to go in the trailer, so they could change into shorts and fix their makeup. Mabs and Dottie entered the house with Monica and Alecia and were led to a room reinforced with plywood with a bed in it. According to court documents, as the group entered, Coddington barged into Mabs and Dottie as he closed the door behind him and hit Alecia in the face with a rectangular object. He continued to hit Mabs and Dottie in their faces and chests.

Coddington instructed Mabs and Dottie to lie on the floor or he would kill the girls. He then used "FLEX-CUFs" to bind their hands behind their backs and bind their feet. According to court documents, Dottie begged not to be killed and Mabs offered herself and her money for the girl's safety. Coddington then placed a pillowcase over Mabs head and put a FLEX-CUFF around her neck. Mabs asked Coddington to loosen it. Within minutes Mabs was gagging from not being able to breathe, fell on her side, and died. Coddington then murdered Dottie the same way.

The court document states that Coddington then made Alecia and Monica lay over the legs of their chaperones and used more FLEX-CUFs to bind their hands behind their backs and their feet together. Coddington then put a jacket over Alecia's face and placed her on the bed. He put a pair of shorts over Monica's face and put her on the floor next to the bed.

Both girls then heard what sounded like bodies being dragged and rustling plastic. Monica believed Mabs and Dottie were taken out of the room.

Coddington returned to the room where Alecia and Monica were being held and unbound, their wrists from behind their backs. Using belts, Coddington retied their hands in front of them. He put a ski-mask over Alecia's eyes and tied a rope around her neck to secure it. Alecia could see Coddington cleaning up a red stain on the floor and asked him what he was doing. Coddington told her he spilled Kool-Aid and was cleaning it. Monica was also able to see Coddington clean what she described to be a dark brown stain on the carpet.

Coddington eventually allowed Alecia and Monica to take off their masks and bindings. He told them he may hold them for a ransom. Monica asked if he had planned to kill them. In response, Coddington brandished a pistol with a silencer and stated that if he wanted to kill them, he could have already. He then gave them some water and put pillowcases on their hands. Coddington would then bring them fruit and magazines. Alecia noticed a mailing address on the magazine and ripped it off and saved it. The girls would spend the night in the trailer.

In the morning, Coddington made Alecia and Monica take vitamins and fed them eggs and strawberries. Both girls recalled Coddington was wearing something over his face and had seen orange hair sticking out. The girls were allowed to watch TV in the living room for a bit. After some time, Coddington told them he was going to work out and told them to go into the other room to change clothes, so they could work out too.

Coddington exercised in the next room and then took a shower. He then played an exercise video and forced the girls to work out. Afterwards, Coddington told the girls they could shower, which they declined.

Coddington then told Alecia and Monica a fabricated story. He said they would have to make a sexual tape with an 18-year-old boy that his friends had kidnapped. Coddington did not have friends over and there was not a kidnapped boy.

He blindfolded them and told them they would have to take their clothes off. Alecia asked Coddington if he was going to rape them, to which he said no. He added that he would hurt the boy if he hurt them. According to court documents both girls were put on the bed.

Coddington told the fake-kidnapped boy to be gentle. He would then pretend to be the kidnapped boy and use a fake voice to sound like a younger male. Coddington climbed on top of Monica and started whispering in her ear as the kidnapped boy and told her he was scared. He also said there were people were who had guns in the house. Coddington sexually assaulted Monica for approximately 30 minutes before asking the fake boy to stop and to get dressed.

Coddington turned his attention to Alecia. He would use the fake voice again and pretended to be a kidnapped boy who was being forced to sexually assault. According to court documents, he would kiss her entire body for about 20 minutes. Alecia asked him to stop, which he did.

He let both girls get dressed and go into the living room. Coddington told the girls they would have to make another video since the one they made was "not worth two cents". He told the girls he would release them after another 10 minutes and forced them to go back into the bedroom.

Once in the bedroom, he blindfolded them, put Monica on the bed, and Alecia on the floor. The girls continued to hold hands. Coddington would pretend to be a British man and spoke using a British accent. He stated that the video was no good and another one would have to be made.

Coddington would remove Monica's clothing again and raped her.

Alecia and Monica asked to call their parents. Coddington did not let them, but told them he would allow them to record a message for them. The girls watched TV later that night and would eventually fall asleep.

In the morning, Coddington told the girls he was going to take them to a payphone so they could call the police. He told them when they spoke to the police, they were to say they had been kidnapped and taken to Sacramento, where they were held in a 2-story blue house. Coddington threatened the girls' families if they did not stick to the story

Meanwhile Alecia's stepfather had reported his daughter missing to the police. They had then broken into Mab's studio and were led to Jennifer K., the teenager who Coddington deemed too old for his film. Jennifer relayed the license plate she remembered. The license plate did not read "TVTEEN" as Jennifer remembered, but "TEVEN", which was a car dealership in South Lake Tahoe.

Detectives located the Teven dealership and learned the owner had given a friend a license plate to use on his BMW until he got it registered. He confirmed his friend was Herb Coddington by a sketch shown to him and provided authorities with Coddrington's address.

Teven, the owner of the dealership, then called Coddington to inform him that he had sold his car for him (a business deal they had made prior). He also informed him there was a police wanted picture of him in the post office and asked if he had been involved in the kidnapping. Coddington replied "that he had done much worse".

Detectives put surveillance on the trailer and followed Coddington to the post office. They watched him as he looked at the board where the wanted poster was pinned. Coddington returned to the trailer at 9:00 p.m. At 9:03 a man who identified himself as Coddington called the FBI and acknowledged that he was wanted by the FBI. The agent took the caller's name, number, and address.

While in the trailer, Coddington told the girls he had been found and was attempting to wash off evidence from the girls' clothing. FBI agents knocked on the door and asked to speak to Coddington. Coddington stated he wanted to speak over the phone and not in person and turned the lights out. The FBI called the trailer and told Coddington to do as they instructed and open the door for the agents at the door. Coddington told the FBI agent over the phone that the girls were in his trailer, and he wanted to go to the hospital.

Agents entered the trailer by force through the door. An agent outside broke a window and ordered Coddington to lie on the floor until other agents entered and took him into custody. While being searched, he told agents the girls were okay, but he was sick. He added that Mabs and Dottie were in the back room and he had placed them in bags because he did not want any "mess" He stated he killed both women and he was sick.

Investigators found both women with their hands bound, wrapped in plastic garbage bags in a back room of the trailer. The medical examiner determined Mabs and Dottie both died from "ligature neck compression" that was the cause of death.

Later medical examinations of Alecia determined she had been sexually assaulted. There was "bluish bruising in the vaginal area and torn necrotic tissue hanging from the hymen". Monica also showed evidence of a sexual assault.

Coddington told investigators he committed the crimes because "there were too many bad things in the world, too much smoking in the casinos, and too many drunk drivers." He was charged with two counts of murder, forcible rape, oral copulation, and forcible digital penetration.

The case gained a lot of local public attention, so a judge ordered the trial to take place in Placerville, California.

Coddington entered a plea of not guilty by reason of insanity. After the trial concluded, the jury found Coddington to be sane at the time of the murders and sexual assaults; they found him guilty on 6 counts and recommended the death penalty be carried out. In January 1989, Coddington was sentenced to death.

After being arrested for murdering Mabs and Dottie and for sexually assaulting Alecia and Monica, investigators looked into Coddington's history to see if they could link him to any other crimes. During their search, they came across the murder of Shelia Jo Keister.

Shelia Jo Keister, 12, was born on July 8th, 1969, to Auguesta Harrison and William Keister.

Shelia had a twin sister, Sheba, and a younger brother, Stevie.

On August 18th, 1981, Shelia had wanted to use her younger brother's bike, but he would not let her. Instead, she decided to go hang out with a friend who lived in a different section of the trailer park. Shelia left home around 1:30 p.m.

When Shelia did not return home within a few hours, her mother called the police. By the time Shelia's mom reported her missing, target shooters had discovered her body in a desert area near the city. She had been raped and strangled. Investigators also noted there were bite marks on her breasts from which plaster casts were taken.

Shelia's case remained unsolved for 6 years until the bite marks on Shelia were connected to dental casts taken from Coddington.

A warrant for charges of abduction, rape, and murder was served to Coddington while he was in jail in July 1987 although there is no evidence of a trial or whether Coddington was ever convicted and sentenced for Shelia's murder.

He has been serving his time in San Quentin prison. He has appealed his death conviction multiple times; all have been denied.

CHARLES MARK COHEN
Born 1954 – Sentenced to life in prison 1992.

Charles Cohen was 35 and featured widely on US TV and media in 1989 when he was being sought for the murder of Conrad Lutz, a vice president of Wells Fargo Bank with whom he had struck up a gay relationship and moved in with. He had stabbed Lutz to death. After the killing he fled and took various cash paid jobs finally surfacing a year later in New Orleans when he was arrested for attempting to mug a woman at an ATM and not paying a taxi fare.

As he was being charged with those crimes in court he suddenly stood up and told the court that he was also a triple killer having murdered Lutz and killed both his parents the year before by bludgeoning them with a dumbbell before stabbing them both almost decapitating his mother.

He was returned to Delaware in 1992 and received two life sentences plus 60 years for his parent's murder before pleading guilty to the murder of Lutz in California and being sentenced to life in prison for that.

His appeals have all been rejected although he maintains to have found God and become a different Christian person during his years in prison. The parole has also refused commutation of the life sentence.

CARROLL EDWARD COLE

Born May 8th, 1938 – executed by lethal injection December 6th, 1985.

A death wish, once in custody, is not unusual among compulsive killers. Carroll Edward Cole, admitted murderer of thirteen persons, was securely serving out a term of life in Texas, with parole a possibility in seven years, when he elected voluntarily to face a pair of murder charges in Nevada, fully conscious of the fact that he would be condemned to die upon conviction and his wish granted.

Once the sentence had been passed, helped along by his guilty plea, Cole fended off appeals and efforts of assorted liberal groups to act on his behalf and raise appeals. His execution, in December 1985, immediately paved the way for others in the Western states

When Cole was five years old his mother forced him to accompany her on extramarital excursions in his father's absence making him an accomplice to her own adultery. Cole was forced to dress in frilly skirts and petticoats for the amusement of his mother's friends, dispensing tea and coffee at sadistic "parties" where the women gathered to make sport of "mama's little girl."

He was enrolled in elementary school two years behind his peers, mainly at the insistence of social workers and he grew up fearing for his masculinity, brought about by repeated jokes about his 'girls' name.

His first murder was committed aged 9 when he drowned a playmate who had made fun of him by holding him under water until dead. Cole avoided punishment when officers dismissed the murder as an accident. He had begun to be violent and fight habitually at school. He contrived to maim the winner of a yo-yo contest in which Cole had come out second-best while playing near a piece of road repair equipment by crushing his rival's hand inside the dozer's massive treads.

In his teens, Cole had many arrests for drunkenness and petty theft. He joined the Navy after dropping out of high school, but was discharged for the theft of pistols, which he used to fire at cars along the San Diego highways. Back at home in Richmond, California, during 1960, he attacked two couples parked along a dark lover's lane with a hammer. He told psychiatrists later that it was about this time he started having fantasies of strangling girls and women who reminded him of his adulterous mother.

Finally, alarmed by violent fantasies which would not leave him Cole flagged a squad car down in Richmond and confessed his urges to police. On the advice of a police lieutenant, Cole surrendered voluntarily to mental health authorities, and spent the next three years in institutions where he was regarded as an "anti-social personality" who posed no threat to others. Finally discharged in 1963, he moved to Dallas, Texas, and exacerbated matters by immediately marrying an alcoholic prostitute.

Their relationship was doomed to failure, filled with screaming battles, beatings, the occasional resort to weapons, until finally, in 1965, persuaded that his wife was servicing the tenants of the motel where they lived, Cole torched the place and was imprisoned on an arson charge.

On release, he drifted northward, through Missouri, and was jailed again for the attempted murder of Virginia Rowden, age eleven. Cole had chosen her at random, crept inside her room while she was sleeping, and had tried to strangle her in bed; her screams had driven him away, and he was readily identified by the girl and several witnesses as her assailant when police arrived.

Missouri offered Cole more psychiatric treatment through assorted inmate programs, but it didn't help. In 1970, he once again surrendered to authorities -- this time in Reno, Nevada, confessing his growing desire to rape and kill women. Psychiatrists wrote him off as a malingerer looking for a permanent home and set him free with the condition that he left the state. Cole's file contains the telling evidence of psychiatric failure: *"Prognosis: Poor. Condition on release: Same as on admittance. Treatment: Express bus ticket to San Diego, California."*

Within six months of his return to San Diego, Cole would kill at least three women. On the day before his execution in Nevada, he suggested that there might have been two others in this period, the details of their murders blurred by massive quantities of alcohol. His victims, then and later, shared the common trait of infidelity to husbands, fiancées, or boyfriends; each one had approached Cole in a bar, accompanied him to lonely roads for sex, and had laughed and boasted about how they had "put one over" on their regular companions.

Moving eastward, Cole picked off another victim in Casper, Wyoming, during August 1975. Assorted jail terms for minor thefts or assaults often interfered with hunting, but he surfaced in Las Vegas during 1977, staying long enough to kill a prostitute and get himself arrested on a charge of auto theft, which was dismissed. A few weeks later, after days of drinking, Cole awoke in Oklahoma City to discover the remains of yet another woman in his bathtub; bloody slices of her buttocks rested in a frying pan on the kitchen stove.

Going back again to San Diego, Cole remarried, she was Diane another alcoholic, and sought the help of local counsellors to curb his drinking. Given the conditions of his home life, it was hopeless, and the urge to murder was consuming him, inevitably fuelled by the alcohol.

During August 1979, he strangled Bonnie Stewart on the premises of his employer, dumping her nude body in an alleyway adjacent to the store. For weeks, he had been threatening to kill his wife -- the threats had been reported to an officer in charge of supervising his parole -- but when he finally succeeded in September, the authorities refused to rule her death a homicide. Despite discovery of her body, wrapped in a blanket in a closet of Cole's home, despite Cole's own arrest while drunkenly attempting to prepare a grave beneath a neighbour's house, detectives somehow viewed the death of Diane Cole as "natural," related to her own abuse of drink.

Taking no chances, Cole hit the road. He claimed another victim in Las Vegas, and moved on to Dallas where, within eleven days in 1980, he would strangle three more victims. Though discovered at the third murder scene with the victim stretched out at his feet, he was again regarded merely as a "casual suspect" by detectives. Weary at last, Cole sat down with detectives and startled them with his confession to a string of unsolved homicides. He made it known he wanted the death penalty.

At his trial, in 1981, his guilty plea insured a term of life with possible parole, not the death penalty he craved. He was counting down the days to freedom on parole when reports of a extradition to Nevada to face two further murder charges cheered him up. He pleaded not guilty, was found guilty and sentenced to death. His 'death wish' had been confirmed. He even said 'thank you' to the judge when it was handed down.

Cole refused to make any appeals and was killed by lethal injection in Carson City, Nevada on December 6th, 1985.

CHARLES TROY COLEMAN

Born March 15th, 1947 – executed by lethal injection September 10th, 1990

Charles Coleman was born on March 15th, 1947, in Muskogee Oklahoma. He was one of eight siblings born into a low-income family that moved from state to state frequently. His parents spent most of their money on alcohol. Coleman was described as a career criminal who had a lengthy criminal history on his record. This criminal career began age 11 when he stabbed a mule while catching frogs with his brother. He then escaped from jail by slipping through the bars of his cell.
    At age 13, Coleman ran away from home. At age 15, he committed a burglary, and one month later, he escaped from a juvenile court after pulling a gun on an officer. At age 16, he got married, and the couple drifted around all over the country, living in at least twenty different states until the marriage broke down and they separated. Coleman continued to commit crimes and built up a lengthy rap sheet of offenses in multiple states. His offenses included: burglary, grand theft, auto larceny, carrying a concealed weapon, assault with a deadly weapon, and receiving stolen property.
    On August 24th, 1975, 44-year-old Will Stidham was found dead inside his pickup truck in Bakersfield, California. He had been beaten to death with a tyre iron, and his wallet stolen. Stidham was the father of Coleman's then current girlfriend,

17-year-old Shirley Stidham. Authorities suspected Coleman was involved in the murder because Will Stidham had told Coleman not to date his daughter. Coleman's fingerprints were also found on the pickup truck Will's body was found in. One of Coleman's brothers, Abraham Coleman, had allegedly bragged to a woman about being involved in the killing. However, he later denied this and said he had nothing to do with it. He passed a lie detector test, and Shirley Stidham provided Charles Coleman with an alibi, claiming he had been with her when her father had been murdered. However, according to media accounts, several months after the murder, Shirley Stidham had told police that her father had slapped her in front of Coleman. Coleman had then promised her that if she gave him a little more time, her father would not be around any longer. Coleman was prosecuted for the murder but was acquitted in July 1976 through lack of hard evidence. Attorneys who prosecuted him claim his charisma and charm helped him gain an acquittal, but they remained convinced he was guilty of the murder.

In January 1979, while serving time in prison in California for a parole violation, Coleman was released and given a thirty-day travel permit to explore job possibilities in Muskogee County, Oklahoma, his native home county. He returned to his home state but remained there longer than the thirty days he had been given. On February 9th, 1979, Coleman broke into the home of Dale and Delthea Warren in Muskogee County. While burglarizing the home, he was interrupted by 68-year-old John Seward and his wife, 62-year-old Roxie Seward. John Seward was the brother of Delthea Warren. Armed with a .28 gauge shotgun, Coleman took the Seward's hostage and led them into the home's basement at gunpoint. He then fatally shot each of the victims with the shotgun, killing John via a single gunshot wound to the back of the head and killing Roxie via four gunshot wounds inflicted from only a few inches away. Coleman then fled. The bodies of the Seward's were found later that day at around 4:15 p.m. in the basement of the Warren's home. Several items from the house were also determined to be missing, including watches, wallets, and packets of frozen meat.

At around 6:00 p.m., Coleman was stopped by police for a traffic violation. The pickup truck he was driving was searched, and several incriminating items were found. Roxie Seward's wallet was found on Coleman, and the stolen packets of frozen meat were found in the truck. A watch belonging to Delthea Warren was also discovered on his wrist. He was arrested and taken in to custody. In addition, it was later determined that the shotgun used to carry out the murders was very rare, and Coleman was found to own one. Witness testimony also placed Coleman's pickup truck at the Warren's home at around the time the murders were committed. None of the evidence was refuted. Because of the overwhelming amount of evidence against him, Coleman was charged with first-degree murder in the deaths of John and Roxie Seward.

On April 23rd, 1979, while awaiting trial for the murder of the Sewards, Coleman escaped from the Muskogee County jail through cutting a hole in its tarpaper roof. He broke into a home nearby which he burglarized, and then stole the homeowners' car. The following day, Officer Tom Dotson pulled over Coleman for a speeding violation in Luther. An altercation followed, and Coleman stabbed Dotson's throat before stealing his revolver and forcing him into the backseat of his patrol car. Coleman left Dotson for dead and handcuffed him inside his locked patrol car. Two days later, Coleman carjacked Russell E. Lewis Jr. in Tulsa, and fatally shot him in the head with the revolver he had stolen from Dotson. He then dumped Lewis' body down an embankment near Tulsa Park. The body was found two days later by a lineman.

On April 28th, Coleman was pulled over in Tucson, Arizona by Pima County deputy Terry Parish for driving erratically. After the two exchanged words, Coleman took out his gun and kidnapped Parish. He stole Parish's gun, handcuffed him, and drove him out into the desert in his patrol car. Coleman prepared to execute him but changed his mind and left the officer locked in the car out in the desert. Law enforcement had watched the confrontation from a helicopter and were able to direct ground units to Coleman's location. Coleman was arrested by Arizona law enforcement and taken into custody. The revolver, however, that had been used to murder Lewis, was nowhere to be found. Authorities found the weapon in the desert near where Parish had been left for dead three months later.

Following his capture, Coleman was held at the Pima County Jail under maximum security. Mike Turpen, a Muskogee County District Attorney, then began extradition proceedings to bring Coleman back to Oklahoma to face trial for the murder of the Seward's.

Coleman was to be tried in Muskogee County for the murder of John Seward, however, in July 1979 a Muskogee County judge granted a change of venue due to the level of media publicity surrounding the case. As such, Coleman was tried in Tahlequah instead.

Coleman's trial began on September 26th, 1979, with a six-man, six-woman jury selected. The prosecution rested their case on September 29th. On October 1st, the jury found him guilty of first-degree murder in the killing of John Seward and recommended a death sentence. On October 12th, Coleman was formally sentenced to death by District Judge Hardy Summers.

Mike Turpen, who prosecuted Coleman, held the evidence against him in the murder of Roxie Seward in reserve in case another trial was ever needed. Turpen chose not to try Coleman for the murder of Roxie Seward because he felt there was no point, as Coleman had already been sentenced to death for John Seward's murder, and another trial would cost time and public money.

Coleman was also tried for the murder of Russell Lewis. He was found guilty, convicted, and sentenced to death again. However, in 1983, that sentence was overturned, following the discovery that a potential juror had been excluded from the trial after expressing doubts about the death penalty. The charge was not relisted.

In 1987, Coleman was nearly executed, but won a stay of execution at the United States Court of Appeals for the Tenth Circuit with just hours to go. The stay was dismissed by the Supreme Court and he was rescheduled for execution for September 10th, 1990. In the month prior to this scheduled execution, his attorney asked the Oklahoma Pardon and Parole Board to recommend his sentence be commuted to life in prison. However, the board chairman denied Coleman a clemency hearing. A federal appeals court also denied him a further stay of execution.

On September 10th, 1990, Coleman was executed at the Oklahoma State Penitentiary via lethal injection. He was pronounced dead at 12:35 a.m.

Coleman was the first person to be executed in Oklahoma by lethal injection. The lethal injection process consisted of three drugs; the first to be injected was sodium thiopental, followed by pancuronium bromide, and then potassium chloride. Coleman declined a last meal. His last words were, "Just tell everybody I love them. I have peace and a quiet heart."

Since the reinstatement of capital punishment in 1976, Coleman was the first person to be executed in Oklahoma, and the 138th in the United States.

There's an interesting aside to this case:

Twelve years after Coleman's execution in May 1988, the body of a woman was found in the Grand Neosho River beneath Fort Gibson Dam in Cherokee County, Oklahoma. The woman had been murdered and had been attached to a concrete block that had been tied around her waist. Investigators were unable to identify her. But because a daisy tattoo was found on her shoulder, she was referred to as Daisy Doe. Her identity remained a mystery for nearly three decades until March 2015 when the Oklahoma State Bureau of Investigation had prepared a presentation to cold case detectives in regards to the Daisy Doe case. They discovered that her hands had been preserved in cold storage when gathering evidence originally and were still there. New technology allowed the investigators to take fingerprints off Daisy Doe. The fingerprints matched those of a woman who had been arrested in connection with the 1979 murders of John and Roxie Seward. The woman had never been charged in the murders but was identified as Jeanette Ellen Coleman. Jeanette Coleman had been the wife of Charles Coleman and the daughter of Will Stidham, who Coleman was suspected of murdering back in 1975.

  The discovery led investigators to suspect Charles Coleman could have been involved in the Daisy Doe murder. However, it was determined that Coleman had been in jail when Jeanette had been murdered, ruling him out as a suspect. Three men were believed to be responsible, who investigators believe she met at a Muskogee bar before engaging in sexual intercourse near the dam. She then had a concrete block tied to her and was thrown into the river while still alive. One of the suspects was charged with first-degree murder in 2017. A District Attorney said he believes the other two men have since died

DeWITT CLINTON COOK

Born 1920 – executed by asphyxiation-gas at San Quentin Prison on January 31st, 1941.

On the evening of February 24th, 1939, DeWitt Clinton Cook, 20, a former printer for a Hollywood trade paper, clubbed to death Russian born dancer Anya Sosoyeva, 32, on the campus of Los Angeles City College. Cook later told police, "She screeched a little, so I hit her some more. Then she only moaned." She was found by police around 9:15 p.m.

Sosoyeva had been sexually assaulted and lived just long enough to give police a description of Cook. Clues found at the scene consisted mainly of an old pair of shoes retrieved near the scene by a police dog, a pair of gloves, a size 38 blue serge coat and a 30-inch piece of roof beam used to bludgeon the girl as she walked across the campus to attend an evening dramatics class.

Next, Cook clubbed film studio dancer Delia Bogard, 17, on March 28th as she was returning home from an evening at the movies near her Hollywood home, but he was frightened away by her screams before he could further his attack into murder. A piece of wood similar to the Sosoyeva murder was found nearby. Bogard, suffered from a severe head injury, was hospitalized for weeks and later moved in with her parents to care for her.

On Thursday night, August 24th, 1939, Cook went on to club and rape Myrtle Wagner, 17, a domestic working for Mr. and Mrs. M. W. Lippman at their residence in Hollywood as she was crocheting a towel in their kitchen. Wagner's head injuries were so severe she had to use a cane for weeks after the assault. Police patrols were increased in the Hollywood area by LAPD Homicide Captain Dalton R. Patton and Deputy Chief Homer B. Cross.

Four nights later Mr. and Mrs. W. Warnock were relaxing at their home on Oakwood Avenue in Hollywood. According to Mrs. Warnock, "We were going out to play badminton. My husband was in the front room with our little daughter and our dog. When I finished dressing in the bedroom I went to the front room to leave but at the last moment decided to return for a hat. In the bedroom I saw a man in a brown suit standing in front of the dresser. I screamed and he jumped out of the window which had been opened. My husband came running but the burglar was gone."

Cook was arrested by LAPD Sergeants E. L. Berger and A. D. McCoole a short distance from the Warnock home. An eighteen-inch piece of two-by-four, a long screwdriver, a pocket knife and several pairs of gloves were found on him. He was also wearing tennis shoes that matched a footprint left at the scene of the Wagner assault. At a search of his home the police also found a pair of moccasin shoes "whose soles matched perfectly the unusual pattern found beside Miss Bogard's unconscious form."

Cook confessed on August 29th to the Sosoyeva murder and the Bogard/Wagner assaults in the presence of LAPD homicide officers and a representative from the district attorney's office. After his confession he had lunch with the officers at a Sunset Boulevard coffee shop, where he ate a plate of spaghetti, ravioli, spinach and mashed potatoes.

During lunch, Cook estimated that he had committed approximately three hundred burglaries in two years. After finishing lunch the group proceeded to the three crime scenes and Cook re-enacted each of his attacks for police and reporters. Cook was then given a physical and psychiatric exam before spending the night at Central Jail in downtown Los Angeles.

The next day he entered a plea of guilty to four of the nine felony charges against him. Cook refused, however, to repeat his confession in court on September 1st, and his pleas were set aside for trial by Superior Judge Clarence L. Kincaid.

Born in Waterloo, Iowa, Cook did not finish high school; instead, he served eleven months in the Iowa State School for Boys for petty crime and was paroled. He moved to Los Angeles with his parents at the age of sixteen; shortly afterward his father was killed in a car accident. On June 19th, 1938, he married his first cousin Lorraine Levy in Tijuana, Mexico, and they had another ceremony at a downtown Los Angeles wedding chapel in October. His salary as a printer was twenty-four dollars a week and he lived with his wife and his mother, Mrs. Ruby Cook, 45, at 1300 1/2 North Sycamore Avenue in Los Angeles.

Cook's trial opened on October 4th, 1939. A jury of twelve men was selected. On October 11th the jury and courtroom watched Cook's re-enactment on film taken at the crime scene of the murder of Anya

Sosoyeva. On October 13th the jury took only forty minutes to find Cook guilty.

The case is considered one of the strangest in criminal law at the time because there was no defence offered and Cook never once denied the murder, nor did he himself enter a plea of not guilty.

Members of the jury told the judge afterwards they felt that by seeing the re-enactment of the Sosoyeva murder on film in which Cook answered questions to police about the murder, they were assisted materially in clearing up several points they had under discussion.

Cook was sentenced on October 18th to the gas chamber at San Quentin. On October 26th, 1939, Cook was transported by train to San Quentin Prison. His appeal was turned down, and his wife obtained a marriage annulment on May 24th, 1940.

Cook received a temporary reprieve from Governor Olson on November 25th, 1940, and filed for clemency on December 30th which was denied on January 5th, 1941.

On January 31st, 1941, DeWitt Clinton Cook was executed at 10:02 a.m. in the San Quentin gas chamber. All night long in his death cell he had played a small radio, making no attempt to sleep. He ate no breakfast. He told a guard 'I have made up my mind I have to go; that is all there is to it.'

WILLIAM E. COOK Jr.

Born 1929 – executed by asphyxiation-gas in San Quentin Prison on December 12th, 1952.

It started simply enough. On Dec. 28th, 1950, a Texan named Lee Archer picked up a young hitchhiker near Lubbock, Texas. The next morning, near Oklahoma City, the squinty-eyed youth overpowered Archer and locked him in the car's trunk. Unfamiliar with the manual transmission on the stolen car, the young man got it stuck in a ditch, and then he flagged down what was later identified as a blue, 1949 Chevrolet sedan.
Archer freed himself from the trunk and called police. By the time they arrived, the Chevy, with the young man inside, had disappeared westward on U.S. 66.
Inside Archer's car, police found a duffel bag with clues as to who the hitchhiker was. Using newspaper wire photo machines, officials soon had pictures and the Missouri penitentiary records of William Cook, 5 feet 6 inches tall, 145 pounds, tattooed, with a right eye that never closed thanks to a botched operation to remove a congenital growth from the eyelid.
At that time, December 29th, the case was one of highway robbery – a known criminal stealing a car.
Then on January 3rd, 1951, things changed. A blue 1949 Chevrolet sedan was found in a ditch 3 miles northwest of Tulsa, Oklahoma. The interior was splattered with blood.

That car belonged to Carl Mosser, 33, who with his wife, Thelma, was making a Christmas trip from their home in Atwood, Illinois, to Albuquerque, N.M. with the couple's their three children - Ronald Dean, 7, Gary Carl, 5, and Pamela Sue, 3.

Relatives who had been expecting the Mossers for several days had not heard from them and reported them missing. Lawmen feared the worst.

Within hours, the largest manhunt in United States history up to that time had begun, with 2,000 law enforcement officers brought in. They were joined by thousands more police, game wardens and private citizens.

Rescue of the Mossers was not in the minds of the police. In fact, a later reconstruction of the family's last days was quite awful. From central Oklahoma, Cook forced Mosser to drive to Wichita Falls, Texas; then to Carlsbad, N.M.; back east to Houston; then north to Winthrop, Arkansas.; and finally back to Joplin. There, between 1:30 and 2:30 a.m. on January 2nd, 1951, Cook, who became panicked by a passing police car, shot each member of the family and dropped their bodies down a mine shaft in the Chitwood section of town.

Cook then fled to Tulsa, abandoned the car, and managed, by bus and hitchhiking, to reach Blythe, California, by January 6th. There he kidnapped a deputy sheriff, stole his patrol car, and used it to pull over a car driven by Robert Dewey, 32.

Cook killed Dewey, took his car, and crossed into Mexico, where he kidnapped two other Americans, James Burke and Forrest Damron, amateur prospectors and kept those two men with him for the next week, crisscrossing Baja California. The two captives said they were afraid to try an escape because they never could tell when Cook was asleep because his right eye remained open.

Finally, on January. 15th, Mexican police recognized Cook from the thousands of FBI posters that had been posted in the search area and he was arrested at gunpoint in a cafe.

That same day in Joplin, Police Chief Carl Nutt and Detective Walter Gamble played a hunch. Laboratory tests of mud found in the Mosser car showed a heavy shale content. Shale and zinc mining went together. Cook had been raised around Second and Oliver streets, where there were abandoned zinc mines. They checked each one and in one of the flooded shafts floated the bodies of the Mosser family.

Cook was brought back to Oklahoma and tried under federal kidnapping statutes. Since the Lindbergh kidnapping, such charges had almost automatically meant the death penalty. Cook told his jailers that he expected to be hanged.

The judge, trying the case without a jury, gave Cook 300 years. But that included the possibility of parole. The public was outraged. The media flayed the judge.

Just hours after the verdict the U.S. Justice Department announced it would honour a request by California to try Cook in Imperial County. Prosecutors there maintained they had an open and shut case for the murder of Dewey. They were right.

In November 1951, a jury took 50 minutes to find Cook guilty. Cook, a smirk on his lips, got the death sentence.

On December 12th, 1952, his appeals exhausted, a sullen Cook was strapped to the chair in San Quentin's gas chamber and made a point of eagerly inhaling the cyanide fumes.

Three days later his body went on display at a Comanche, Oklahoma, funeral home. The sight of his 'open eye' attracted fifteen thousand people to view the body before relatives put a stop to it. A few days later, well after dark, Cook was buried in Peace Cemetery in Joplin.

DONNELL CLYDE COOLEY

Born December 17th, 1910 – sentenced to life in prison. Died in prison November 23rd, 1969.

Donnell Clyde 'Spade' Cooley was an American Western Swing musician, a big band leader, actor, and television personality. His career ended when he was arrested and convicted for the murder of his second wife, Ella Mae Evans.
Cooley's 18 month swing band engagement at Santa Monica's Venice Pier Ballroom was record breaking for the early half of the 1940s. His "Shame on You" record, released on Columbia's OKeh label, was recorded in December of 1944, and was No. 1 on the country charts for two months. It was the first in an unbroken string of six Top Ten singles including "Detour" and "You Can't Break My Heart".
Cooley appeared in 38 westerns, both in bit parts and as a stand in for cowboy actor Roy Rogers. He also hosted a Los Angeles based syndicated television show from 1949 until 1959 called The Hoffman Hayride, which was so popular that an estimated 75 percent of all televisions in the L.A. area were tuned into the show each Saturday night. In 1950 Cooley had significant roles in several films, and starred in two film shorts: "King of Western Swing" and "Spade Cooley & His Orchestra".
He would often bill himself as the 'king of western swing'. His sound was closer to conventional dance-oriented pop orchestras than that of others in the genre, which accounts for his work having been

more popular with mainstream audiences during his 1940s and 1950s heyday.

Alcohol began to take a detrimental effect on his life with many arguments both at home and with band members many of whom left. The emergence of rock n'roll pushed his style of music out of favour and he got passed over for the big TV shows and concert bookings dried up. He was still immensely rich but craved the recognition of the past, it wasn't there anymore and the drinking got out of hand.

In 1961, his second wife of eleven years expressed her wish to be divorced from him because of his infidelities. Cooley responded by beating her and stomping on her body until she died in front of his 14 year old daughter.

During the subsequent trial Cooley suffered a heart attack in court while he was being given his prison sentence of life.

After serving his time for a while, the state of California granted him a temporary release in order to play a benefit concert for the Deputy Sheriffs Association of Alameda County at the Paramount Theatre in Oakland. After the performance, he suffered another heart attack in the backstage area. This time it was fatal. He was 59.

KEVIN COOPER

Born 1957 – sentenced to death May 15th, 1985.

On October 8th, 1982, Kevin Cooper robbed a Pennsylvania home and kidnapped and raped the high school student who interrupted him. He was convicted of two other burglaries in Los Angeles and began serving his sentence at the California Institution for Men (CIM) in Chino on April 29th, 1983, under the alias David Trautman. On June 1st, he was transferred to the minimum-security portion of the prison and escaped on foot the very next day.

Four days later, on the morning of June 5th, 1983, Bill Hughes arrived at a semi-rural home in Chino Hills, California where his 11-year-old son Christopher had spent the night on a sleep-over. Inside, he found Douglas and Peggy Ryen, their 10-year-old daughter Jessica and his own son dead. They had been chopped with a hatchet, sliced with a knife, and stabbed with an ice-pick. Josh Ryen, the 8-year-old son of Douglas and Peggy, had survived. His throat had been cut. The mother's purse was in plain sight on the kitchen counter, but no money had been taken. The family station wagon was missing; it was discovered several days later in Long Beach, California, about 50 miles west of Chino Hills.

The San Bernardino County Sheriff's Department deputies who responded to the call decided almost immediately that Kevin Cooper was the likely killer. He had admittedly hidden out in the vacant rental house next door, 125 yards away, for the two days 2nd and 3rd June. He had made repeated calls from this house to two female friends asking for money to help with his escape, but they had refused. Cooper later testified at trial that he had left that house as soon as it got dark on June 4th and had hitchhiked to Mexico. It was established that Cooper checked into a hotel in Tijuana, about 130 miles south of Chino Hills, at 4:30 pm on June 5th.

There, Cooper befriended an American couple who owned a boat, and hitched a ride on the boat with them; he was arrested shortly after when the boat sailed to Pelican Bay near Santa Barbara.

A blood-stained khaki green button identical to buttons on field jackets issued at the state prison from which Cooper escaped was found on the rug at the rental house; tests revealed the presence of blood in the shower and bathroom sink; hair found in the bathroom sink was consistent with that of Jessica and Doug Ryen; a hatchet covered with dried blood and human hair that was found near the Ryens' home was missing from the rental house, and the sheath for the hatchet was found in the bedroom where Cooper had stayed; Cooper's semen was found on a blanket in the closet of the rental house; plant burrs found inside Jessica's nightgown were similar to burrs from vegetation growing between the rental house and the Ryen house as were two burrs found on a blanket inside the closet where Cooper slept at the rental house, and in the Ryen station wagon; two partial shoe prints and one nearly complete one found in or near the Ryens' house and in the rental house were consistent with Cooper's shoe size and Pro-Keds Dude tennis shoes issued at CIM that Cooper did not deny having; a hand-rolled cigarette butt and "Role-Rite" tobacco provided to inmates at CIM were in the Ryens' vehicle.

On Cooper's defence attorney's motion, the court changed the venue of the trial from San Bernardino County to San Diego County. Cooper pleaded guilty to the charge of escape from prison.

In videotaped testimony, survivor Josh Ryen said that the evening before the murders, just before the family left for the Blade barbecue, three Mexicans came to the Ryen home looking for work. Ryen did not identify Cooper as the killer, but said in an audiotape with his treating psychiatrist that he saw the back of a single man attacking his mother. Ryen told a sheriff he thought the three men might have done it because "I thought it was them. And, you know, like they stopped up that night," but he did not actually see three people during the incident.

Cooper testified in his own defence. He admitted escaping from CIM, hiding out and sleeping at the rental house, but denied committing the murders or of being in the Ryen house at any time. Cooper said he left the rental house on foot, hitchhiked, stole a purse, and eventually made his way to Mexico. The defence pointed out the inconsistencies in Ryen's testimony, presented evidence of other events apparently not involving Cooper that might have had something to do with the killings, and presented an expert witness that criticized the forensic investigation as untrustworthy.

A jury convicted Cooper of four counts of first degree murder and one count of attempted murder with the intentional infliction of great bodily injury, and then imposed the death penalty.

Appeals were made and local people and celebs raised doubts about the evidence in many ways including Josh's recollection of three men in the house. However all appeals were denied. As of now Cooper sits on death row.

JOSEPH CORBETT Jr.

Born October 25th, 1928 – sentenced to life in prison March 29th, 1961. Paroled June 15th, 1978. Committed suicide August 24th, 2009.

During the weeks leading up to February 1960 a canary yellow 1951 Mercury automobile had been a regular visitor around the Rocky Mountains not far from Denver. People noticed the car, and the man who drove it often enough to make one suspicious local man take a mental note of the license plate number.
Lucky he did, because that car would later become the key to solving the murder of Adolph Coors 3rd. Known as Ad, the 44-year-old was heir to the Coors beer empire started by his grandfather in 1873. Coors was president of the company, which he ran with his brothers William and Joseph.
Married for 20 years and the father of four children, Ad Coors' reputation was of someone quiet, competent, and reserved, a good businessman and a good family man.
In all, a good target for a big ransom.
A little before 8pm on the morning of February 9th 1960, Coors got into his International Travelall station wagon and started out on the 12-mile trip from his ranch in Morrison to the brewery in Golden, Colorado.
Three hours later, a milkman found the green-and-white car, with its motor still running, abandoned

on a rickety wooden bridge over Turkey Creek, two miles north of Coors' home.

Blood stains were on the road near the car and a railing on the bridge. Down below, on the creek bank, searchers found the baseball-style cap that Coors was wearing when he left home that morning, and the plastic-rim glasses that he always wore because he was nearsighted.

The police had no doubt that this was the work of professional kidnappers.

"I cannot be emotional about this," the missing man's father, Adolph Coors II, told reporters. "The crooks have something I want to buy, my son. The price is secondary."

The next day, FBI agents recovered a letter at the Morrison post office, addressed to Coors' wife, Mary. It demanded $500,000, in tens and twenties, and instructed her to advertise a tractor for sale in the Denver Post, and then to wait for the call. "Call the police or FBI: he dies. Co-operate: he lives," the kidnapper wrote.

Mary Coors placed the ad, as instructed, and waited. But there was no call, nor any word or whisper of what had happened to her husband. In the weeks to come she would receive more than 50 ransom notes, all cruel hoaxes. But there was no call from the real kidnapper.

With little to go on, the FBI focused on a few slim clues. Most of the attention was aimed at the canary yellow Mercury and the memory of the man who remembered that the license plate had an "AT" and the numerals "62."

Based on that alone, FBI agents traced the car's owner to be Denver resident Walter Osborne, who had, until recently, been working in a local paint factory.

Further investigation matched a fingerprint from Osborne's driver's license application form they retrieved from the files to that of a convicted murderer who had escaped from a California prison five years earlier named Joseph Corbett Jr. age 31.

Born in Seattle, the son of a newspaper editor and his wife, Corbett had an average upbringing and as a child, he seemed to have a bright future.

But by 1950 his behaviour was changing. He began to unravel completely when his mother fell from a first floor balcony at the family home and died.

Six months later, for no reason, Corbett shot a hitchhiker in the head, and was sent to prison for life. Corbett cut short the sentence himself in 1955, when he escaped from a minimum-security cell in Chino.

Within the year, a man calling himself Walter Osborne showed up in Denver. Corbett had assumed an alias, Walter Osborne.

A few days after Adolph Coors disappeared, the FBI arrived at the Denver apartment Osborne had rented, but he was already gone. The landlord said that his quiet tenant explained he was going to Boulder, Colorado, to finish his studies, then packed and left.

Around the same time, police in New Jersey found a smouldering burnt-out canary yellow 1951 Mercury car in an Atlantic City dump, its motor number matching that of the car purchased by Corbett, using his alias Osborne.

On March 30th, Corbett appeared on the FBI's 10 Most Wanted List. But through the summer, despite a gigantic manhunt, there was no sign of the fugitive nor the missing beer magnate.

Then, on Sept. 11th, a pizza truck driver went out for some target practice near a dump in the Rocky Mountain foothills southwest of Denver. He found a pair of trousers, with a label that read, "Expressly for Mr. A. Coors, III" and a penknife in the pocket with the inscription "A.C. III." He called the police.

About 500 yards away, they found human bones, from a man about six foot one, which was Coors' height, and a skull. Dental records would later confirm Coors remains had been found.

Coors had been shot twice in the back, at close range.

Corbett's picture was spread around the world through newspapers, magazines, and thousands of "Wanted by FBI" posters. In Toronto, someone saw Corbett's picture in a Reader's Digest article, and told police that he looked very much like a former co-worker.

The hunt moved north, but by the time the FBI made it to Toronto, Corbett had fled again.

It would be October 29th before the law would catch up with him in Vancouver, British Columbia, given away by another bright automobile. For his dash to the north, Corbett had rented a fire-engine red Pontiac, the kind of car no one could ignore.

In the end, there were no shoot outs, no desperate attempts at flight, just a knock on the door. "I'm your man," Corbett said as he gave himself up.

No one had actually seen the killing of Adolph Coors, but prosecutors had a strong case based on circumstantial evidence. Co-workers told of the defendant's boasts that he was planning "something big" and it would net him a million dollars. Forensic scientists showed that the ransom note came from a typewriter Corbett had purchased.

The star witness, however, was the yellow Mercury car. By examining dirt on the undercarriage and wheel arches, investigators drew a map of the car's journey. There were four layers. One contained dirt and particles matching those in the Atlantic City dump. But the others contained pink feldspar and granite, the kind of rocks and minerals found at the site where Coors' body had been found and on the roads around the Coors ranch.

On March 29th, 1961, the jury found Corbett guilty.

Although sentenced to life, Corbett, a model prisoner, was paroled near 20 years later in December 1980. He took a job in Denver as a truck driver for the Salvation Army, and lived quietly, kept himself to himself and rarely spoke of the case. In a 1996 interview with the Denver Post, one of the few times he broke his silence, he insisted he was innocent and that the FBI had framed him.

On Aug. 24th, 2009, the body of the frail 80-year-old, with a self-inflicted gunshot wound to the head, was found in the apartment where he had lived in near-seclusion for the past 29 years.

JUAN VALLEJO CORONA

Born February 7th 1934 – died in prison March 4th, 2019

Juan Vallejo Corona was a Mexican serial killer who was convicted of the murders of 25 migrant farm workers found buried in peach orchards along the Feather River in Sutter County, California, in 1971.

Until the discovery of Dean Corll's's victims two years later, Corona was the deadliest known American serial killer.

Corona was convicted of 25 counts of First-degree murder in 1973. An appellate court overturned the conviction in 1978 on the basis of incompetent legal representation and granted him a new trial. In 1982, he was again found guilty on all counts. He served a life sentence in California State prison, Corcoran, and died in 2019 age 83.

In January 1956, after what was thought to be a schizophrenic episode, his brother, Natividad, had 22year old Corona committed to DeWitt State Hospital in Auburn, California, where he was diagnosed with "schizophrenic reaction, paranoid type." He received 23 electroconvulsive sessions before he was declared recovered and released three months later and deported to Mexico as an 'illegal'.

In 1962, Corona was given a green card and returned to the United States legally, where he was regarded as a hard worker. He suffered with schizophrenic episodes and a violent temper. He became a licensed labour contractor, in charge of hiring fruit ranch workers. His violent outbursts continued and In March 1970, he was again admitted to Dewitt for treatment. In March 1971, he applied for but was denied welfare.

On May 19th, 1971, a farm owner who had used Corona to contract field workers noticed a freshly dug hole in his peach orchard, which was filled in when he checked the next day. In the hole was the body of a man who had been stabbed and hacked. The police used cadaver dogs to sniff out other graves. In one, deputies found two meat receipts bearing Corona's signature. In another two graves, there were two crumpled Bank of America deposit slips printed with Corona's name and address. This circumstantial evidence later supported the state prosecutor's case.

Witnesses later told police that some of the victims had been last seen riding in Corona's pickup truck.

In the early morning hours of May 26th, 1971, police entered Corona's Yuba City home with a search warrant and arrested him. Evidence indicating his guilt was discovered and seized, such as two blood-stained knives, a machete, a pistol, and blood-stained clothing. There was also a work ledger that contained 34 names and dates, including seven of the known victims' names. The ledger came to be referred to as a "death list" by the prosecution, who alleged it recorded the dates the men were murdered.

Corona had been supplying workers to the ranches where the victims were discovered. He housed many of the men who worked for him in a bunkhouse on the Sullivan Ranch, where most of the victims were discovered.

All of Corona's victims, except for three, were middle-aged Caucasian male drifters between the ages of 47 and 64; most of them had criminal records, and all but one were stabbed or slashed with a knife or machete.

Corona was provided legal aid and assigned a public defender, Roy Van den Heuvel, who hired several psychiatrists to perform a psychological evaluation of Corona. Although the sheriff, Roy Whiteaker, said the prisoner was in no apparent or immediate danger from his fellow townsmen, Corona was moved to the new and larger county jail in Marysville on May 30th, 1971, for his own protection.

On June 2nd, Corona was returned to Sutter County for the arraignment hearing, which was closed to the media and public. A plea of not guilty was entered, and a date was set for Corona's preliminary hearing.

By the time the search for bodies finished on June 4th, a total of 25 male victims had been discovered. Four of them were unidentified.

On June 14th, Van den Heuvel was replaced by Richard Hawk, a privately retained defence attorney. In return for his legal representation, an agreement was made granting Hawk exclusive literary and dramatic property rights to Corona's life story, including the proceedings against him. Under the agreement, Corona waived the attorney-client privilege. Shortly after taking over the defence and even before seeing Corona's medical record or reading it Hawk fired the psychiatrists.

Corona complained of chest pain from his cell in Yuba City on June 18th and was taken to the hospital, where he was diagnosed with having had a mild heart attack. The grand jury returned a 25-count murder indictment against him on July 12th. In early August, Corona was hospitalized again after complaining of chest pain and saying he had not been able to sleep because of it.

It took over a year after the murders were discovered for the case against Corona to come to trial. The California Supreme Court voided the death penalty in the state on February 18th, 1972, ruling it unconstitutional, cruel and unusual. Therefore, it would not be a capital case. Hawk succeeded in getting a change of venue from Sutter County to Solano County.

The trial began on September 11th, 1972, at the courthouse in Fairfield, California, more than 60 miles from Yuba City. Jury selection took several weeks, and the trial took another three months.

Though Corona denied all culpability, he was not called to the witness stand to testify in his own defence, and no defence witnesses were called. The jury deliberated for 45 hours and returned a verdict on January 18th, 1973, finding Corona guilty of First-degree murder on all 25 counts charged. The judge, Richard Patton, sentenced Corona to 25 terms of life imprisonment, to run consecutively, without the possibility of parole.

Because of his heart irregularities Corona was first incarcerated at Vacaville's California Medical Facility's, nine miles from Fairfield. In 1973, he was stabbed 32 times in his cell because he had bumped into a fellow inmate in a corridor and failed to say "excuse me." Of the five men questioned, including the one involved in the bumping incident, one identified as the bumped man's sexual partner, and three inmates identified as friends of the partner, four were charged with assault with a deadly weapon.

Corona was transferred to the Correctional Training Facility (CTF), in Soledad, California. In 1974 his wife filed for divorce, which was granted on July 30th.

On May 18th, 1978, the California Court of Appeal granted Juan Corona a new trial based on his appeal and petition for the writ of habeas corpus filed by new lawyers, Alan Exelrod and Michael Mendelson. The Appeals Court based its decision on two primary issues raised by his counsel: first issue, the previous trial counsel did not do the requisite legal and factual investigations required; and the second issue, that the trial counsel's obtaining publication rights as part of his fee created an impermissible conflict between trial counsel and Corona.

The second trial began on February 22nd, 1982, in Hayward, California. Corona's defence suggested that the real murderer of the ranch workers was most likely his brother, Natividad Corona, a known homosexual who was accused of attacking Romero Raya at his cafe in Marysville and, after losing the lawsuit Raya filed, had fled back to his native Mexico. Natividad had died in 1973 in Guadalajara.

This time, more than 50 defence witnesses were called to the stand by yet another lawyer, Terrence Hallinan. Corona was also called in his own defence. He was asked only two questions through an interpreter, taking only two minutes. "Do you understand the state has accused you of killing 25 men?" "Yes," Corona answered, almost inaudibly. "Did you have anything to do with killing those men?" "No," Corona replied. Hallinan then, unexpectedly, turned Corona over to the prosecutor, Ronald Fahey, for cross-examination. Startled prosecution attorneys requested a brief recess to gather their wits and prepare some of the more than 630 exhibits for their cross examination. Later, Fahey questioned Corona about the various vans and cars he used at the ranch where he worked and lived and where some weapons were found.

The trial lasted seven months. Corona was again convicted of the crimes on September 23rd, 1982, and returned to prison after the strategy failed to persuade the jury of his innocence. Afterwards, the foreman told the press that the most incriminating piece of evidence against Corona was his work ledger, for which the labour contractor had "no reasonable explanation." He said the jury had dismissed the defence's contention that Natividad committed the murders. "He wasn't in Marysville enough to have committed the bulk of the killings," he said.

In 1992, Corona was transferred from CTF at Soledad to Corcoran State prison, Corcoran, California where he served his sentence in the Sensitive Needs Yard because he had dementia. He was denied parole eight times.

Corona died in prison on March 4th, 2019, aged 85, from natural causes.

ANTONE CHARLES COSTA

Born August 2nd 1944 – sentenced to life in prison 1969, committed suicide in prison May 12th, 1974.

Antone Charles "Tony" Costa, sometimes referred to as the Cape Cod Vampire or the Cape Cod Cannibal was a serial killer who was active in and around the town of Truro, Massachusetts during 1968 –1969. The dismembered remains of four women were found in or near a forest clearing where Costa grew marijuana for his own use. His crimes gained international media attention when the district attorney falsely eluded them to cannibalism.

Tony Costa was born in Cambridge, Massachusetts, on August 2nd, 1944. He committed his first violent offence in November 1961 at age 17, when he broke into a house and attacked the occupant, a teenage girl. He was charged with burglary and assault, and sentenced to three years' probation and a one-year suspended sentence.

Costa was married in 1963 and had three children, but the marriage failed over his drug use and he left for California in 1966. In the summer of 1968, Costa returned to Massachusetts where he stole thousands of dollars of medical equipment from various hospitals by wearing a porter's uniform.

On February 8th, 1969, a search was organized for two missing women, Patricia Walsh and Mary Anne Wysocki in a woods where Walsh's Volkswagen van had been abandoned. During the search, police discovered the remains of Susan Perry, who had been missing since September 1968. Perry's body had been cut into eight pieces. About a month later, parts of Wysocki's body were found, and then Walsh and the rest of Wysocki's body were found in a nearby forest clearing. The latter two women had been mutilated with a knife and apparently died of gunshot wounds to the head. Beneath these remains, police found the dismembered body of Sydney Monzon. The bodies showed signs of necrophilia.

Police knew that the clearing where the bodies were found was used by Costa for growing marijuana, making him their main suspect. Costa also knew the four women, who had all disappeared after his return to Truro, and his fingerprints were on the torn cover of the Volkwagen owner's manual, which was found discarded in the woods near the bodies.

The case gained international attention when district attorney, Edmund Dinis, in comments to the media, claimed of Walsh and Wysocki, "The hearts of each girl had been removed from the bodies and were not in the graves ... Each body was cut into as many parts as there are joints." Dinis also claimed that there were bite marks found on the bodies. These claims, although totally untrue, drew national and international media outlets to Province town, Massachusetts.

In all, Costa was considered as a potential suspect in the deaths of 16 women on the US West Coast. This included Bonnie Williams and Diane Federoff, hitchhikers he had picked up while crossing the country in 1966, and his girlfriend in San

Francisco, Barbara Spaulding. However, all three women were later found alive.

On June 12th, 1969, Costa was arraigned on charges of murder for three of the deaths. In May 1970, he was convicted for the murders of Wysocki and Walsh and sentenced to life in prison at Massachusetts' Walpole Correctional Institution. On May 12th, 1974, Costa died from an apparent suicide by hanging himself in his cell, though this was later rumoured as a possible murder. No evidence supported that rumour.

FERNANDO VELAZCO COTA

Born 1946 – committed suicide to avoid arrest October 14th, 1984.

At 8:00 p.m. on October 14th 1984 two officers of the California Highway Patrol noticed a white van that was weaving erratically in the fast lane of Highway 101, some fifteen miles north of San Jose.
They stopped the van and approached the driver who seemed very nervous. When they asked him to open the back of the van to look inside the suspect held up a pistol and started shouting, "Kill me! Kill me! I'm very sick. If you don't kill me, I'll kill myself!" With that, he jammed the barrel of the gun inside his open mouth and fired a single shot killing himself.
Inside the van was a coffin shaped wooden box that held the body of a young, dead woman. She was nude except for panties and a pair of stockings; chains and rope secured her hands. Medical examination found she had been raped and strangled. Subsequent investigation named the victim as Kim Dunham, 21, reported missing one day earlier.
The driver of the van, and Kim's apparent murderer, was local resident Fernando Cota. An examination of his record showed a rape conviction from El Paso, Texas, during 1975 when Cota had attacked a nurse, and two days later mailed her a note which read: "Sorry about the argument we had. Still loving you."

Cota was sentenced to twenty years in prison for that attack, eight of which he served before parole released him in September 1983. By then his wife had left him, taking their children with her. Cota did his time, and on full release he moved to California, settling in San Jose.

A young woman and her daughter moved in with Cota in May 1984, but they soon departed, citing his behaviour as "too weird."

Kim Dunham's murder, and the killer's wild "confession," before killing himself, prompted local homicide investigators to review other open murder cases in their files. They began to see a common thread linking other recent sex-related murders.

On September 10th, Kelly Ralston, 21, was stabbed to death by an intruder in her San Jose apartment.

One day later, housewife Gwendolyn Hoffman, 57, disappeared from her home in Campbell, a San Jose suburb; on September 13th, her strangled body was recovered from the trunk of her own car, two miles from her home.

Tania Zack disappeared on September 15th, when her car ran out of gas near Los Gatos. Her body was recovered on October 5th, discarded in a roadside ditch; she had been raped and bludgeoned, rope burns on her wrists suggesting she was held alive for some time after her abduction.

Lori Miller, 20, was the manager of a cafe in San Jose. She was reported missing by her live-in boyfriend on September 26th when he came home from work to find their phone off the hook, eggs burning on the stove and the smoke alarm buzzing in an empty house. That afternoon, he told detectives, someone posing as a plumber had come knocking at their door, but Lori, learning that her landlord had no knowledge of the visit, told the man to leave. Her semi-naked corpse was found October 6th, in a ravine a few miles south of San Jose. She had been bound and tortured, strangled and raped. Detectives established that Fernando Cota had resided in a block of apartments directly behind Miller's home.

Joan Leslie, 28, a transient, had been stabbed to death, her corpse recovered in a subdivision near Aptos, fifteen miles due south of San Jose.

And there were other victims, tentatively added to the list.

In San Jose itself, on September 30th, a group of children had reported rancid odours coming from an empty house within two blocks of Lori Miller's home. Inside, police discovered the remains of 29-year-old Teresa Sunder, first reported missing two weeks earlier. She had been raped and beaten brutally by her assailant.

Fernando Cota, having spared the residents of California an expensive trial by his suicide in the van, is definitely linked by evidence with only one of eight crimes in the five-week murder rampage. However detectives were convinced, by the proximity of times and places that Cota was responsible for all the homicides mentioned.

TIEQUON AUNDRAY COX
(with Darren Williams)

Born December 1st, 1965 – sentenced to death 1986.

Early in the morning of August 31st, 1984, 58-year-old Ebora Alexander, her twenty-four-year-old daughter, Dietria Alexander, and two visiting grandsons, thirteen-year-old Damani Garner and eight-year-old Damon Bonner were shot and killed in their beds in Elbora's south central Los Angeles home.

Sometime earlier, between 5:00 and 6:00 a.m. on the same day, DeLisa Brown and Ida Moore were at Moore's home on Third Avenue in Los Angeles when Tiequon Cox, 18, a casual acquaintance of Moore's, arrived with Horace Burns, 20. Cox made a telephone call. Burns then left, but returned 20 to 30 minutes later with another man, Darren Williams. Cox asked Moore to drive him, Burns and Williams to "some lady's house" to "pick up some money."

The group left in Moore's van, with Moore driving, Brown in the front passenger seat, and the three men in the back. Moore needed gasoline for the van and asked the men for money to pay for it. They said they had none, so Moore used her own money to pay for $2 worth of gasoline. Cox told Moore to drive to 59th Street. On the way, Brown heard one of the men say something about "killing everybody" in the house. On 59th Street, Cox kept checking a piece of paper with an address written on it.

Near the corner of 59th and Main Streets, Cox directed Moore to pull over but to keep the motor running. He told Burns to stay in the van with the two women. Williams and Cox got out and walked toward a house on 59th Street. Cox was carrying a jacket with something wrapped up inside it. When Moore asked Burns what Cox and Williams were going to do, Burns replied that they were going to "shoot it up" to "scare people to make sure" they would hand over their money. Moments later, gunshots rang out.

Around 7:30 a.m. on August 31st, 1984, 17-year-old LaShawn Driver was returning to her 59th Street home when she saw two men walking toward the Alexander house. Driver entered her own house. A couple minutes later, she heard gunshots and ran outside. Within a minute or so, Driver saw Williams walking down the Alexanders' driveway. She heard a second volley of shots and Cox ran out of the Alexander house carrying a rifle.

Moore and Brown estimated that Williams was gone from the van for just a few minutes. When he returned, he was carrying a handgun. He held the gun up, spun it around, blew on its barrel, and said he had only one bullet left. About three minutes later, Cox came back with a rifle. As he jumped in the van, he exclaimed, "I just blew the bitch's head off."

Williams directed Moore to drive to the corner of Gage and Vermont Avenues. Williams told the two women not to say anything about what had just happened. Then, accompanied by his two male companions, he went into an establishment known as the Vermont Club. Moore and Brown returned to Moore's house.

A short while later, Williams telephoned Moore's house and asked that Brown drive his car to the Vermont Club. On the way, Brown picked up Cox at a gas station and drove him to the back of the Vermont Club. Someone handed Cox the same rifle that Brown had seen him with on 59th Street, and Cox put it in the car trunk. Brown then drove Cox to 10th Avenue. Taking the rifle with him, Cox went into an apartment building and returned five minutes later without the rifle.

Sometime between 10:00 and 10:30 a.m. on August 31st, 1984, Brown and Moore met with Williams at the house of a mutual acquaintance. Williams removed new clothes from a shopping bag, handed Moore $50 and asked her to buy him some toiletries. He also gave Moore $5 for the gasoline she had paid for earlier, and he gave Brown $20.

Later that same day, Cox bought a 1975 Cadillac for $3,000, paying for it in $100 and $20 bills. The next day, Williams made a $1,500 cash down payment on a used car for his wife.

When police entered the 59th Street home of Ebora Alexander, they found four people dead from gunshot wounds. Ebora Alexander died from multiple gunshot wounds to the head whilst sitting at the kitchen table having breakfast. The other three murder victims were shot in their beds, execution style: Dietria Alexander had three gunshot wounds to the head and neck, while the two young boys, Damani Garner and Damon Bonner, each died from a single gunshot wound to the head. Two persons who were present in the Alexander household during the shooting survived. One of them was Neal Alexander, a son of Ebora Alexander and a brother of Dietria Alexander. Awakened by screaming, Neal had run from his bedroom to Dietria's bedroom and saw an intruder holding a rifle. Neal then ran out of the house. The other survivor was 14-year-old Ivan Scott, a grandson of murder victim Ebora Alexander who was asleep in his Uncle Neal's room when he was awakened by gunshots and screams. He immediately hid in a closet, and came out only after the gunfire had stopped.

Police ballistics experts identified bullet fragments and casings recovered from the Alexander home as having been fired by an M-1 carbine rifle. On September 27th, 1984, after a tip off, police recovered an M-1 carbine from James Kennedy, who lived in an apartment on 10th Avenue. Kennedy said that Tiequon Cox had left the weapon at his apartment early one morning. Although Kennedy could not recall the exact date, he did remember seeing a young woman sitting in a car in front of his building, waiting for Cox. Ballistics tests of the M-1 carbine retrieved from Kennedy and the bullet fragments and casings recovered at the murder scene established that some of the fragments and casings had come from the M-1 carbine. Others could also have been fired from the M-1 carbine, but were so damaged that ballistics experts could not say with certainty that they had come from that particular rifle, although nothing linked the fragments to any other weapon.

On February 28th, 1985, two detectives from the Los Angeles Police Department arrested Williams in Richmond in Northern California for the murders of the four members of the Alexander family. Williams waived his rights and agreed to talk to the officers. In his tape-recorded interview, which was played at trial, Williams gave several contradictory statements. He first said that he had heard about the murders and understood that the gunmen had gone to the wrong house. He denied any involvement. Later, he admitted he was present at the Alexander house, but insisted that he had run away as soon as Cox started shooting. Williams said that he had heard that a man named "Jack" from the Vermont Club had hired Cox and Burns to kill a young woman who was suing the club for injuries sustained in a shooting at the premises.

Williams presented an alibi defence. Mary Alford, his cousin, testified that around 3:30 a.m. on August 31st, 1984, he came to her house, and she allowed him to sleep on the couch. Between 6:30 and 8:30 a.m., Alford and two other people saw him asleep on the couch. He was still at Alford's between 10:00 and 10:30 a.m. when another cousin, Willie Morris, talked to him.

At 6:00 p.m. that evening, William's wife, Cheryl Williams, picked him up at Alford's home. They were separated but were trying to reconcile. They spent the next two nights in a motel in El Monte in Southern California. The next day, Williams made a cash down payment on a used car for Cheryl. He had recently made $2,000 from a furniture sale, and still had most of $2,523 he had won a month earlier at the Hollywood Park race track.

Detective David Crews investigated the Vermont Club in connection with this case and heard that there had been a "contract" to kill a young woman named Valarie Taylor, who was injured in a shooting incident at the Vermont Club. Taylor had filed a suit against several people she alleged were involved in the shooting and had also named as defendants the club and its owner, Ossie Jackson.

Williams and Cox were sent to trial with Williams being found guilty of abetting murder and sentenced to life in prison. Cox, who committed the killings with the rifle was charged with four counts of first-degree murder and receiving the death sentence on each.

It was later found out that the killers had the correct house number but were on the wrong street block. A mistake that cost the death of four innocent people.

LOUIS CRAINE

Born 1957 – sentenced to death. Died of AIDs complications in prison 1989.

Louis Craine was an American serial killer who committed at least four rape-murders in South Los Angeles, in the period between 1985 and 1987. He was convicted for these crimes in 1989, and was sentenced to death. It was later determined that at least five other serial killers operated in the same area during the 1980s and 1990s, collectively known as The Southside Slayers and Craine was suspected of several more murders by police. At the same time, his guilt was controversial, as he was diagnosed with signs of intellectual disability.

Craine was born on January 6th, 1957, in Los Angeles, the third in a family of four children. Early in his school years, he showed signs of intellectual disability. He left school after finishing and passing the 4th grade, entering into social conflict with the rest of his family.

In the early 1970s he left his parents' home and became a drifter. Without a qualified profession, Craine was forced to engage in low-skilled labour over the next years, and took several jobs in the construction industry. At the time of his arrest in 1987 he was unemployed.

Craine was arrested on May 29th, 1987, on charges of killing a 29-year-old prostitute named Carolyn Barney. She had been raped and sodomized before being strangled.

Her corpse was found in an empty house, not far from where her parents, and Craine's brother, lived. After finding the body, the police noticed Craine, who, due to the area being cordoned off, was intently watching their actions, behaving in an inappropriate manner. He was arrested, taken to the police station and subjected to long hours of questioning, during which he confessed to the murder of Barney and two other women: 24-year-old Loretta Perry, killed on January 25th and Vivian Collins, killed on March 18th. Both of the women, like Barney, had been strangled and raped before death.

During his interrogation, Craine claimed that Collins was murdered by his older brother Roger after they had paid her for sex. According to his story, Roger strangled her while having sex with her; however, relatives, including their mother, provided an alibi for Roger on the day of the murder, which resulted in no charges being brought against him. Subsequently, Craine was charged with the murder of two more women: 24-year-old Gail Ficklin and 30-year-old Sheila Burton, who were killed on August 15th, 1985, and November 18th, 1984. Their bodies were also found not far from where the other victims' corpses had been located, all of whom were near to the house where Craine's parents lived.

Craine's trial began in early 1989. The main material evidence was a blood-stained shirt, on which was found the blood type of one of the victims.

Testimony from Craine's relatives, included that of his mother, told the court that he had repeatedly expressed aggressive behaviour towards prostitutes and was spotted in a bloodied shirt after one of the murders.

Other evidence pointed to him as well, including his confession of killing Loretta Perry. Initially, it was believed that she had died from a drug overdose, but after Craine's testimony, her body was exhumed and subjected to a thorough pathological study the results of which validated Craine's claims to be the killer.

Craine himself, over the course of the trial, insisted on his innocence. He repudiated his earlier testimony, stating that he had been pressured into confessing. He also stated that the bloodied shirt in which, according to his relatives he had committed the murder, did not even belong to him.

He accused his family of perjury. His lawyers insisted that on the basis of various tests, Craine showed signs of intellectual disability, with a threshold of intelligence coefficient of 69 points, a tendency to exaggeration and high susceptibility to outside suggestions. As a result, they requested a forensic psychiatric examination, but their application was rejected. On May 16th, 1989, he was found guilty of four murders and acquitted of Burton's killing; on June 6th of that year, the court sentenced him to death.

After his conviction, Craine was transferred to the San Quentin State prison to serve his sentence, but due to health problems, he was taken to a prison hospital near the city of San Rafael, where he died on November 3rd, 1989, from AIDS complications.

THE FEMALES

MARIA del ROSIO ALFARO

Born October 12th, 1971 – sentenced to death July 14th, 1992.

Maria Alfaro was raised in the Spanish area in Anaheim, California, near Disneyland. She became a drug addict at 13, a prostitute at 14, a single mom at 15, and mother to 4 children at 18. Eventually, she became a murderer at 18 while pregnant with twins, and the first woman in Orange County, California to get the death penalty at 20.

On June 15th, 1990, Autumn Wallace, aged 9, was home alone in Anaheim, California; she was waiting for her older sister and mother to return from work. Rosie Alfaro was high on cocaine and heroin and needed a fix. She knew the Wallace family and was friendly with one of the older daughters. She thought they were out and that she would be able to steal items from the home to sell so she could buy her drugs.

Autumn opened the door for Alfaro, her sister's friend, who asked to use the bathroom. She took a knife from the kitchen before proceeding to the bathroom located at the back of the house. She then asked Autumn into the bathroom on a ruse, and stabbed her over 50 times. Alfaro then ransacked the house for anything she could steal to acquire drug money. The stolen property was later sold for about $300.

Alfaro confessed to the crime during a police-taped interview, stating she was high on heroin and cocaine when she stabbed Autumn. Later she changed her story and alleged an unidentified man "forced" her to stab the little girl. Still later Alfaro told police that two men drove her to the Wallace home, and one of the men came into the house and forced her to kill Autumn. She refused to identify the man. The evidence from the crime scene indicated that only members of the Wallace family and Alfaro (based on her fingerprints and a matched bloodstained shoe print) were present in the home that day.

She was tried and convicted of first-degree murder with special circumstances. At the end of the penalty phase of the trial, the jury deadlocked 10-2 on the sentence of death. The penalty phase of the trial was then declared a mistrial. A second jury unanimously voted to recommend the death penalty. The trial judge upheld the jury's recommendation and sentenced Alfaro to death.

In August 2007, the California Supreme Court voted unanimously to uphold Alfaro's death sentence.

In 2017 the U.S. 9th Circuit Court of Appeals overturned a previous U.S. District court allowing an appeal. The appeal continues.

JULIA ROTHON ANDREWS.

Born July 21st, 1954 – sentenced to 44 years in prison August 8th, 2013.

In August 2013, a jury of six women and three men sentenced Julia Andrews, 59, of Vidor to 44 years in prison for the murder of 42-year-old Randy Peddy also of Vidor in November 2012. She could have received up to 99 years in prison for the first degree felony charge.
Following a guilty verdict Andrews took the stand.
"I am so sorry," she said tearfully. "I shot my best friend. I lost him too so I know what you all are going through."
Randy Peddy's father, Jack Peddy, only shook his head side to side while looking at the ground as if unable to look at the woman who killed his son.
The events leading up to Randy Peddy's death began when he went to Andrews' house in November 2012 on the premise of repairing a broken exhaust on her car. Andrews had discovered Peddy was drinking vodka when a bottle fell out of his pocket. From experience, she said she knew that was not a good thing and took him back to his father's house. Peddy returned later in the day still intoxicated.
At first he was visiting with other family members. But, he approached her when he wanted to talk about his relationship with her daughter. She didn't think that was a good idea and had told him so.

Later, court testimony would reveal, Andrews had been involved with Peddy in a relationship herself. When the pair were together, they were said to be very openly affectionate. But, on Andrews' birthday in July, instead of attending her party he went to the beach with her daughter Jackie Uzell. They soon began dating and he ended the relationship with Andrews.

"Her feelings were hurt," said Kailee Hunt, 21, during testimony.

When Uzell called the residence on the day of the murder Andrews told her Peddy was there. Uzell, concerned about her mother, called for police to go check on her mother at the residence.

When the officer arrived in the 1400 block of Terry Road, Andrews told him "everything was OK." So, the officer left.

After the police were called, Randy Peddy became angry and the situation got out of hand.

About an hour later, Peddy went outside and began hitting and damaging the bodywork on Andrew's vehicle. She attempted to stop him but in her statement told officers he pushed and hit her. She also stated Peddy had never hit her before.

Andrews said she repeatedly told him to stop destroying her vehicle.

She went into her house and retrieved a .22 rifle which had been kept loaded behind her bedroom door and went back out onto the porch.

"When I went to get the gun, I wasn't going to shoot him. I just wanted to scare him," Andrews said. "All I wanted was for him to just leave."

When Peddy saw the rifle, he dared her to shoot him.

Andrews stated Peddy began coming towards her and she just "started shooting."

Andrews fired three shots. Witnesses testified the shots were only seconds apart. But, Andrews in her taped statement said she first fired a "warning shot." The first shell casing was found near the front door. The second shot was closer to the railings of the porch. The third shell casing was found a few months later on the porch.

"I was just trying to get him to quit destroying my car," Andrews said.

According to evidence and court testimony by pathologist Dr. Robert Lyons, Peddy was shot in the heart by a single bullet which also penetrated his spine. His blood alcohol level was 0.261 and he had a small amount of diazepam, a muscle relaxant, in his system.

Orange County Assistant District Attorney Cory Kneeland, used a tape measure to show jurors how far Andrews was from Peddy when she shot him. Peddy was about 35 feet away from the side of the porch when the gun was fired.

She will have to serve 22 years before she is first eligible for parole. This is not the first time Andrews faced felony charges. She was already on felony probation from a charge in Hardin County. Andrews stated she had given someone money to purchase a prohibited substance which was going to be given to an inmate in jail that resulted in the charges. Her appeals continue.

SHAJIA AYOBI

Born 1966 – sentenced to 26 years in prison on June 15th, 2013.

Shortly after midnight on December 18th, 2011, whilst sitting in the passenger seat of his van, Ghulam Ayobi was shot in the head three times and died. At trial, Ghulam's wife and the driver of the van, testified she had hired her classmate, Jake Clark, to kill her husband and Clark had done so after hiding in the back seat while the couple visited with friends. At trial, Ayobi relied principally on an imperfect self-defence.
Because defendant and the victim share the same surname, we shall refer to the victim by his given name, Ghulam.
In previous statements, Ayobi reported the shooting to be a carjacking and a CIA assassination.
Ayobi was born in 1966 in Afghanistan near the Pakistani border. She was one of 11 children. Between the ages of four and 14, she witnessed her father beat her mother on multiple occasions. When she was 12 years old, the Soviet Union invaded Afghanistan. During the occupation, she recalls a bombing of her school, seeing her neighbours butchered, and being personally assaulted by the Taliban.
At 17, Ayobi immigrated to California. Although she wished to attend college and medical school, her family forced her into an arranged marriage with her first husband, a marriage that

included coerced abortions, physical abuse, and an eventual divorce.

To mitigate the personal shame that her culture and family placed on divorce, Ayobi married Ghulam Ayobi after knowing him for only two hours. After a good first year of marriage, Ghulam became abusive. For the next 17 years Ghulam physically and emotionally abused her and their four children.

In 2010, Ghulam took a job in Louisiana and returned home only occasionally. After a visit that summer in which Ghulam threatened Ayobi with a gun, she purchased her own gun for self-protection. During this two-year period, she became more and more fearful that Ghulam would harm her or their children. When away from home, he repeatedly made threatening phone calls to the family. When at home, his behaviours escalated including one incident in which he got mad and etched Farsi letters onto his body and another in which he attacked the family computer with an axe because his son, who was at the computer at the time, had been playing too many video games.

Ayobi testified that about two months before Ghulam's visit in December 2011, he became more secretive. Ghulam told her not to tell anyone he was coming and he would be arriving at any time with military personnel via helicopter. She became fearful and began preparing herself for something "tragic."

On December 15th, 2011, the day before Ghulam's visit home, Ayobi asked a classmate, Jake Clark, to kill Ghulam for $10,000. Ayobi and Clark met the next day; together they purchased a prepaid phone, and Clark told her to call when she was ready for him to kill Ghulam.

Ayobi told Clark that the intended victim was the brother-in-law of a friend of hers who had raped her friend's daughter. She never did disclose the actual intended victim was her husband.

At about 10:00 p.m. on December 16th, Ghulam called from the airport, three hours earlier than expected. After arriving home that night and shortly after going to bed, Ghulam got up and began searching the house. Ayobi feared he would find her gun in the garage. Between 4:00 and 5:00 a.m., Ghulam roused the children and announced to them and Ayobi that "death can come at any time" and "death is coming. It's very close." He also talked to them about a prayer from the Koran he wanted to be buried with.

At about 5:00 p.m. on the evening of December 17th, an hour before Ayobi and Ghulam were due for dinner at a friend's house, Ayobi received a phone call from Clark. She told Clark there was a 50/50 chance she would go through with it, gave him the address of where they would be, and described the van. She told him this was "not the final instruction for him to proceed." Clark told her to make sure the gun, along with a knife and a flashlight, were in the back of the van, which she did.

Ghulam insisted on wearing his old, faded army pants to the friend's dinner because the pants gave him pride; he added that he wanted to be buried in them. Throughout the evening, he was not himself; he appeared more serious than usual and did not joke with his friends as he normally would. At this point Ayobi called Clark and told him the plan was on.

Ayobi went outside to unlock the van at about 9:30 or 10:00 p.m. She had previously left the gun, the knife, and the flashlight in the back of the van.

At about 11:45 p.m., Ayobi and Ghulam got into the van to head home. As Ayobi drove Clark emerged and held the gun to Ghulam's head and told her to get onto the freeway. Ghulam started to hand Clark his wallet, and then tried to tackle Clark. Ayobi heard one gunshot, and then two more. She pulled over to the side of the road to let Clark out. Clark told her he had taken everything with him, and she should get back on the freeway and report the shooting as a carjacking: which is what she did.

She was not believed by the police and broke down during their questioning implicating Clark. Both were arrested and charged with murder.

At trial, Rahn Minagawa, Ph.D., testified as an expert in clinical and forensic psychology, with experience and expertise in the areas of traumatic child abuse and domestic violence. He testified that individuals who have been exposed to multiple traumas throughout their life can develop a particular mood disorder called "complex trauma." Examples of the types of traumas that can lead to complex trauma include witnessing domestic violence between parents, witnessing war as a child, and physical or sexual abuse. Symptoms of complex trauma include distortions in thinking that make individuals interpret everything around them as a threat or a potential trigger for violence to occur. Complex trauma can result in poor decision making, hypervigilance, and dissociation.

After interviewing Ayobi and members of her family, Dr. Minagawa diagnosed her as having complex trauma disorder. Dr. Minagawa was certain that the diagnosis was present when Ghulam was killed.

"Hypervigilance" is a condition in which individuals have an automatic response to external sensations such as a combat veteran diving to the ground when a car backfires. "Dissociation" is when an individual feels like they have separated from their body in order to psychologically protect themselves from an event.

Dr. Minagawa also diagnosed Ayobi with post-traumatic stress syndrome and major depressive disorder.

In addition to his testimony regarding complex trauma, Dr. Minagawa testified that it is common for victims of domestic abuse to stay with or return to their abusive partners—especially when there are children involved. He also testified that domestic violence is a socially acceptable expectation in some Middle Eastern cultures. While Dr. Minagawa testified regarding the effects of domestic abuse, he did not describe or provide a diagnosis of intimate partner battering or battered women's syndrome.

Throughout his direct examination of Ayobi and Dr. Minagawa, and in his closing argument, Ayobi's defence counsel relied on a theory of complex trauma disorder. Counsel did not rely on intimate partner battering or battered women's syndrome as a separate defence. Instead, he used the evidence of domestic violence, along with Ayobi's lifetime of traumatic experiences—i.e., the evidence of complex trauma disorder in Ayobi—to develop imperfect self-defence. Further, in closing argument, counsel conceded that, based on the evidence presented, perfect self-defence was "a pretty big stretch of reality in this case."

In line with the theory of complex trauma supporting imperfect self-defence, the defence counsel stated in their closing argument, "And there are some people, ladies and gentlemen, who actually experience this trauma. And they experience it not once, not twice, but over and over and over again. And those people suffer from complex trauma disorder, just like Shajia Ayobi does. The defence is not speculating what was in Ayobi's mind. I'm telling you, showing you, giving you evidence of what was in her mind, because what was in her mind is the only important issue here in this case." Defence counsel continued in closing, "Now, the law also recognizes that there are times when people in good faith believe something, but the rest of us wouldn't"; and Shajia Ayobi "had an actual belief, in her need to defend, because she was traumatized, because she suffered from complex trauma, and because her husband was an erratic brute."

Jake Clark denied being in the van and stated that Ayobi had indeed offered him $5,000 to kill her husband which he rejected. His activity, if any, in the killings is unknown.

It took 4 days for the jury at her trial to convict Ayobi, 46, of first degree murder on December 18th, 2011 and she was sentenced to 26 years to life in prison. Jake Clark, 36, was convicted with aiding and abetting a murder. Their testimonies disputed each other's. The jury obviously believed Ayobi was the shooter.

VIOLET JOHN BERLING

Born 1928 – sentenced to life in prison on April 28th, 1951.

Kay Frances Erickson was only 10 years old on the morning of October 12th, 1950, when police in Long Beach, California., received a frantic call. It was her music teacher, Violet John Berling, 32, screaming that the child was not breathing.

Berling told police she had been asleep when, around 6 a.m., she was awakened by the child crying, "Take the accordion off me."

But this was no nightmare. The child had been strapped into a straight-backed chair, her hands and feet bound, and an accordion strap wrapped around her shoulders. She had died when she regurgitated food and choked on it, unable to move in the makeshift torture rack.

As to how the child got strapped into the chair? Berling said Kay had done it herself. Berling said that lashing herself to furniture was just one of the child's weird habits.

Another was self-mutilation, which explained the assortment of scars and bruises, old and new, that the coroner's autopsy found on her body.

Berling insisted that Kay inflicted these wounds in a frenzy of masochism. Hurting herself and magically making it all better was the only way she could convince non-believers the she had special powers, Berling told detectives.

While agreeing that some of the wounds could have been self-inflicted, the coroner said that somebody else had been responsible for most of them. He also said that the girl had died several hours before Berling had called for help.

Police also found several bloodstained accordion straps in the studio.

The death was ruled a homicide. Berling was arrested and charged with murder.

Berling told detectives that Kay had been one of her many pupils, but that the girl had come to live with her when Kay's family fell on hard times during the summer.

Harry Erickson, the girl's father, was a Navy electrician, a career that kept him away from home. The mother, Beatrice Erickson, had decided to take classes to become a nurse's aide, in the hope of improving the family's situation.

Berling told Beatrice Erickson that Kay had a real talent on the accordion and that it would be a shame if the budding virtuoso didn't live up to her potential.

The only way to do this would be to practice night and day. Berling said she'd be happy to keep the child living at her studio to give her the attention and training she needed.

So Kay went to live with her teacher, cutting nearly all ties with her parents. Berling told the Ericksons that it was better if they stayed away so the girl would have nothing to distract her from her instrument. Every time the parents showed up Kay played the accordion badly and the teacher said, "she had just lost her touch" on the accordion for several days.

The mother agreed not to attend her child's recitals.

"I didn't go to the programs she was in because Miss John (Berling's professional name) told me parents were not invited and the programs were private."

The parents had no idea that their daughter was spending much of her time tied to a chair, sometimes gagged, often with an accordion strapped to her front.

Erickson insisted that Kay was a normal child. But further questioning would reveal that the mother had an odd idea of what constituted 'normal'.

Long before she introduced her daughter to the accordion, Erickson took the girl to faith healing services and to churches that practiced "cosmic ray" healing, in which heavenly cures were conveyed through copper wires on the ceilings.

By the time Kay played her first note, the girl was possessed and prone to tantrums and trances, or so Berling said.

At least twice, Berling recalled, Kay stopped mid-chord, saying the spirit of her dead grandfather had ordered her to do so. The only way to keep her from mutilating herself was to watch her constantly, or tie her up.

"I was out of the studio about 20 minutes," Berling told the court during her trial, which started on January 3rd, 1951, and would drag on to the end of April mainly because Berling kept fainting and had to be carried from the courtroom. Prosecutors did their best to make Berling out to be a "witch woman," even introducing a photo of the teacher in a "weird topknot," and suggesting that it was indicative of more than just a bad hair day. They called on other of her accordian pupils, who took the stand, and told of abuses they had seen. One 9-year-old girl said she saw Berling kick Kay, hit her with a ruler or bind her face with elastic bandages.

Berling's other students said that they had often seen Kay tied to the straight-backed chair. Berling said it was for the girl's own good because Kay's behaviour was so erratic and dangerous. Former pupils showed up and testified that the teacher had hurt them as well. Another 9-year-old told the court "sometimes I think I'd like to see her die in the gas chamber."

The week before Kay's death, Berling said, the child had been sleepwalking, lapsing in and out of trances, and talking about death.

Berling said she called Erickson that week to tell her that her daughter was out of control. Erickson offered a simple explanation. She said a family friend "was performing black magic on Kay."

It took the jury nine days of stormy deliberation to reach the verdict of guilty.

The judge sentenced her to life in prison. A year later, Berling's lawyers used a bizarre argument to win her a retrial. They said that because she had fainted so often during the first trial, she was "mentally absent," from the proceedings. In his decision, the judge wrote: "The conviction cannot be approved because of the violation of the defendant's fundamental right to be present physically and mentally and fully conscious during all stages of the trial."

The second trial was swift. In May 1953, after a one-day retrial without a jury, the judge upheld her conviction and sent her back to prison.

ROSEMARIE DIANE BJORKLAND

Born 1941 – Sentenced to life in prison, 1959. Paroled in 1966.

On February 2nd, 1959, the body of August Norry, a 28-year-old landscape gardener, was found in a remote area of Daly City. Norry had been shot more than 15 times. He had been shot from the driver's side of his car and then shot from the passenger's side of the car and then the body had been dragged out of the car and shot some more. A Korean War veteran and former dance instructor, Norry seemed to have no enemies. His father described him as "a clean, upstanding boy."

There were only two clues: a witness reported seeing a young blond woman speeding away from the scene in the victim's car that was later found abandoned and the unusual make of the bullets used in the murder.

Two and a half months went by as San Mateo Sheriff's Department detectives Milt Minehan and Willam Ridenour tracked down the manufacture of the bullet mold to a New Jersey company, of which only 10,000 of that kind were sold, and narrowed it down to Bay Area purchasers. Then one by one, Minehan and Ridenour checked out each buyer, often taking samples of the gun enthusiast's fired bullet to analyze and compare with the bullets taken from the crime scene.

Eventually Inspectors Minehan and Ridenour questioned twenty-three year old Daly City mechanic

Lawrence Schultze about his reloading practices. After taking samples of Schultze's bullets and comparing it against the Norry bullets, they came up with a match.

On April 14th, 1959, Minehan and Ridenour confronted Schultze with the evidence; he confessed that he had indeed made the bullets and loaded them into a live cartridge. Then Schultze went further. He told the detectives that he had sold a box of fifty wad-cutter bullets to his eighteen year old blonde-haired friend, Rosemarie "Penny" Bjorkland of Daly City.

When interviewed by the detectives they discovered an "18-year-old blond who killed a man to satisfy an 'urge' to find out if killing somebody would haunt her conscience." She shot Norry, whom she barely knew, "and then calmly drove away in his blood-stained, bullet-shattered car." She openly confessed to the crime. The sheriff wanted to know more of the motive. Penny stated: "I know the answer. I know why I did it. But I won't talk about it." Later, of course, she did talk about it: "I figured it could have been anybody...but it couldn't have been anybody I know. It had to be a stranger."

She was more than helpful to the authorities, even directing them to the exact sewer in San Francisco where she had thrown the gun.

She had no police record and had only one school violation: smuggling vodka into her high school.

She had little regard as to how the crime and following arrest would affect her family: "I guess this does affect my parents, but that's not my concern."

Later she would be even more vehement, telling the San Francisco Chronicle: "All I can think of is hatred toward my family. I'm just going to sit in court hating them."

In the Redwood City courtroom, Judge Frank B. Blum said Penny "had the mental ability to premeditate the killing." He sentenced her to life with the possibility of parole in just seven short years.

Penny did indeed go to prison but quickly convinced her jailers that she was insane and so she was shipped off to a secure mental facility. Once there she re-convinced the facility's administrators that she had been faking her insanity, on the belief that if she was subsequently judged sane they would be forced to free her. It didn't work that way.

But she did have one more trick up her sleeve. She vanished. She apparently was paroled after about seven years and, once freed, disappeared from history. She may have changed her name and lived a long life – she may be alive today and reading this.

But what is definitely known is that she killed a man as a theoretical experiment and thought she would get away with it, but didn't.

AMBER MERRIE BRAY

Born 1977- sentenced to life in prison without parole on June 30th, 1998.

Amber Bray, 20, and her boyfriend, Jeffrey Ayers, 23, were charged with murder and conspiracy to commit murder in the beating and stabbing to death of Bray's mother in January 1996.

Bray and her mother, Dixie Hollier, had a strained relationship, and prosecutors claimed that Bray coerced Ayers into killing her mother with promises of marriage and his share of an inheritance worth $300,000. In addition, prosecutors said Bray told Ayers that she would kill herself if he did not kill her mother.

In a videotaped confession, Ayers admitted to his role in the murder and insisted that although Bray knew about his intentions, he alone planned the crime. During his confession, Ayers said that he decided to kill Hollier when Bray threatened to kill herself because her mother allegedly abused her so much. Ayers's attorneys argued that Bray manipulated his love for her and forced him into the killing.

On the other hand, Bray contended that Ayers decided to kill Hollier entirely on his own. Bray's defence claimed that she is only guilty of associating with Ayers.

The victim, Dixie Hollier, was a divorced single mother who was a manager of special projects at Warner Brothers Studios and was involved in management of the Red Hot Chili Peppers rock band. She lived with her two teen-age daughters and five-year-old son in a modest duplex in Burbank.

According to Bray's younger sister, Bray and Hollier fought about issues such as curfews and household chores. Their relationship became increasingly strained in the autumn of 1995, when Bray began missing school often and was transferred to Monterey Continuation High School, a school geared towards students with academic or attendance problems. Sometimes the arguments between Bray and her mother escalated into shoving matches, as they fought over Bray's schoolwork and the people she associated with.

It was around this time, Bray started dating Jeffrey Ayers, a high school dropout who lived with his mother and was an avid "Dungeons and Dragons" fan. Ayers soon became Bray's confidant, especially after numerous fights with her mother. Eventually, Ayers became convinced that Hollier was abusing Bray and became concerned for her mental well-being. According to friends of them both, Bray and Ayers began making plans to marry and live together.

On January 16th, 1996, Ayers entered Bray's house just before 5 am. Police suspected later that Bray met him at the door and let him in. Ayers then entered Hollier's room and fired five shots at her. Two bullets hit Hollier, grazing her forehead and shattering her upper right arm. When Hollier started yelling for help, Ayers began to beat her on the head with the butt of the gun. Then Ayers went into the kitchen, grabbed three knives, and stabbed Hollier 24 times.

Awakened by the gunfire, Bray's younger sister ran out of her room to find Ayers attacking her mother. She tried to call 911, but Bray pulled out the phone cord. The younger sister put the plug back in, but Bray then allegedly pulled the phone out of the wall and ordered her to look after her younger brother. As the attack continued, Bray barricaded herself and her siblings in the back bedroom.

A neighbour had heard the gunfire and called the police. When they arrived, they saw Ayers through a window still straddling Hollier and continuing to stab her. With Hollier's blood covering his hands and clothes, Ayers surrendered without resistance to police. He confessed to the murder on video three hours later. Police began to suspect Bray's involvement after her sister told them that she had pulled out the phone cord when she tried to call them during the attack. The authorities also found various letters between Bray and Ayers in Bray's bedroom that outlined their plan to kill Hollier.

In one of the letters between Ayers and Bray, dated "Someday in November," Bray suggested that she and Ayers arrange to have her sister and mother killed while they take her younger brother out to a movie. "I come home and discover them, call the police...and it goes on record as another unsolved homicide," she writes. In that letter, Bray also discusses how she and Ayers would spend her inheritance from her mother. Ayers responded to the letter by writing, "Your mother and sister will trouble you no more."

Bray and Ayers were tried together in front of two different juries. Ayers's confession was not shown to Bray's jury. Prosecutors attached two special circumstances to the defendants' indictments or first-degree murder and conspiracy to commit murder: (1) the murder was intentional and carried out for financial gain (2) Bray killed the victim while lying in wait.

If convicted of first-degree murder under special circumstances, Bray and Ayers faced life in prison without parole. If found guilty of murder without special circumstances, they faced sentences ranging between 25 years-to-life in prison. Prosecutors chose not to seek the death penalty against the defendants because neither of them had prior criminal records.

On Feb. 5th, 1998, Amber Bray was found guilty of first-degree murder and conspiracy to commit murder. The next day, Jeffrey Ayers was also convicted of the same charges. Both were also found guilty of committing the crimes under special circumstances under state law. Bray and Ayers have both been sentenced to life in prison without parole.

ELIZABETH ANNE BRODERICK

Born 7th November, 1947 – sentenced to two consecutive terms of 15 years to life, February 7th, 1992.

Growing up in Eastchester, New York, Elizabeth Broderick was the third of six children born to devout Roman Catholic parents Marita and Frank Bisceglia. Her mother was Irish-American and her father was Italian; he founded a plastering firm with his brothers. Her parents taught her that her role in life was to become a good wife and mother.
Elizabeth attended and later graduated from the College of Mount Saint Vincent, a small Catholic women's college in Riverdale, New York.
In 1965, Elizabeth met her future husband, Dan Broderick, eldest son in another large Catholic family at a college party. They then began dating and, not long after, became engaged.
Dan was from Pittsburgh, Pennsylvania. When the couple became engaged, Dan was attending the Cornell University Medical School located in New York City. The couple were married on April 12th, 1969, at the Immaculate Conception Church in Eastchester in a lavish ceremony planned by Elizabeth's mother. They honeymooned on a Caribbean cruise and later stayed with friends in St. Thomas.
She returned from her honeymoon pregnant with her first child, daughter Kim, and continued to work until the day before she gave birth. Afterward,

she continued to hold down several jobs and devoted herself to home and family, which, she stated, had always been her only ambitions. She gave birth to four more children: a daughter called Lee, two sons named Daniel and Rhett, and an unnamed boy who died two days after birth. During the couple's early years before Dan became a successful attorney, they were virtually destitute, living for a time on food stamps, moving in and out of dormitories and apartments. Elizabeth held down a multitude of jobs to support the family, even resorting to selling Tupperware door to door in the cold of winter, while holding her babies in her hands.

After Kim's birth, and after completing his medical degree, Dan announced that he didn't want to proceed with his medical training and that he intended to combine it with a law degree. He enrolled at Harvard Law School while Elizabeth held down a variety of jobs to support his studies.

In 1973, after Dan graduated from Harvard Law School, the family moved to the La Jolla area of San Diego, where Dan eventually became a success as a medical malpractice attorney. Money did not come pouring in quickly, as Dan's initial salary at the law firm where he got a job was quite low. In time, Elizabeth urged Dan to go into practice for himself, which he did. Shortly afterwards, Dan enjoyed much success virtually overnight, after he won his first million-dollar case The Brodericks became bona fide millionaires, and it appeared that after years of hard work and sacrifice, they had finally made it. The couple was well known within San Diego social circles and enjoyed a life of increasing affluence. Elizabeth was finally able to quit working and reap the benefits of all of her hard work.

At the same time, the already-problematic marriage was further deteriorating. Elizabeth continually complained that Dan was an absent father and husband, spending too much time working and socializing with fellow attorneys. She protested that she felt like a single parent of four children.

In the early 1980s, Dan hired Linda Kolkena, a former airline attendant who had become a receptionist, as his assistant, and began a secret affair with her that lasted the next three years.

Elizabeth long suspected the affair although Dan denied it for some time. During one incident after which Elizabeth waited all day and night at Dan's law office to celebrate his 38th birthday, only to find out that he was out with Linda, she drove home in a rage and burned all of Dan's expensive custom-tailored suits.

The marriage continued to deteriorate with Elizabeth constantly suspecting Dan's affair and Dan repeatedly denying it. Dan finally moved out of the family home, bought a house of his own, and eventually, to Elizabeth's surprise, willingly took custody of the four children. Shortly afterward, he admitted to the three-year affair, got a restraining order against Elizabeth and filed for divorce. There followed a lengthy, complex, acrimonious divorce in which Elizabeth felt that she was unfairly treated, owing to Dan's extensive legal connections and influence. Broderick vs. Broderick became one of the ugliest divorces in the United States, gaining so much notoriety that the Oprah Winfrey Show even contacted Elizabeth to secure an interview on a show whose topic was ugly divorces. Elizabeth declined the interview.

After Dan left Elizabeth she became obsessed with her anger toward her husband. Among other behaviours that later worked against her in court, she repeatedly left obscene messages on his answering machine and frequently abused him and Linda Kolkena in recorded telephone conversations with her children, of whom she made demands regarding their behaviour and attitude towards their father and Kolkena.

One particularly notorious incident involved her driving her vehicle through the front door of Dan Broderick's new house after he sold the family house from underneath Elizabeth without her consent. She also smeared a Boston cream pie all over Dan's clothing when she entered his home one day unannounced, spray painted his walls, and broke his windows. Throughout the divorce, Elizabeth's behaviour became increasingly violent. The only way she knew how to fight back against her estranged husband was to vandalize his home, leave him vulgar phone messages, and complain to all of her friends about his philandering.

Dan, on the other hand, was able to keep a cooler head and regularly used his legal acumen against her. Dan repeatedly had her hauled into court on "Orders to Show Cause" whenever Elizabeth would violate the restraining order Dan had against her. After one hearing, she was imprisoned for three days. To many onlookers, Dan was egging Elizabeth on, exacerbating her already unstable demeanour, instead of showing her sympathy and assisting her in getting the help she needed. At the time, Dan was paying Elizabeth $9,000, and then later $16,000, per month in alimony, and was living with Linda Kolkena. Throughout it all Elizabeth was hopeful that Dan would return home.

The long drawn-out Broderick divorce was finalized in 1989, four years after Dan filed for it. By many accounts, Dan dragged the divorce out for four years on purpose. In California, there was a little-known legal concept called "Epstein credits" which worked to thwart any financial settlement entitled to Elizabeth. By the time the divorce trial came to fruition, because of Epstein credits, Elizabeth's share of community property had been substantially reduced. Epstein credits are a provision under California divorce law which says that the supporting spouse, in this case Dan, may charge the dependent spouse, Elizabeth, for one-half of all community debts accumulated from the date of separation. If there is a substantial amount of time in the interim, a dependent spouse may actually accumulate enough Epstein credits to effectively cancel out any share of the community property which might have been forthcoming had the divorce been finalized immediately after separation.

In the case of the Brodericks, legal manoeuvrings and delays by Dan postponed the divorce trial time and time again. Finally, at the divorce trial, Elizabeth represented herself without an attorney. In what many believed was outrageously unfair and what only solidified Dan's clout in the local legal arena, the Broderick divorce trial was completely sealed off from the public at Dan's request. The courtroom door windows were covered up with paper. At the end of the eight day trial, Judge William Howatt accepted all of Dan's proposed numbers and ruled that Betty owed Dan $750,000 in Epsteins and cash advances, all accrued between the time Dan moved out and the date the divorce was final on January 30th, 1989.

In the end, Dan Broderick, multi-millionaire and the father of Elizabeth's four children, was ordered to pay his wife of 20 years less than $30,000 in cash. In addition, Dan was re-awarded custody of the children. Elizabeth was completely devastated and felt that her life was over.

On April 22nd, 1989, ten days after what would have been Dan and Elizabeth's 20th anniversary, Dan and Linda were married.

One month before Dan was to marry Linda, claiming the need for protection as she was now living alone as a single woman, Elizabeth bought a Smith & Wesson revolver. She took shooting lessons and, by some accounts, carried the gun with her most of the time and made many threats to shoot Dan.

Eight months after buying the gun and seven months after Dan and Linda were married Elizabeth shot and killed the couple while they slept. The murder occurred at approximately 5:30 am on the morning of November 5th, 1989, two days before Elizabeth's 42nd birthday.

This followed a letter from Dan's lawyer to Elizabeth's lawyer that contained allegations that Elizabeth was mentally unstable, as well as threats of incarcerating her into a psychiatric facility. Elizabeth had gained entry to her ex-husband's home in Marston Hills with a key that she had taken from the purse of her eldest daughter, Kim Broderick.

At her trials, she was harmed by the fact that she had removed from the bedroom a telephone that the apparently still-living Dan Broderick could have used to call for help. Elizabeth shot all five bullets from her gun. Two bullets hit Linda in the head and chest, killing her instantly, one bullet hit Dan in the chest as he apparently was reaching for a phone, one bullet hit the wall, and one bullet hit a night stand. Dan was 44; Linda was 28.

After the shooting, Betty turned herself in to the police, never denying that she had indeed pulled the trigger five times. But at her trials, she denied that she had any intention of murdering the couple when she broke into their house.

When asked why she had brought a handgun into the home that night, she replied "because I wanted him to listen to me." She claimed that her intention was to make him listen to her, and if he wouldn't, she would commit suicide and "splash her brains all over his goddamn house." When pressed for an answer as to why she did not commit suicide after shooting Dan and Linda, she stated that she didn't have any bullets left. She claimed that she had shot her ex-husband in the heat of passion as soon as she entered the bedroom and saw Linda screaming, "Call the police!"

Elizabeth's explanation at both trials was that she had never planned to kill Dan and Linda and her crime was never one that was premeditated. Her account of the murders, at her second trial, was that, "The movement that I made into their bedroom woke them up, and they moved and somebody screamed 'Call the police!' and I said 'No!' and I just fired the gun and this big noise went off, and then I grabbed the phone and got the hell out of there. But I wasn't even in that room . . . I mean, it was just an explosion. Just, I moved, they moved, the gun went off, and it was like AHHHH! And it was that fast." She alleged that she was startled by Linda screaming, "Call the police!" and with no thought process or plan, she immediately fired the gun, unaware at that moment, in the dark bedroom, that any of the bullets hit the couple.

The jury at her second trial found Elizabeth Broderick guilty on two counts of second degree murder and she was sentenced to two consecutive terms of 15 years to life plus two years for illegal use of a firearm. Since then she has been refused parole on each occasion for not showing any remorse and not acknowledging her wrongdoing. Two of her children have spoken against her release at each parole hearing. She will be 84 years old when next up for parole in 2032. At the time of writing she is in the California Institution for Women in Chino, California.

CAROL MARY BUNDY
See under **Douglas Daniel Clark**

Born August 26th, 1942 – sentenced to 27 years to life on May 31st, 1983. Died in prison December 9th, 2003.

SOCORRO CARO

Born March 27th, 1957 – sentenced to death April 5th, 2002.

Socorro Caro, 44, was a woman who decided the best way of getting back at her estranged husband was to murder three of her children, boys aged 11, 8 and 5 on November 22nd, 1999. A fourth infant was unharmed.

According to court documents Caro was upset that her husband was preparing to leave her so she shot dead her three young children. Caro would then shoot herself in the head in a suicide attempt which failed. She has said that she has no memory of the night of the triple murders and considering she underwent two brain surgeries to fix the damage the self-inflicted bullet caused this is plausible. However the California jury did not think so and found her guilty on all three counts and sentenced her to death, she remains on California Death Row

CELESTE SIMONE CARRINGTON

Born 1961 – sentenced to death November 23rd, 1994.

The offences of which Celeste Carrington was convicted arose out of four separate incidents. Most of the facts underlying these offences were admitted by Carrington in her statements to the police which she made shortly after her arrest. The first incident involved the burglary of a Dodge dealership located at 640 Veterans Boulevard in Redwood City on the night of January 17th, 1992. In her statement to the police, Carrington admitted the following. She previously had been employed as a janitor for several companies and, having worked in this dealership building, she was aware that the back entrance was often left unlocked. She went to that location with gloves and a crowbar, which she used to force open several interior doors. Among other items, she stole a .357 magnum revolver and five bullets.

The second incident involved the burglary of a building located at 1123 Industrial Road in San Carlos and the murder of Victor Esparza, 34, on the night of January 26th, 1992. In her statement Carrington admitted the following. That she previously had worked on the premises as a janitor and had retained a key to the building. She borrowed a car from her neighbour and drove to the location, armed with the .357 magnum revolver she had stolen from the Dodge dealership. She used her key to enter the building, accidentally setting off the alarm. Victor Esparza, who was cleaning the facility, observed her in an office cubicle. She told him that she worked in the building and must have accidentally set off the alarm. Esparza asked her to call the building manager to report the alarm, took out his wallet, and handed her a telephone number. Carrington produced the gun and took his wallet, which contained about $45 or $55 in cash. She also demanded the personal identification number (PIN) for his automated teller machine (ATM) card, which he wrote down. As she walked out of the cubicle, she turned around and shot Esparza. She later attempted to use his ATM card, but the PIN he had given her was invalid.

Carrington admitted that she intended to kill Esparza, and that the experience was exciting and made her feel powerful. The forensic pathologist who performed the autopsy on Esparza testified that Esparza died of a gunshot wound to the head, inflicted from a distance of approximately six inches. He also concluded that the angle of the gunshot wound was not inconsistent with the victim having been shot while kneeling and looking up at the shooter, nor was it inconsistent with the possibility that the victim was standing.

The third incident involved the burglary of an office building located at 777 California Street in Palo Alto in Santa Clara County and the murder of Carolyn Gleason, 36, on March 11th, 1992. In her statement to the police, Carrington admitted the following. That she previously had worked as a janitor in the building and had retained a key. A neighbour gave her a ride to the premises from her apartment in East Palo Alto. She brought with her a pair of gloves, a screwdriver, and the same .357 magnum revolver she had used to kill Victor Esparza. Her key would not open the door. She observed two cars in the parking lot and two janitors working in the building so she waited for these individuals to leave before using the screwdriver to open the door. Carrington then walked through the facility looking for money but found none. She heard Caroline Gleason enter and go into an office. Carrington watched her and eventually encountered her in the copy room where she displayed the gun. Gleason begged her to put it away. According to Carrington, she did not want to hurt Gleason, but she became nervous and accidentally pulled the trigger. After shooting Gleason, she took Gleason's keys and about $400 from her desk. She went outside to the parking lot and entered Gleason"s car, where she found Gleason's purse, which contained her ATM card and PIN. Carrington drove the car to a bank in Palo Alto, where she made two unsuccessful attempts to withdraw money from Gleason"s account, but was able to withdraw $200 from an ATM at a 7-Eleven store and another $100 from a second bank. She left the car in a hospital parking lot and took a taxi back to her apartment. An autopsy indicated that Gleason died as the result of a single gunshot to the head fired from a very close range.

The fourth incident involved the burglary of a medical office building located at 80 Brewster Street in Redwood City and the attempted murder of Dr.

Allan Marks on the evening of March 16th, 1992. Carrington, in her statement to the police, admitted the following. As in two of the earlier incidents, she brought with her a key she had retained from her prior employment at the building as a janitor, a pair of gloves, and the same .357 magnum revolver. The doors to the building were unlocked when she arrived at 5:30 p.m. After discovering that she was unable to open any of the internal offices with her key, she hid in a closet for a few hours. She emerged from the closet and spent some time in the building before observing Dr. Marks leaving his office after a late appointment. She decided to rob him and pulled out the gun. The two struggled over the gun. During the struggle she pulled the trigger three times, resulting in one misfire and two shots. Marks managed to force her out of the office and locked the door. Carrington fled the building, taking with her some access cards and prescription drugs. Dr. Marks testified at Carrington's trial to a somewhat different version of the shooting. According to his account, as he was about to leave his office Carrington pushed the door open and came "barrelling through," causing the door to push him to the side. He recognized her as a former janitor in the building and began shouting and waiving his hands. Carrington was standing about three feet from him, holding a gun in her right hand. She pointed it at his upper body, and he heard gunshots. He was shot in the left shoulder, left thumb, and right forearm. After being shot, Marks collapsed to his knees and Carrington left the office. He closed the door behind her and called 911.

Carrington was arrested a few days later. Her apartment in East Palo Alto was searched pursuant to three warrants obtained by the Los Altos, Palo Alto, and Redwood City Police Departments. The police found evidence that connected Carrington to all four incidents: the keys to the Redwood City Dodge dealership; the gun that had been taken from the dealership, which was the weapon used to shoot Esparza, Gleason, and Marks; Gleason's pager and purse, and the key to the building in which Gleason was shot; a box from Gleason's office that held petty cash; a piece of paper with Gleason's PIN on it; and a drug kit taken from a doctor's office in the medical building in which Marks was shot. After the search was completed, police officers from each of the three police departments interviewed Carrington, at which interviews she confessed to being the perpetrator in each of the four incidents.

The defence at her trial presented no evidence at the guilt phase of the trial. In closing argument, defence counsel conceded that the crimes occurred as Carrington had described them in her statements and argued that the murders were not executions. Defence counsel argued that with respect to the charge involving the robbery of Gleason, the jury should return a verdict of guilty on the lesser offence of theft and should find not true the allegation that the murder of Gleason took place during the commission of a robbery. Defence counsel also urged that as to the charge involving the attempted murder of Marks, the jury should return a verdict of guilty on the lesser offense of assault with a firearm. The defence was clutching at straws.

Carrington was found guilty of all three murders and sentenced to death on November 23rd, 1994. Age 30 at the time of her crimes she is now 60 and sits on death row in Central California Women's Facility, inmate number W55311.

CYNTHIA LYNN COFFMAN
See under **JAMES GREGORY MARLOW**

Born January 19th, 1962 – sentenced to death August 31st, 1989.

CHERYL CHRISTINA CRANE
(daughter of actress Lana Turner)

Born July 25th, 1943 – killed John Stompanato April 4th, 1958 which was ruled a justifiable homicide, released 1961.

At approximately 8:00 p.m. on April 4th, 1958, eight days after the Academy Awards ceremony, John Stompanato, a member of the Cohen Crime Family and actress Lana Turner's boyfriend, arrived at her rented home at 730 North Bedford Drive in Beverly Hills, California, which Turner had begun leasing a week prior. The two began arguing heatedly in the bedroom, during which Stompanato threatened to kill Turner, her daughter and her mother, as well as making "gangster threats" that involved breaking Turner's bones and slashing her face with a straight razor so she would never work again. Turner's daughter, Cheryl Crane, 14, had briefly entered the room during the argument, but was urged by Turner to stay out of it. In the midst of the ensuing argument,

Turner broke off her relationship with Stompanato and asked him to leave the house.

Fearing that Turner's life was in danger, Crane, who had been watching television in an adjacent room, grabbed a kitchen knife and ran to her mother's defence. Crane recalled the incident in 2012:

"There's a knife on the kitchen counter. I picked it up ran back up the stairs. Her door suddenly flies open. I see John coming toward me. He's got his hand up... I raised the knife and he walks right into it. And he looked at me. And he said, 'My God, Cheryl, what have you done?'"

Turner corroborated this, stating that Crane, who had been listening to the couple's fight behind the closed door, stabbed Stompanato in the stomach when Turner attempted to usher him out of the bedroom. Turner initially believed Crane had punched him, but realized he had been stabbed when he collapsed and she saw blood on his shirt. Official police accounts state that Crane then left the room, placing the knife on a "small marble-topped table" and rushed to phone her father, Joseph Stephen 'Steve' Crane. Meanwhile, Turner called for a doctor, who arrived at the house shortly after; the doctor attempted to revive Stompanato with an adrenaline injection and an artificial respirator. Unable to obtain a pulse, the doctor called for emergency services, thereby notifying the police, and Stompanato was subsequently pronounced dead at the scene.

An autopsy conducted shortly after revealed Stompanato's death was caused by a single knife wound that penetrated his liver, portal vein and aorta, resulting in massive internal haemorrhaging.

Police chief Clinton Anderson, who arrived at Turner's home shortly after the emergency medical services, stated that Turner had pleaded to him, "Please, let me say I did it," after Crane had confessed to the stabbing to her father, who had also arrived at the house. Within one hour of the homicide, Turner and her ex-husband had retained attorney Jerry Giesler to represent their daughter.

In the early morning hours of April 5th, Crane was surrendered at the Beverly Hills Police Department, where she was booked on a holding charge. She gave a formal statement detailing her hearing Stompanato's threats against her mother, and her subsequent stabbing of him in the bedroom doorway. After Crane had provided her statement, Turner, Stephen and Giesler left the station house at the insistence of the police department, as the press had already "gathered like vultures outside." In the interim pending further legal proceedings, Crane was interned in a juvenile remand hall.

On April 7th, 1958, a juvenile pre-detention hearing was held under Judge Donald O'Dell, it was closed to the public, and was attended by Turner, her mother Mildred and ex-husband Stephen. The same day, Turner attempted to file an application for Crane's release into the custody of Mildred, Crane's grandmother. Turner's application was denied, however, as the judge felt that Crane would "be better protected by remaining in custody pending the hearing for Stompanato's murder."

A follow-up juvenile detention hearing was scheduled for April 24th in Santa Monica to determine whether Crane would permanently remain a ward of the juvenile court. During the ruling Crane took the decision "without any show of emotion." Upon her dismissal, she was again relocated to a juvenile detention centre pending further proceedings.

Due to Turner's high profile and the fact that the killing involved her teenage daughter, the case quickly became a cause celebre. Over one hundred reporters and journalists attended the April 11th, 1958, coroner's inquest, described by attendees as "near-riotous".

Cohen, Stompanato's friend and crime associate, was called as the first witness, but refused to provide testimony as he feared he might be implicated in the crime, he also refused to identify Stompanato's body in photographs. While Cohen was questioned, Stephen Trusso, a spectator and friend of Stompanato, interrupted the proceedings by screaming, "I want to testify!" He went on to claim that Crane killed Stompanato in a lover's quarrel because she was infatuated with him, and that she was jealous of her mother. Trusso's request to testify on the stand was denied by the judge. The second witness, Beverly Hills police chief Clinton Anderson, testified that he was "satisfied" with Crane's confession to the killing. Joseph B. Payne, a Beverly Hills police officer who was dispatched to the residence on the night of the killing, also testified; on the stand, he recounted his arrival at Turner's home that night, where he was met by Crane's father, who had placed a call to the police himself.

Additional testimony was provided by Crane's father and her grandmother Mildred. Stephen testified that he had received a frantic phone call from Crane the night of the stabbing, and quickly drove to Turner's home. Mildred, whose own husband, Turner's father, had been murdered in 1930, also briefly took the stand, but was so visibly upset that she was excused from further testimony. Beverly Hills police captain Ray Borders provided further testimony regarding Crane's official statement given at the Beverly Hills police station house. Several law enforcement officials, as well as Turner, Stephen and Giesler, were present, and Borders attested that the version of events as told by Crane was consistent when repeatedly questioned. Cheryl Crane herself did not attend the inquest. In her absence, a written statement was read aloud, which recounted her overhearing of the argument, her acquiring the knife from the kitchen and the eventual stabbing of Stompanato in her mother's bedroom. "He kept threatening her and I thought he was going to hurt her, so I went into the room and I stuck him with the knife," she said. "He screamed and asked what I was doing. I ran out of the room."

Despite the voluminous testimony from others, a report of the inquest in The Philadelphia Examiner noted that Turner's was "the highlight of a circus-like hearing." When Turner took the stand a "hush fell over the crowd as the famous actress sat down, removed one white glove, and filled her lungs with a deep, steady intake of air." She began her testimony by recounting a shopping trip she had taken with Stompanato around 2:00 p.m. on the day of his death, culminating in the argument between them that began around 8:00 p.m. in her home.

Recalling the moment Crane stabbed him, Turner stated: "I was walking toward the bedroom door, and he was right behind me, and I opened it, and my daughter came in. I swear, it was so fast, I—I truthfully thought she had hit him in the stomach. The best I can remember, they came together and they parted. I still never saw a blade." Throughout her 62 minutes of testimony, Turner was noted by reporters as nearly collapsing from anxiety. She described Stompanato's final moments, which consisted of "the most horrible noises in his throat and gasping." Upon finishing her testimony, Turner returned to Giesler, collapsing in tears.

After four hours of testimony and approximately 25 minutes of deliberation, the coroner's jury deemed Stompanato's killing a justifiable homicide, and Crane would not be prosecuted. Crane remained a temporary ward of the court until April 24th, when a juvenile court hearing was held, during which presiding Judge Allen T. Lynch expressed concerns over her receiving "proper parental supervision." This hearing, unlike the coroner's inquest, was closed to the public. Crane was ultimately released to the care of her grandmother Mildred, and was ordered to regularly visit a psychiatrist alongside her parents.

Though Crane was cleared of wrongdoing, Stompanato's ex-wife filed a wrongful death lawsuit in June 1958 on behalf of herself and Stompanato's 7 year old son, against Crane, her father Steve Crane, and Lana Turner, seeking $750,000 in damages. The lawsuit was eventually settled out of court in 1962 for a sum of $20,000.

In the intervening years, Stompanato's homicide has been subject of conspiracy theories, the main one being that Turner had in fact stabbed him, and that Crane had taken the blame to protect her mother, though Crane has always denied this.

THE END

Thank you for buying or borrowing this book. There are two more that complete the California Killers series. To keep up with my new releases and other information on my talks, what book festivals I am attending and other useless information about me please become a friend on my Barry Faulkner Facebook page. I don't have a website, not enough time, but all my books, true crime and crime fiction are on the Barry Faulkner Amazon page for the country you are in together with the first pages of each as a taster. You can also order them at your local library or book shop if they don't have them already.

DCS Palmer books (crime fiction)

Future Riches

The Felt Tip Murders

Killer is Calling

Poetic Justice

Loot

I'm With The Band

Burning Ambition

Take Away Terror

Ministry of Death

The Bodybuilder

Succession

The Black Rose

Laptops Can Kill

Screen 4

Underneath The Arches

Numbers

Ben Nevis and the Gold Digger

(PE thrillers)

Turkish Delight

National Treasure

Chinese Takeaway

Double Trouble

The Pyramid

True Crime Series

London Crime 1930s-2021 (factual)

UK Serial Killers 1930-2021

UK Killers Vol. 1. A to E.

UK Killers Vol. 2. F to M.

UK Killers Vol. 3. N to Z

USA Killers Vol. 1. Alabama

USA Killers Vol.2 Arizona A to L

USA Killers Vol.3 Arizona M-Z

plus The Ladies.

USA Killers Vol.4 Alaska & Arkansas